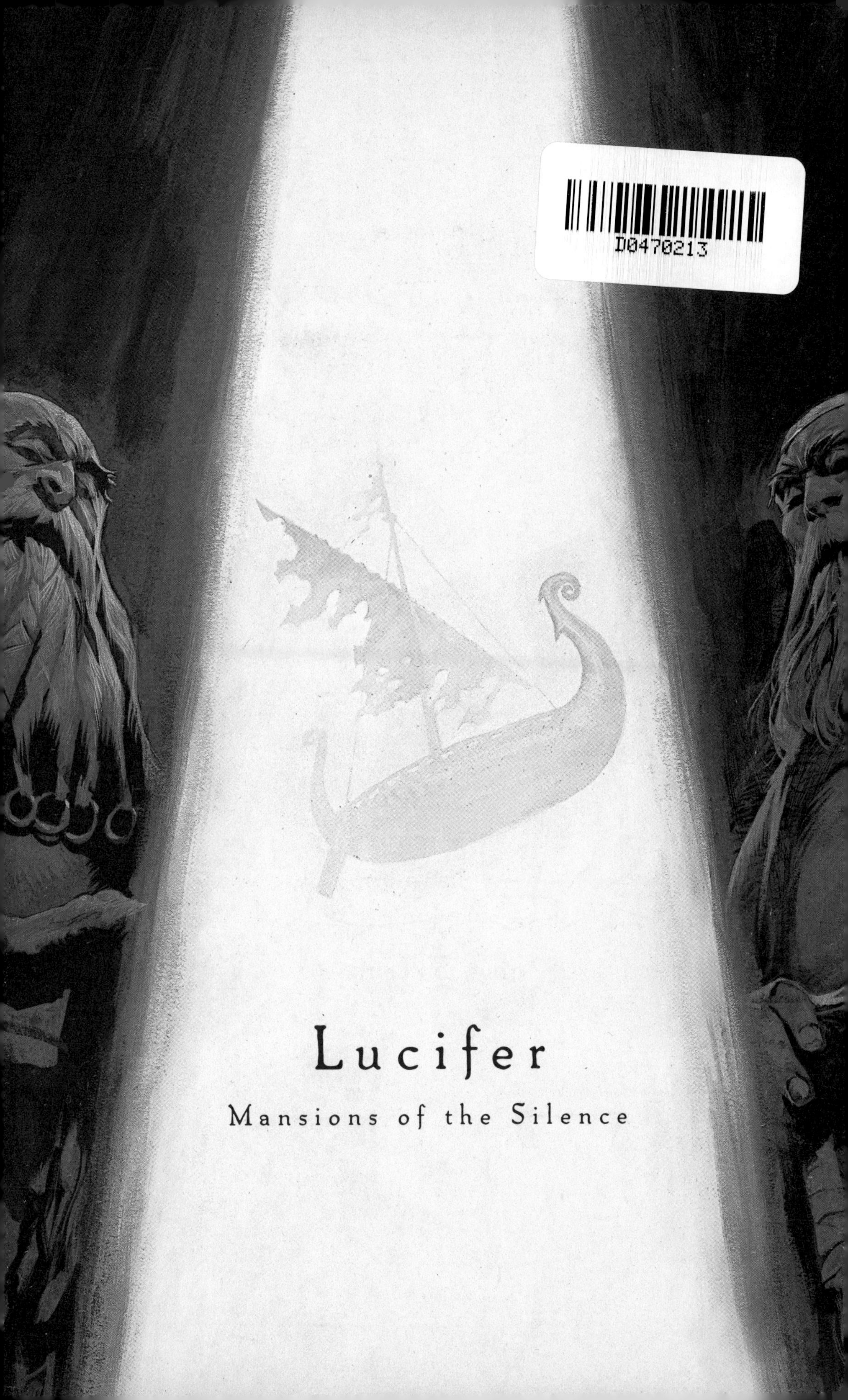

# Lucifer

## Mansions of the Silence

# Lucifer

## Mansions of the Silence

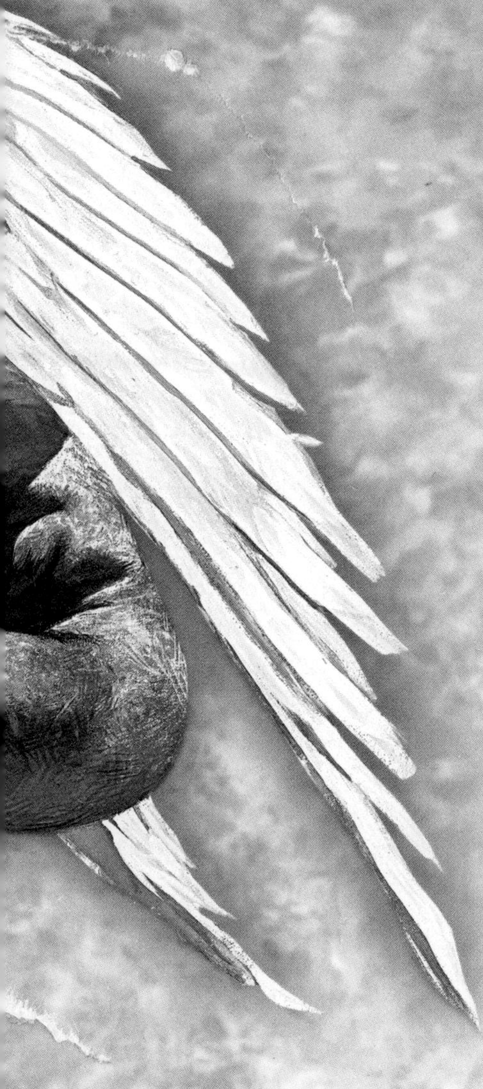


Mike Carey
Writer

Peter Gross    Ryan Kelly
Dean Ormston    David Hahn
Artists

Daniel Vozzo
Colorist

Comicraft
Letterer

Christopher Moeller
Original Series Covers


Based on characters created by
Neil Gaiman, Sam Kieth and Mike Dringenberg

LUCIFER: MANSIONS OF THE SILENCE

Published by DC Comics.

Cover and compilation copyright © 2004 DC Comics.
All Rights Reserved.

Originally published in single magazine form as LUCIFER 36-41.
Copyright © 2003 DC Comics. All Rights Reserved.
All characters, the distinctive likenesses thereof and related elements
featured in this publication are trademarks of DC Comics.
The stories, characters and incidents featured in this
publication are entirely fictional.
DC Comics does not read or accept unsolicited
submissions of ideas, stories or artwork.

DC Comics, 1700 Broadway, New York, NY 10019
A Warner Bros. Entertainment Company
Printed in Canada. Second Printing.
ISBN:1-4012-0249-7
Cover illustrations by Christopher Moeller
Logo design by Alex Jay.

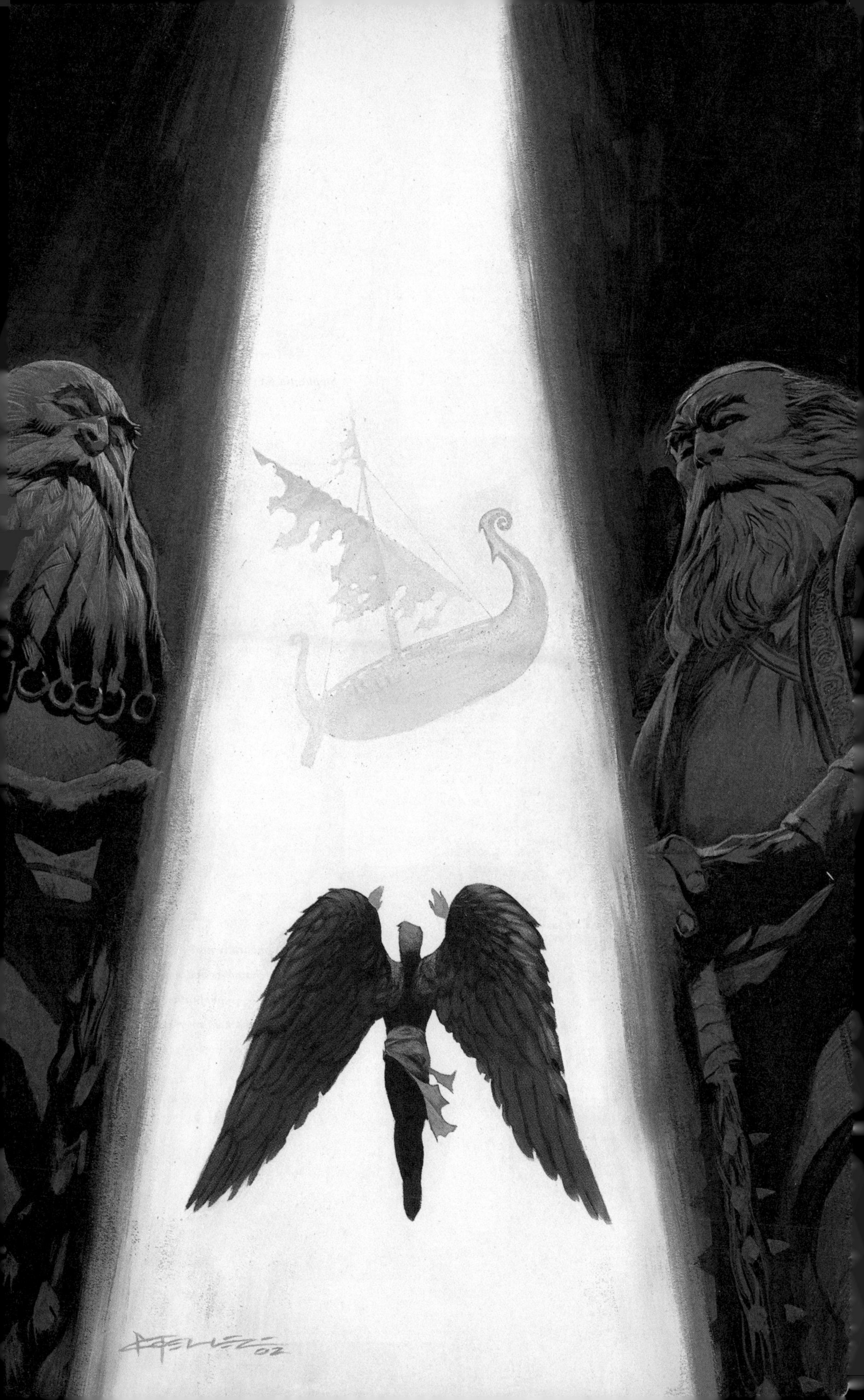

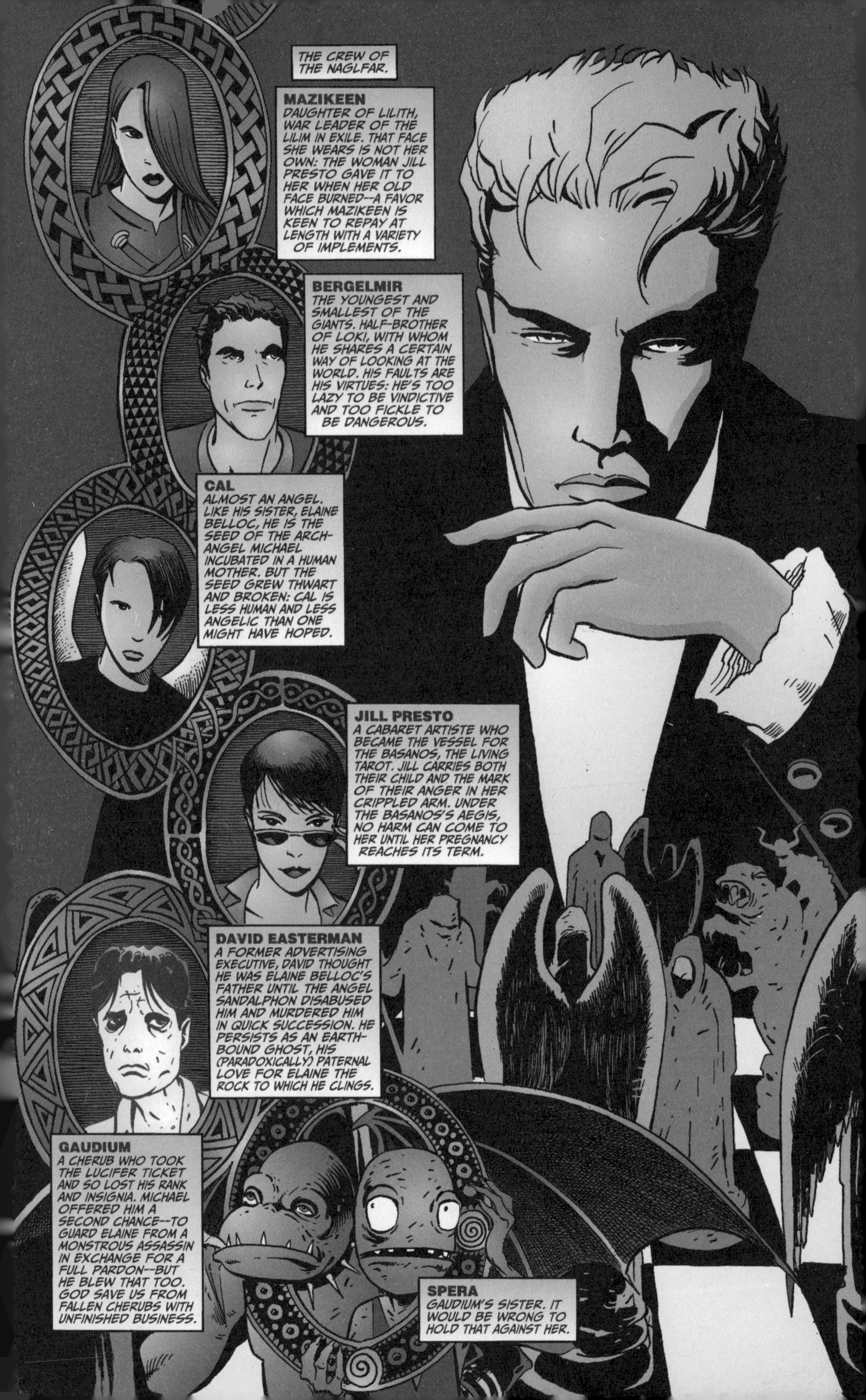
THE CREW OF THE NAGLFAR.
MAZIKEEN
DAUGHTER OF LILITH, WAR LEADER OF THE LILIM IN EXILE. THAT FACE SHE WEARS IS NOT HER OWN: THE WOMAN JILL PRESTO GAVE IT TO HER WHEN HER OLD FACE BURNED--A FAVOR WHICH MAZIKEEN IS KEEN TO REPAY AT LENGTH WITH A VARIETY OF IMPLEMENTS.
BERGELMIR
THE YOUNGEST AND SMALLEST OF THE GIANTS. HALF-BROTHER OF LOKI, WITH WHOM HE SHARES A CERTAIN WAY OF LOOKING AT THE WORLD. HIS FAULTS ARE HIS VIRTUES: HE'S TOO LAZY TO BE VINDICTIVE AND TOO FICKLE TO BE DANGEROUS.
CAL
ALMOST AN ANGEL. LIKE HIS SISTER, ELAINE BELLOC, HE IS THE SEED OF THE ARCH-ANGEL MICHAEL INCUBATED IN A HUMAN MOTHER. BUT THE SEED GREW THWART AND BROKEN: CAL IS LESS HUMAN AND LESS ANGELIC THAN ONE MIGHT HAVE HOPED.
JILL PRESTO
A CABARET ARTISTE WHO BECAME THE VESSEL FOR THE BASANOS, THE LIVING TAROT. JILL CARRIES BOTH THEIR CHILD AND THE MARK OF THEIR ANGER IN HER CRIPPLED ARM. UNDER THE BASANOS'S AEGIS, NO HARM CAN COME TO HER UNTIL HER PREGNANCY REACHES ITS TERM.
DAVID EASTERMAN
A FORMER ADVERTISING EXECUTIVE, DAVID THOUGHT HE WAS ELAINE BELLOC'S FATHER UNTIL THE ANGEL SANDALPHON DISABUSED HIM AND MURDERED HIM IN QUICK SUCCESSION. HE PERSISTS AS AN EARTH-BOUND GHOST, HIS (PARADOXICALLY) PATERNAL LOVE FOR ELAINE THE ROCK TO WHICH HE CLINGS.
GAUDIUM
A CHERUB WHO TOOK THE LUCIFER TICKET AND SO LOST HIS RANK AND INSIGNIA. MICHAEL OFFERED HIM A SECOND CHANCE--TO GUARD ELAINE FROM A MONSTROUS ASSASSIN IN EXCHANGE FOR A FULL PARDON--BUT HE BLEW THAT TOO. GOD SAVE US FROM FALLEN CHERUBS WITH UNFINISHED BUSINESS.
SPERA
GAUDIUM'S SISTER. IT WOULD BE WRONG TO HOLD THAT AGAINST HER.

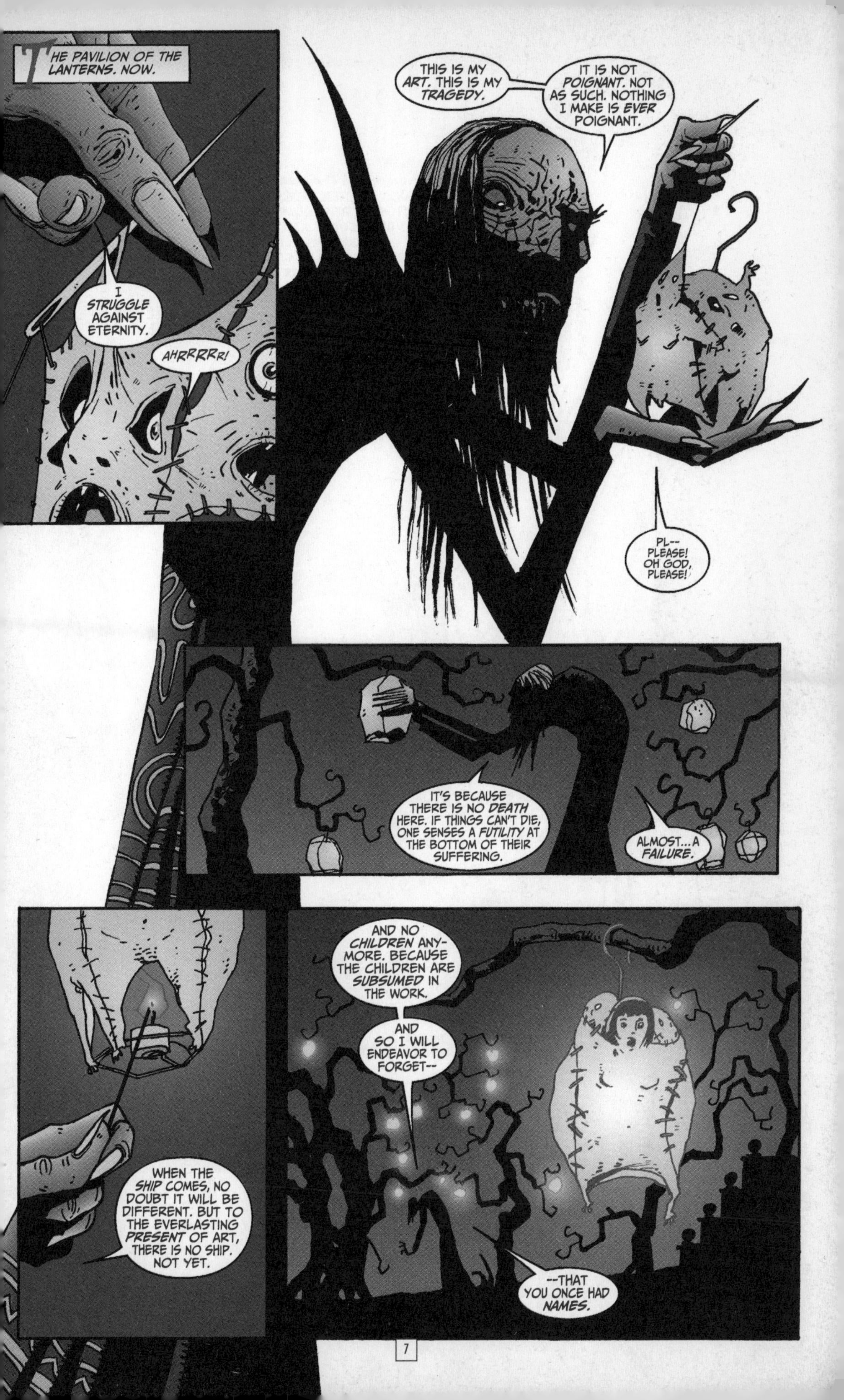
THE PAVILION OF THE LANTERNS. NOW.
I STRUGGLE AGAINST ETERNITY.
AHRRRRr!
THIS IS MY ART. THIS IS MY TRAGEDY.
IT IS NOT POIGNANT. NOT AS SUCH. NOTHING I MAKE IS EVER POIGNANT.
PL-- PLEASE! OH GOD, PLEASE!
IT'S BECAUSE THERE IS NO DEATH HERE. IF THINGS CAN'T DIE, ONE SENSES A FUTILITY AT THE BOTTOM OF THEIR SUFFERING.
ALMOST...A FAILURE.
WHEN THE SHIP COMES, NO DOUBT IT WILL BE DIFFERENT. BUT TO THE EVERLASTING PRESENT OF ART, THERE IS NO SHIP. NOT YET.
AND NO CHILDREN ANYMORE. BECAUSE THE CHILDREN ARE SUBSUMED IN THE WORK.
AND SO I WILL ENDEAVOR TO FORGET--
--THAT YOU ONCE HAD NAMES.

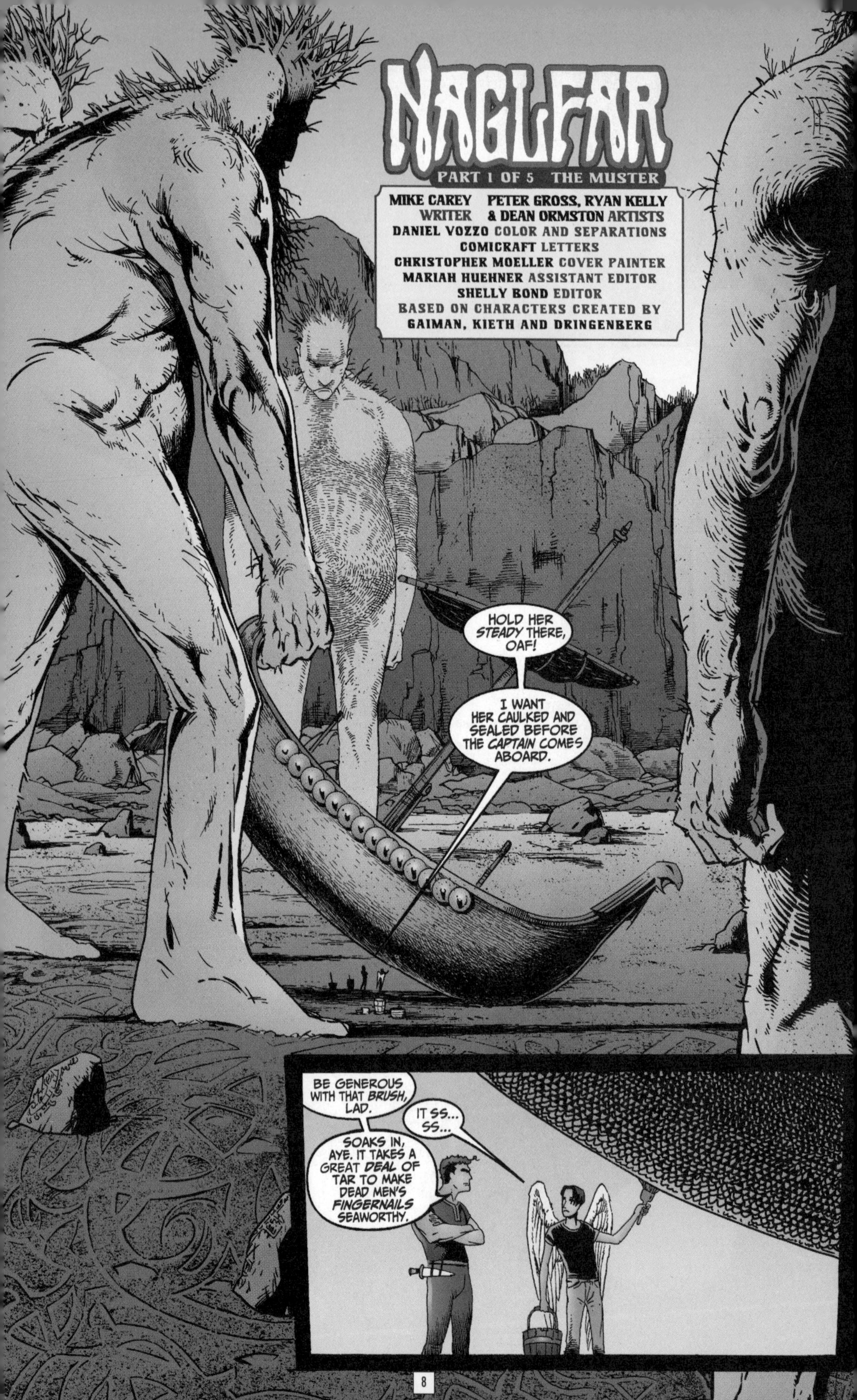
NAGLFAR
PART 1 OF 5 THE MUSTER
MIKE CAREY WRITER
PETER GROSS, RYAN KELLY & DEAN ORMSTON ARTISTS
DANIEL VOZZO COLOR AND SEPARATIONS
COMICRAFT LETTERS
CHRISTOPHER MOELLER COVER PAINTER
MARIAH HUEHNER ASSISTANT EDITOR
SHELLY BOND EDITOR
BASED ON CHARACTERS CREATED BY GAIMAN, KIETH AND DRINGENBERG
HOLD HER STEADY THERE, OAF!
I WANT HER CAULKED AND SEALED BEFORE THE CAPTAIN COMES ABOARD.
BE GENEROUS WITH THAT BRUSH, LAD.
IT SS... SS...
SOAKS IN, AYE. IT TAKES A GREAT DEAL OF TAR TO MAKE DEAD MEN'S FINGERNAILS SEAWORTHY.

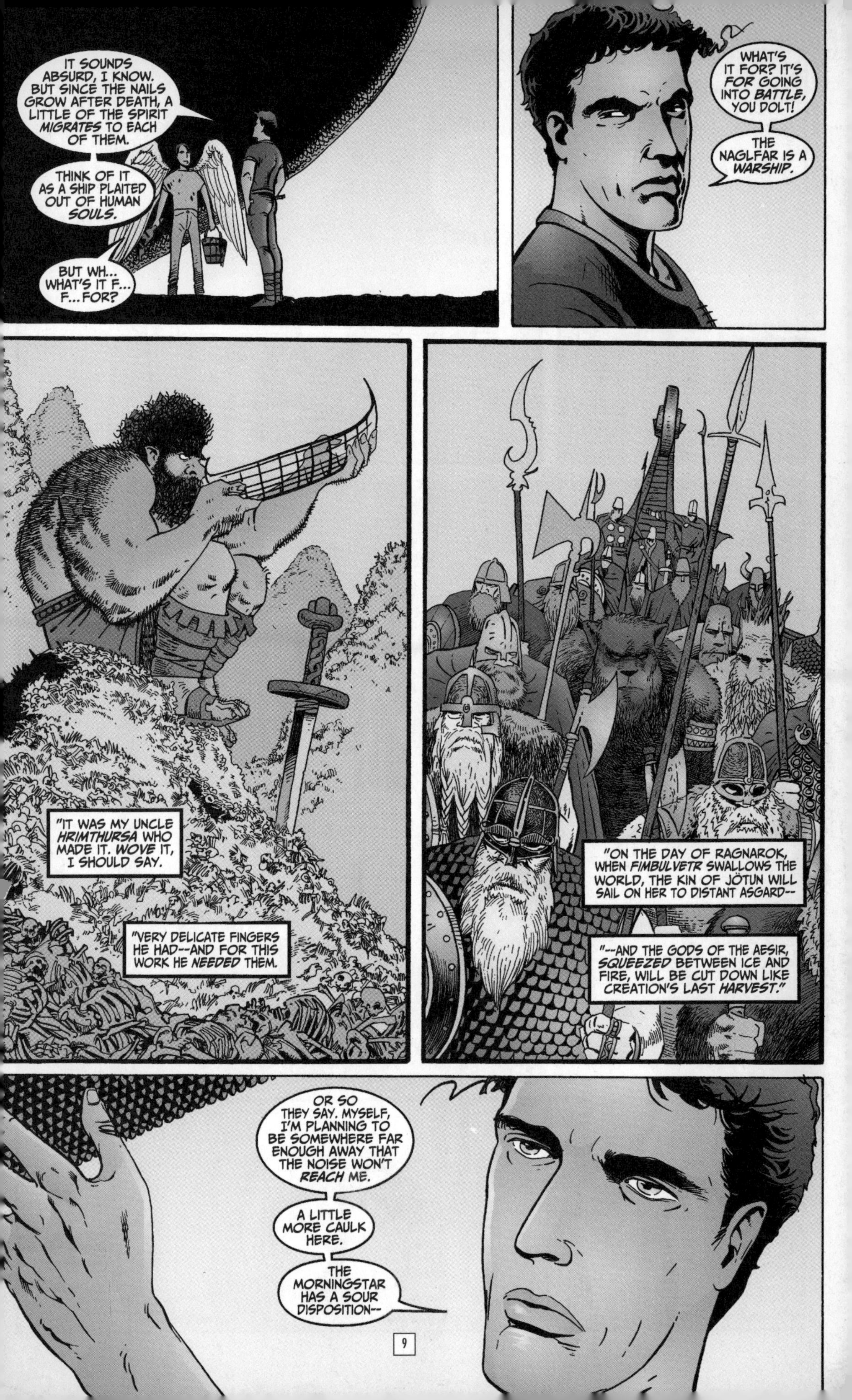
IT SOUNDS ABSURD, I KNOW. BUT SINCE THE NAILS GROW AFTER DEATH, A LITTLE OF THE SPIRIT MIGRATES TO EACH OF THEM.
THINK OF IT AS A SHIP PLAITED OUT OF HUMAN SOULS.
BUT WH... WHAT'S IT F... F...FOR?
WHAT'S IT FOR? IT'S FOR GOING INTO BATTLE, YOU DOLT!
THE NAGLFAR IS A WARSHIP.
"IT WAS MY UNCLE HRIMTHURSA WHO MADE IT. WOVE IT, I SHOULD SAY.
"VERY DELICATE FINGERS HE HAD--AND FOR THIS WORK HE NEEDED THEM.
"ON THE DAY OF RAGNAROK, WHEN FIMBULVETR SWALLOWS THE WORLD, THE KIN OF JÖTUN WILL SAIL ON HER TO DISTANT ASGARD--
"--AND THE GODS OF THE AESIR, SQUEEZED BETWEEN ICE AND FIRE, WILL BE CUT DOWN LIKE CREATION'S LAST HARVEST."
OR SO THEY SAY. MYSELF, I'M PLANNING TO BE SOMEWHERE FAR ENOUGH AWAY THAT THE NOISE WON'T REACH ME.
A LITTLE MORE CAULK HERE.
THE MORNINGSTAR HAS A SOUR DISPOSITION--

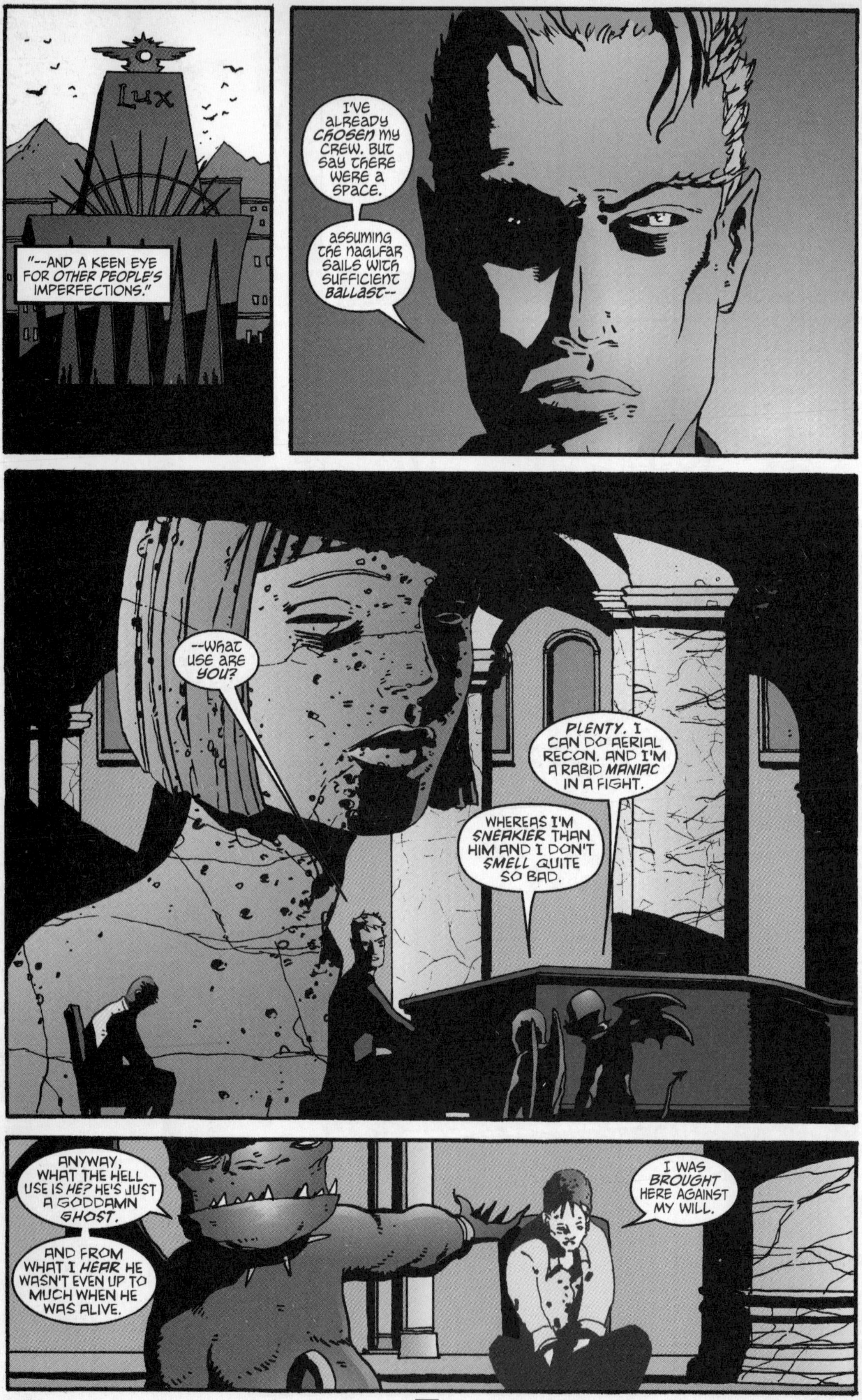

"--AND A KEEN EYE FOR OTHER PEOPLE'S IMPERFECTIONS."
I'VE ALREADY CHOSEN MY CREW. BUT SAY THERE WERE A SPACE.
ASSUMING THE NAGLFAR SAILS WITH SUFFICIENT BALLAST--
--WHAT USE ARE YOU?
PLENTY. I CAN DO AERIAL RECON. AND I'M A RABID MANIAC IN A FIGHT.
WHEREAS I'M SNEAKIER THAN HIM AND I DON'T SMELL QUITE SO BAD.
ANYWAY, WHAT THE HELL USE IS HE? HE'S JUST A GODDAMN GHOST.
AND FROM WHAT I HEAR HE WASN'T EVEN UP TO MUCH WHEN HE WAS ALIVE.
I WAS BROUGHT HERE AGAINST MY WILL.

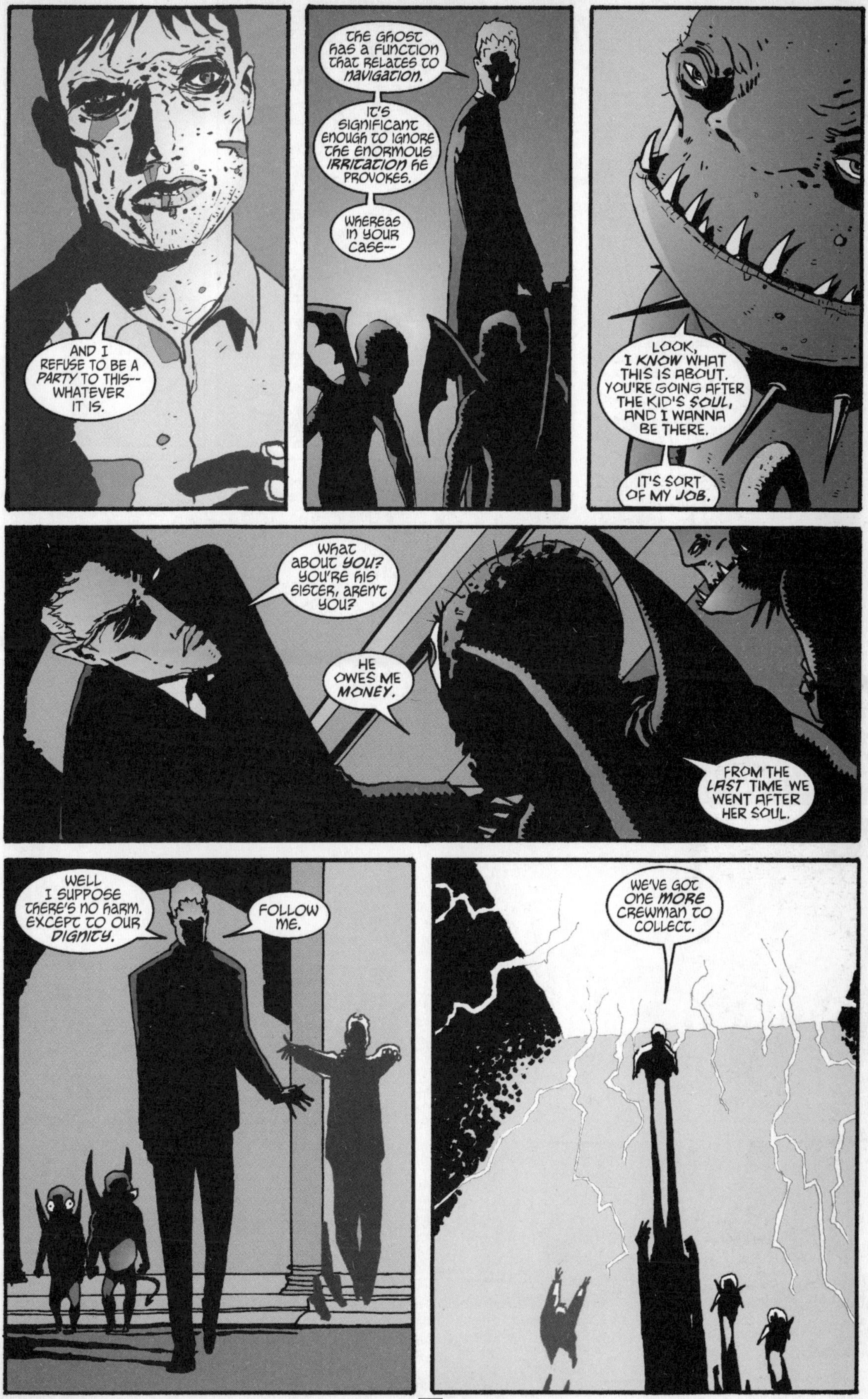
AND I REFUSE TO BE A PARTY TO THIS-- WHATEVER IT IS.
THE GHOST HAS A FUNCTION THAT RELATES TO NAVIGATION.
IT'S SIGNIFICANT ENOUGH TO IGNORE THE ENORMOUS IRRITATION HE PROVOKES.
WHEREAS IN YOUR CASE--
LOOK, I KNOW WHAT THIS IS ABOUT. YOU'RE GOING AFTER THE KID'S SOUL, AND I WANNA BE THERE.
IT'S SORT OF MY JOB.
WHAT ABOUT YOU? YOU'RE HIS SISTER, AREN'T YOU?
HE OWES ME MONEY.
FROM THE LAST TIME WE WENT AFTER HER SOUL.
WELL I SUPPOSE THERE'S NO HARM. EXCEPT TO OUR DIGNITY.
FOLLOW ME.
WE'VE GOT ONE MORE CREWMAN TO COLLECT.

B...BUT WHY ARE YOU C...COMING ON *THIS* VOYAGE? WE'RE NOT GOING TO AS...AS... ASGARD.

NOT BY MY OWN *CHOICE*, CAL.

*HUF!* LORD LUCIFER FELT THAT SINCE I TRIED TO *KILL* HIM, I OWED HIM A SERVICE.

HE PUT THIS POINT OF VIEW MOST *PERSUASIVELY.*

AND *YOURSELF?*

I W... WANTED TO COME. AS SOON AS L...L...LUCIFER EXPLAINED IT TO ME, I B...BEGGED HIM TO TAKE ME.

TO LET ME *HELP* F... F...FIND...

HOLD. WE'VE A VISITOR.

OUR *CAPTAIN*, NO DOUBT.

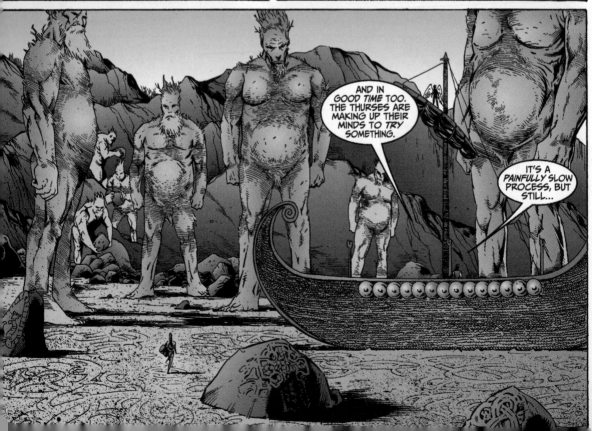

AND IN *GOOD TIME* TOO. THE THURSES ARE MAKING UP THEIR MINDS TO *TRY* SOMETHING.

IT'S A *PAINFULLY* SLOW PROCESS, BUT STILL...

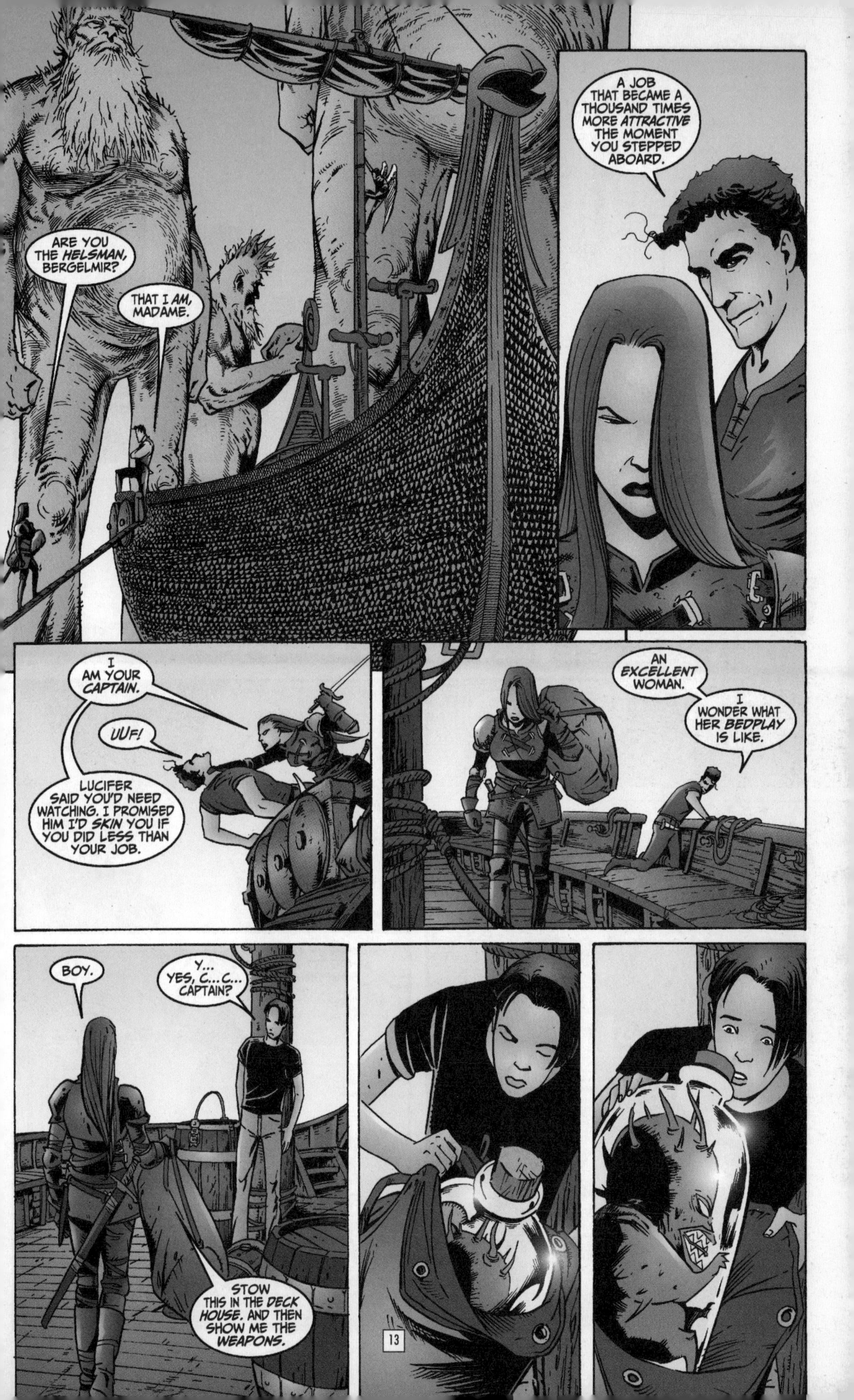
ARE YOU THE *HELSMAN*, BERGELMIR?
THAT I *AM*, MADAME.
A JOB THAT BECAME A THOUSAND TIMES MORE *ATTRACTIVE* THE MOMENT YOU STEPPED ABOARD.
I AM YOUR *CAPTAIN.*
*UUF!*
LUCIFER SAID YOU'D NEED WATCHING. I PROMISED HIM I'D *SKIN* YOU IF YOU DID LESS THAN YOUR JOB.
AN *EXCELLENT* WOMAN.
I WONDER WHAT HER *BEDPLAY* IS LIKE.
BOY.
Y... YES, C...C... CAPTAIN?
STOW THIS IN THE *DECK HOUSE*. AND THEN SHOW ME THE *WEAPONS*.

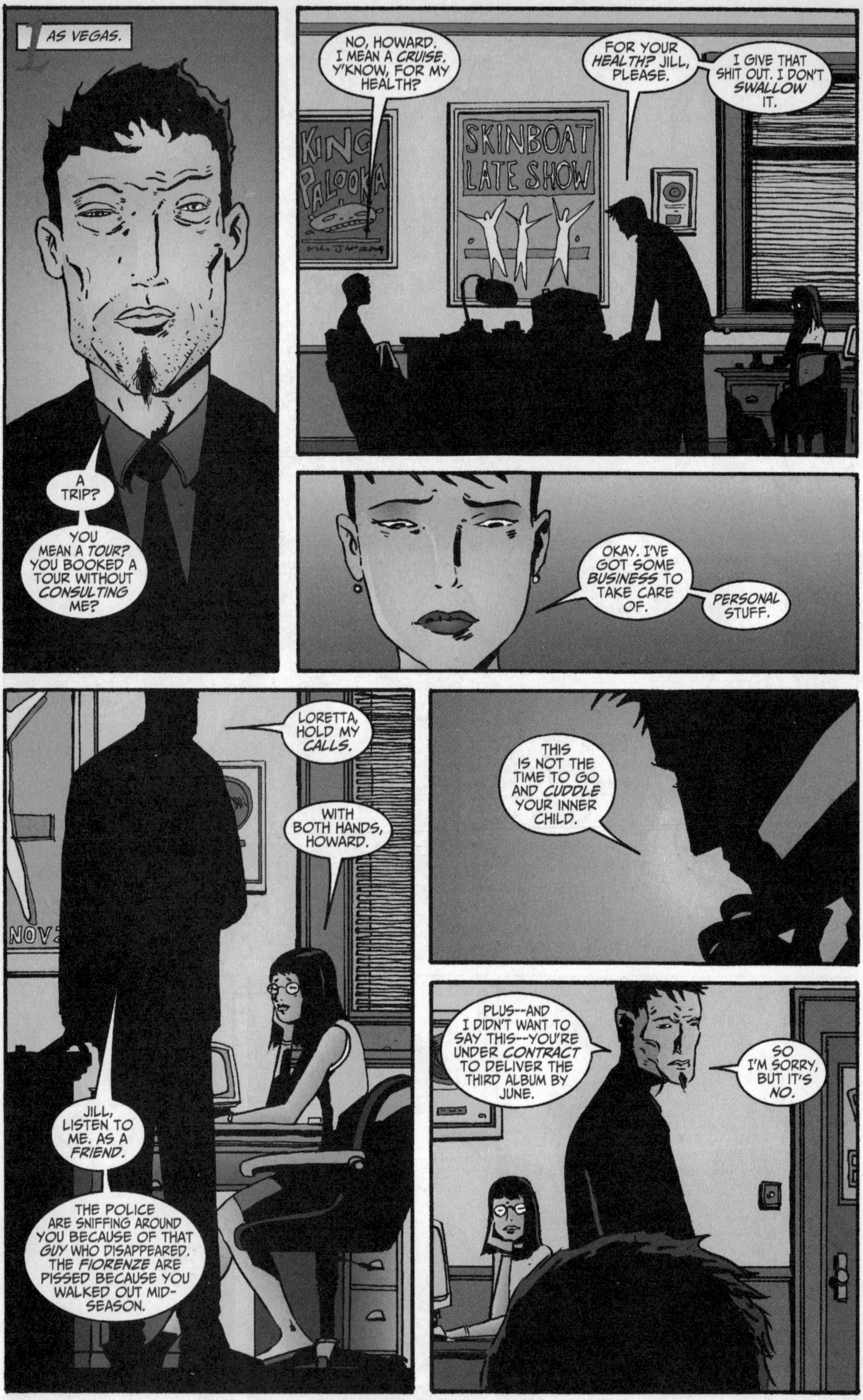

LAS VEGAS.
NO, HOWARD. I MEAN A CRUISE. Y'KNOW, FOR MY HEALTH?
FOR YOUR HEALTH? JILL, PLEASE.
I GIVE THAT SHIT OUT. I DON'T SWALLOW IT.
KING PALOOKA
SKINBOAT LATE SHOW
A TRIP?
YOU MEAN A TOUR? YOU BOOKED A TOUR WITHOUT CONSULTING ME?
OKAY. I'VE GOT SOME BUSINESS TO TAKE CARE OF.
PERSONAL STUFF.
LORETTA, HOLD MY CALLS.
WITH BOTH HANDS, HOWARD.
JILL, LISTEN TO ME. AS A FRIEND.
THE POLICE ARE SNIFFING AROUND YOU BECAUSE OF THAT GUY WHO DISAPPEARED. THE FIORENZE ARE PISSED BECAUSE YOU WALKED OUT MID-SEASON.
THIS IS NOT THE TIME TO GO AND CUDDLE YOUR INNER CHILD.
PLUS--AND I DIDN'T WANT TO SAY THIS--YOU'RE UNDER CONTRACT TO DELIVER THE THIRD ALBUM BY JUNE.
SO I'M SORRY, BUT IT'S NO.

YEAH, WELL I'M SORRY *TOO*, HOWARD. YOU'LL JUST HAVE TO *SUE* ME.

JILL, DON'T DO THIS. IT'S CAREER SUICIDE.

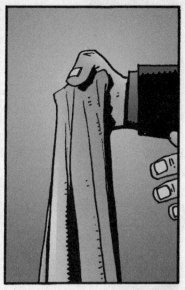

SHIT!

SHIT WITH *ICE CREAM!*

DON'T *STARE* AT IT, OKAY?

FUCK! JUST *STOP!*

I'M GONNA GET THIS *FIXED.*

I'M GOING TO A PLACE WHERE THEY CAN *DEAL WITH* STUFF LIKE THIS.

AND THEN I'LL BE *BACK*, HOWARD. BETTER THAN *EVER.*

YOU TEAR UP THOSE CONTRACTS AND YOU'LL BE WEEPING BLOOD IN A MONTH OR SO.

OKAY, SO SHE KNOWS HOW TO *EXIT.*

YOU WANT TO RECLAIM YOUR LOWER JAW AND CALL *LEGAL?*

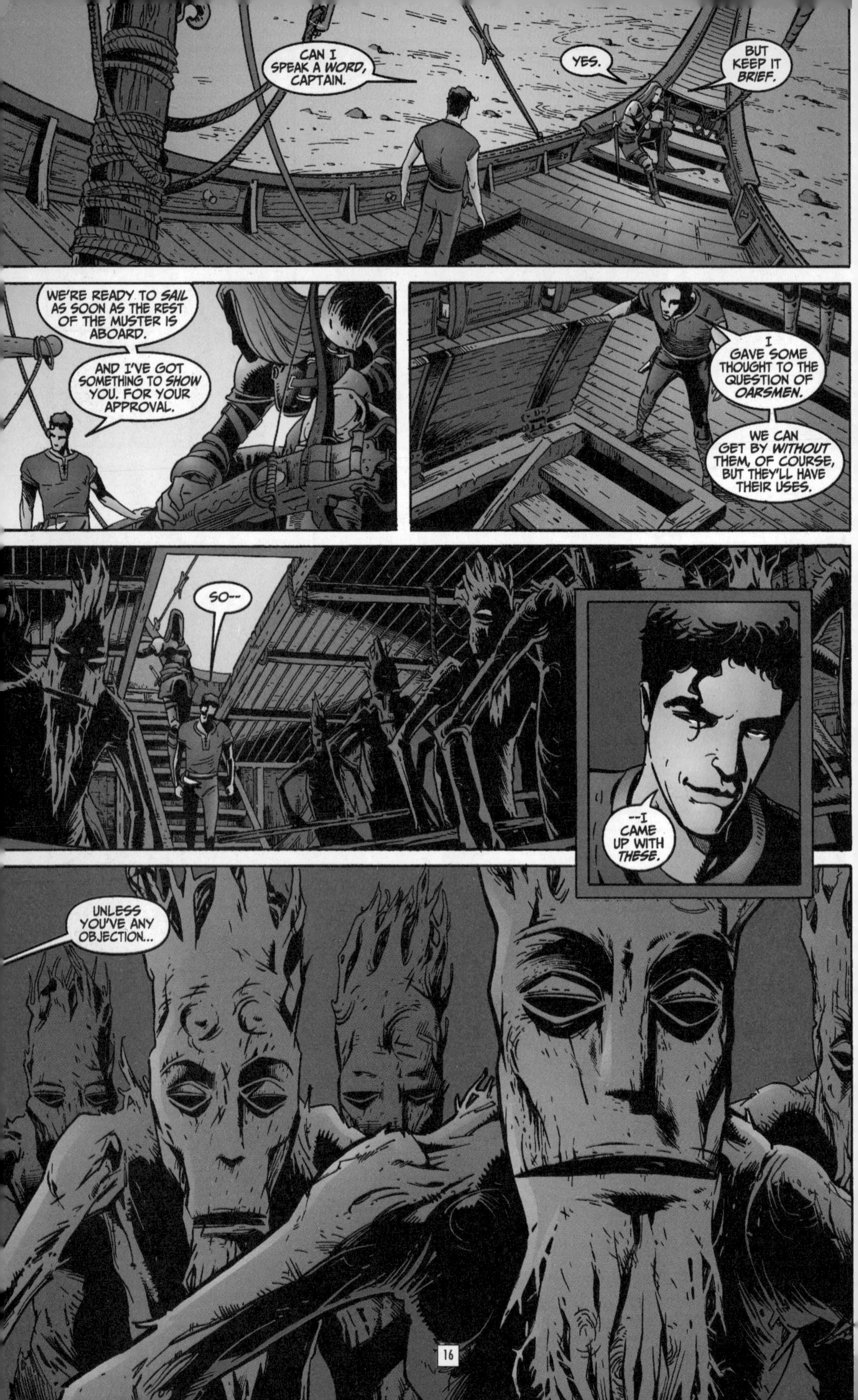
CAN I SPEAK A WORD, CAPTAIN.
YES.
BUT KEEP IT BRIEF.
WE'RE READY TO SAIL AS SOON AS THE REST OF THE MUSTER IS ABOARD.
AND I'VE GOT SOMETHING TO SHOW YOU. FOR YOUR APPROVAL.
I GAVE SOME THOUGHT TO THE QUESTION OF OARSMEN.
WE CAN GET BY WITHOUT THEM, OF COURSE, BUT THEY'LL HAVE THEIR USES.
SO--
--I CAME UP WITH THESE.
UNLESS YOU'VE ANY OBJECTION...

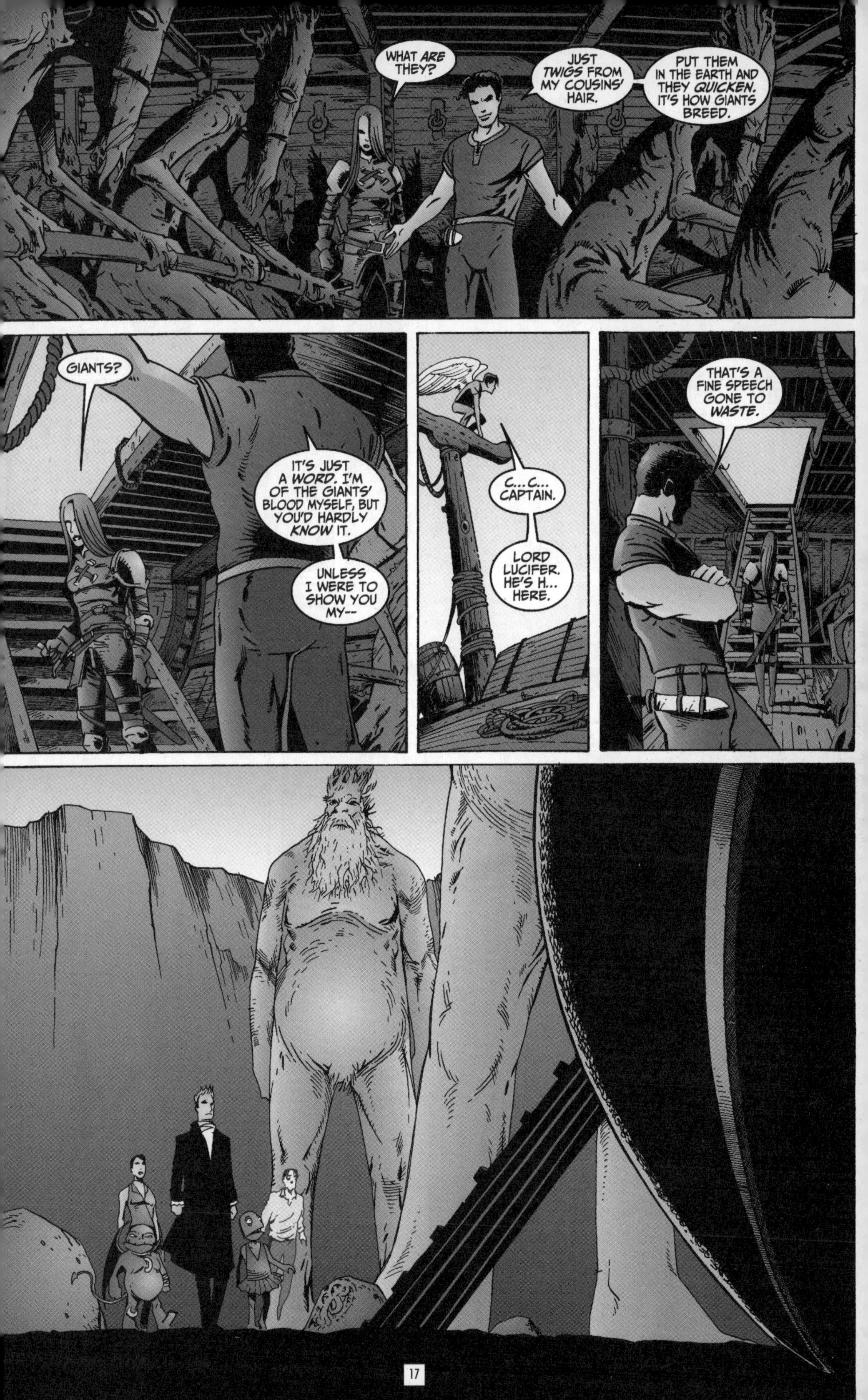
WHAT ARE THEY?
JUST TWIGS FROM MY COUSINS' HAIR.
PUT THEM IN THE EARTH AND THEY QUICKEN. IT'S HOW GIANTS BREED.
GIANTS?
IT'S JUST A WORD. I'M OF THE GIANTS' BLOOD MYSELF, BUT YOU'D HARDLY KNOW IT.
UNLESS I WERE TO SHOW YOU MY--
C...C... CAPTAIN.
LORD LUCIFER. HE'S H... HERE.
THAT'S A FINE SPEECH GONE TO WASTE.

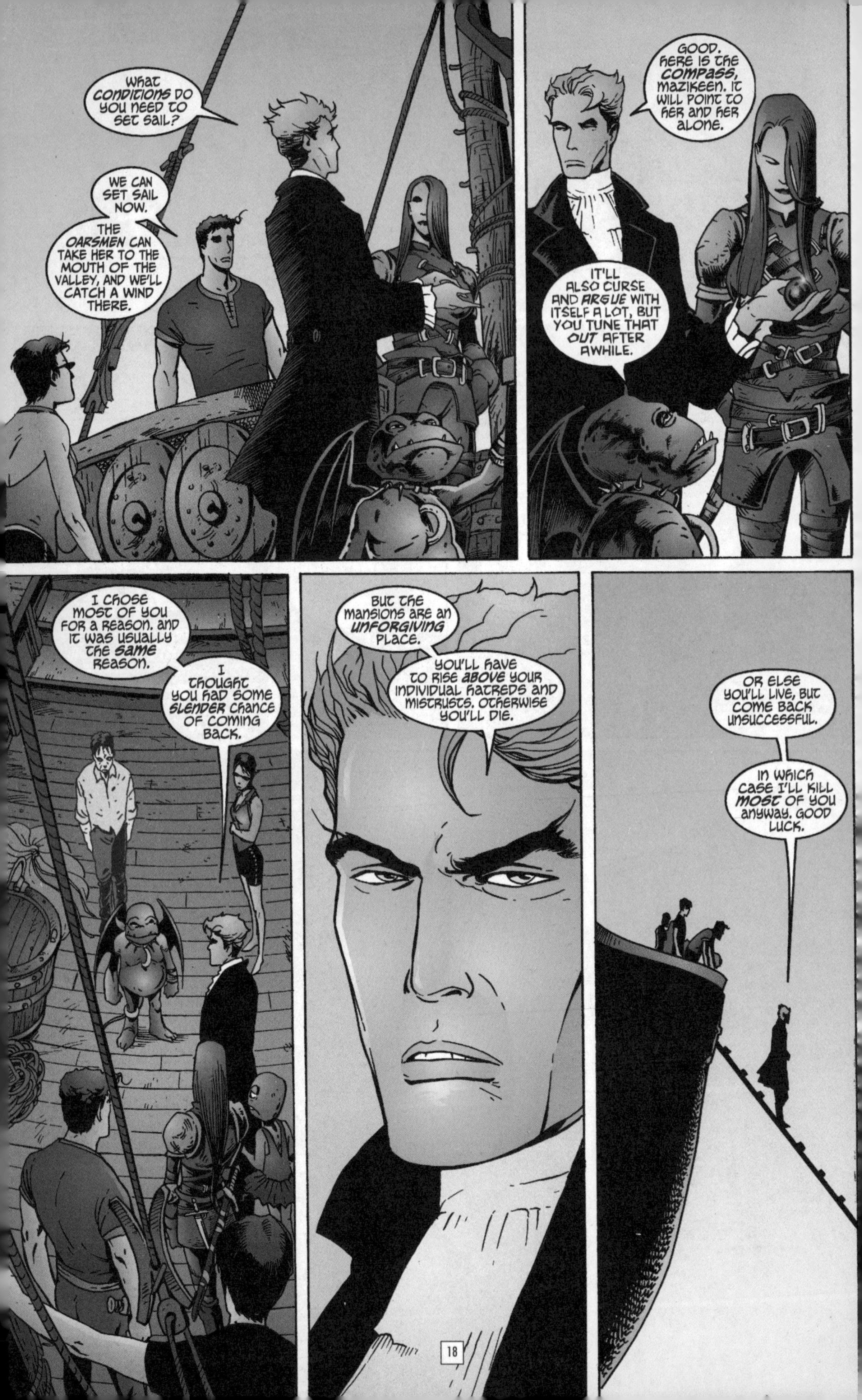
WHAT CONDITIONS DO YOU NEED TO SET SAIL?
WE CAN SET SAIL NOW.
THE OARSMEN CAN TAKE HER TO THE MOUTH OF THE VALLEY, AND WE'LL CATCH A WIND THERE.
GOOD. HERE IS THE COMPASS, MAZIKEEN. IT WILL POINT TO HER AND HER ALONE.
IT'LL ALSO CURSE AND ARGUE WITH ITSELF A LOT, BUT YOU TUNE THAT OUT AFTER AWHILE.
I CHOSE MOST OF YOU FOR A REASON, AND IT WAS USUALLY THE SAME REASON.
I THOUGHT YOU HAD SOME SLENDER CHANCE OF COMING BACK.
BUT THE MANSIONS ARE AN UNFORGIVING PLACE.
YOU'LL HAVE TO RISE ABOVE YOUR INDIVIDUAL HATREDS AND MISTRUSTS. OTHERWISE YOU'LL DIE.
OR ELSE YOU'LL LIVE, BUT COME BACK UNSUCCESSFUL.
IN WHICH CASE I'LL KILL MOST OF YOU ANYWAY. GOOD LUCK.

HE GIVES AN INSPIRATIONAL SPEECH DOESN'T HE?

N... N... N...

JOKE, LAD, JOKE.

PERMISSION TO TAKE HER *OUT*, CAPTAIN?

YES. DO IT.

NOW *ROW*, YOU BASTARDS, ROW!

THE WIND WON'T WAIT FOREVER!

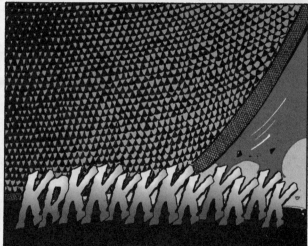

KRKKKKKKKKKK

CHRIST ON A CRUTCH!

THE SUSPENSION ON THIS THING IS *FUCKED!*

19

SLOWER ON THE RIGHT! BRING HER HEAD AROUND YARELY!

WE'RE AFLOOD, CAPTAIN.

AND WE'RE STEADY TO THE WEST.

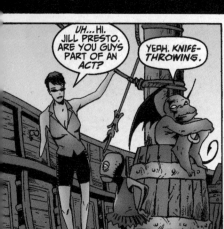

UH... HI. JILL PRESTO. ARE YOU GUYS PART OF AN ACT?

YEAH. KNIFE-THROWING.

WHY STAND YOU SO AMAZED, MAN?

THE BOY WITH WINGS. HE TRIED TO KILL ME ONCE.

DID HE SO?

WELL, NOW THAT YOU'RE DEAD, I'M SURE YOU'LL BE FAST FRIENDS.

WANNA SEE?

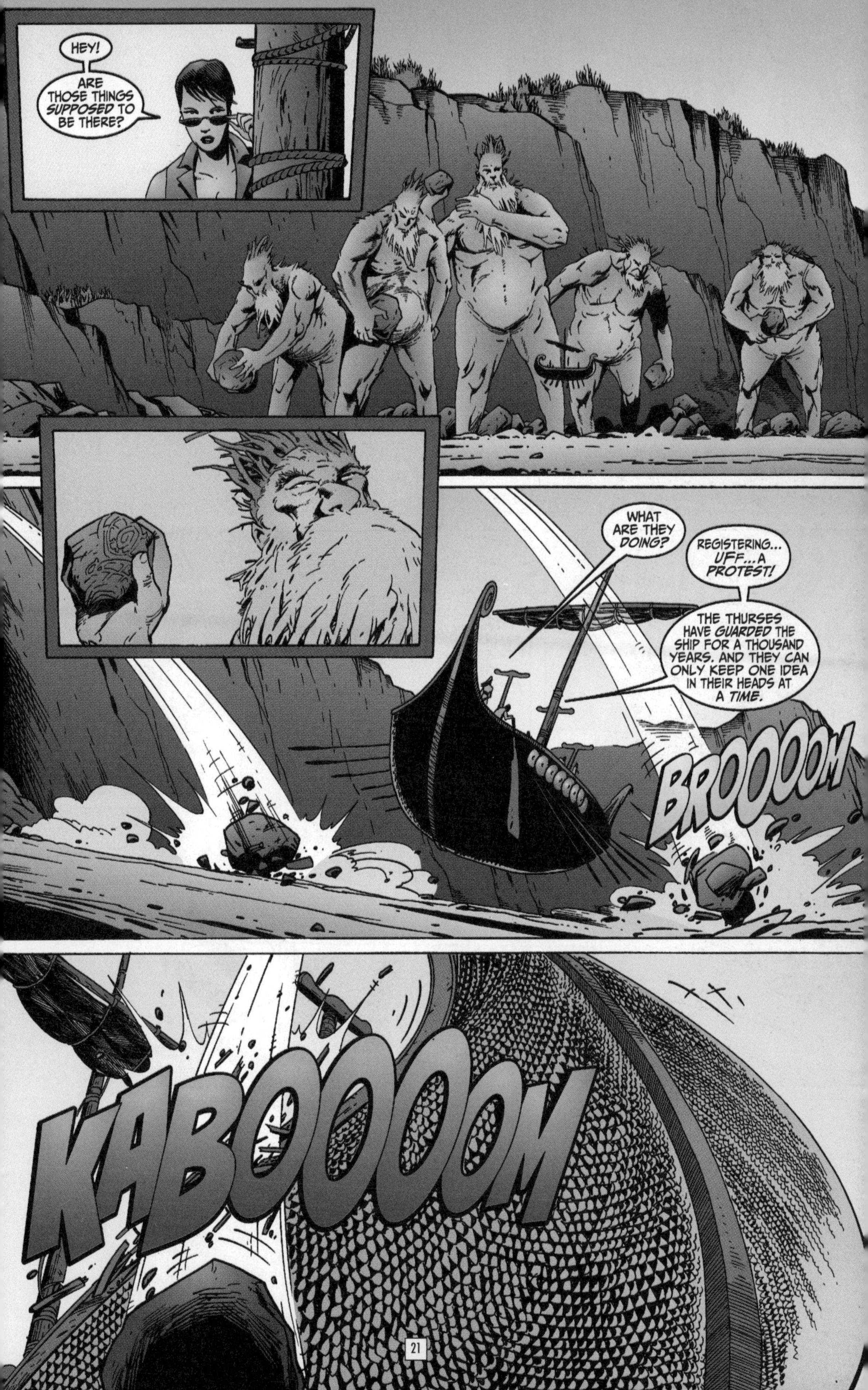
HEY!
ARE THOSE THINGS SUPPOSED TO BE THERE?
WHAT ARE THEY DOING?
REGISTERING... UFF...A PROTEST!
THE THURSES HAVE GUARDED THE SHIP FOR A THOUSAND YEARS. AND THEY CAN ONLY KEEP ONE IDEA IN THEIR HEADS AT A TIME.
BROOOOM
KABOOOOM

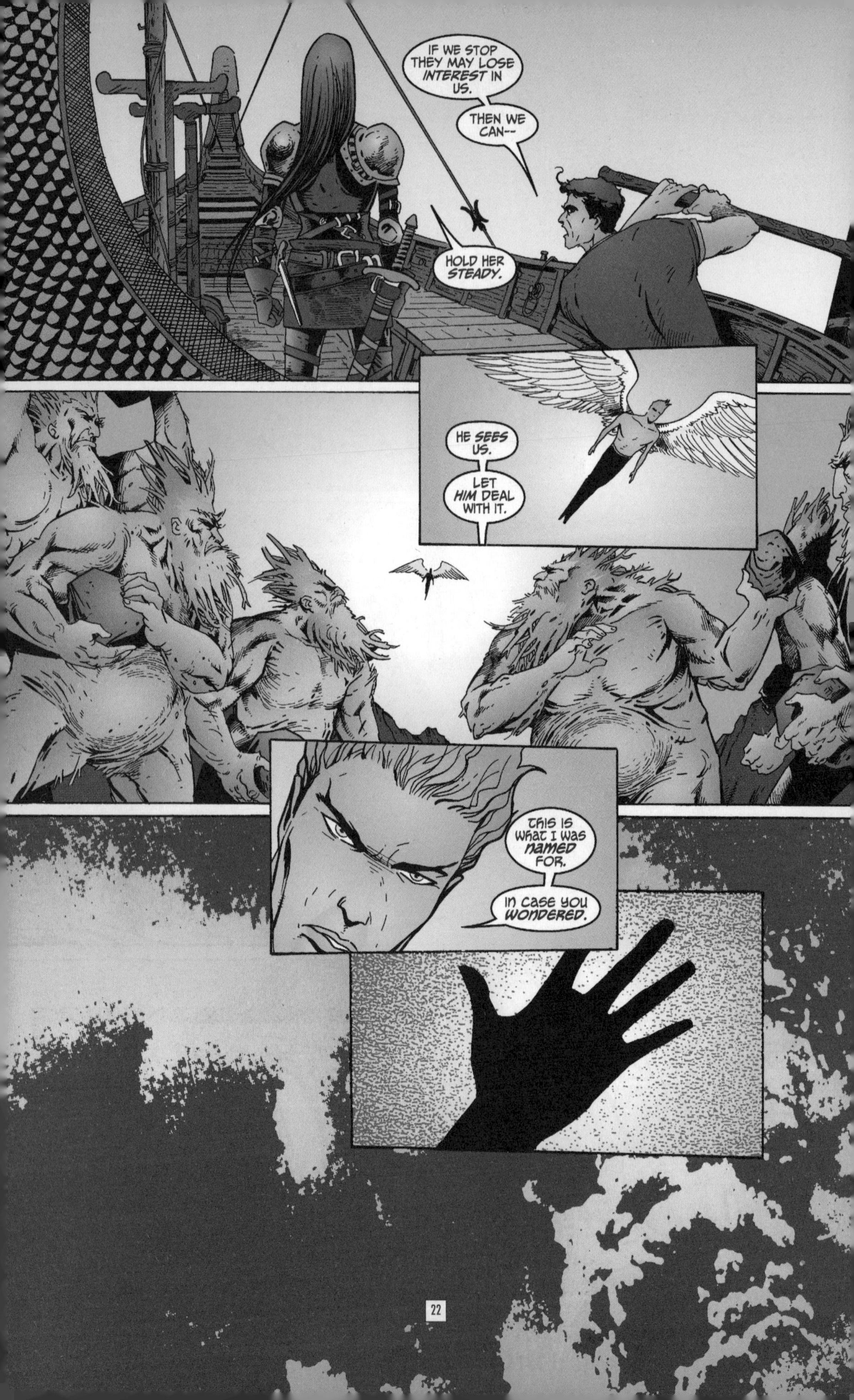
IF WE STOP THEY MAY LOSE INTEREST IN US.
THEN WE CAN--
HOLD HER STEADY.
HE SEES US.
LET HIM DEAL WITH IT.
THIS IS WHAT I WAS NAMED FOR.
IN CASE YOU WONDERED.

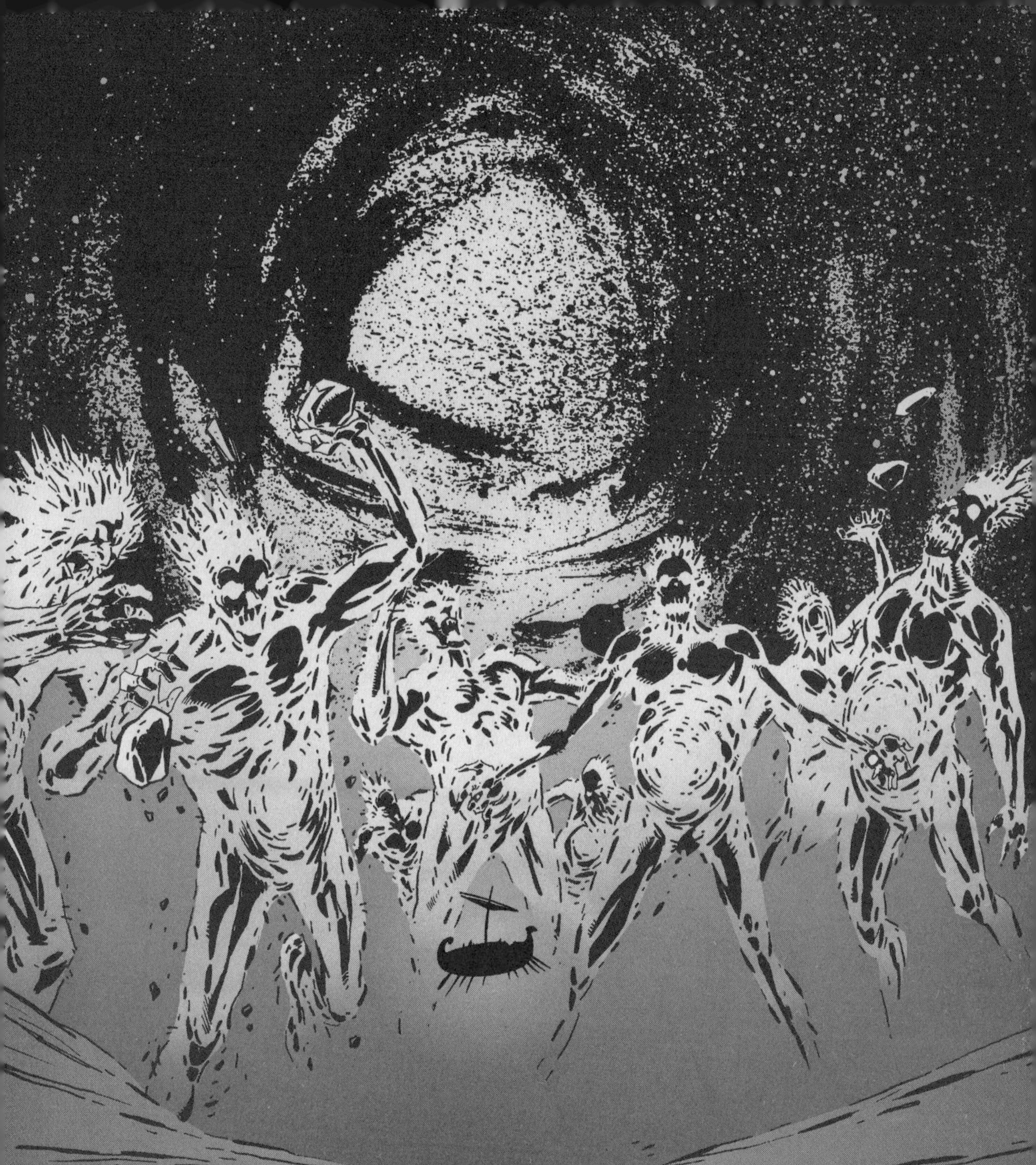

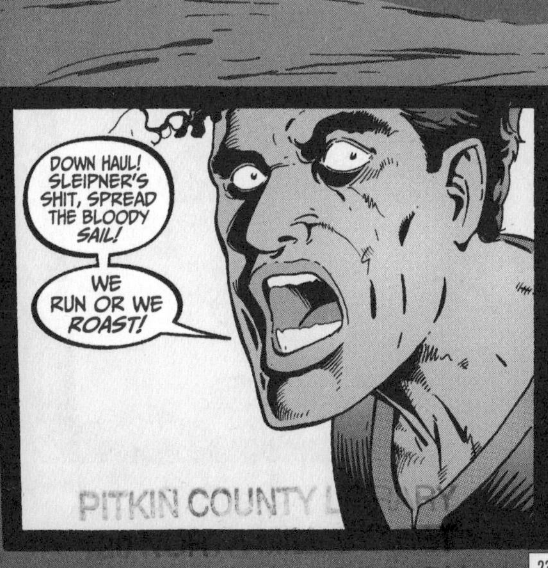
DOWN HAUL! SLEIPNER'S SHIT, SPREAD THE BLOODY SAIL!
WE RUN OR WE ROAST!

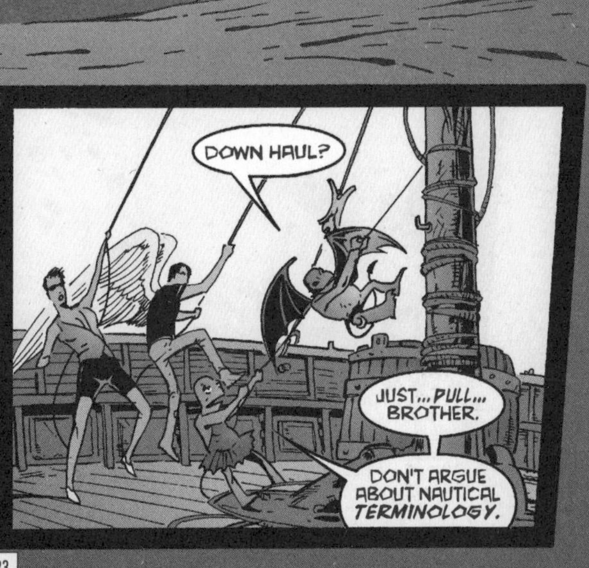
DOWN HAUL?
JUST... PULL... BROTHER.
DON'T ARGUE ABOUT NAUTICAL TERMINOLOGY.

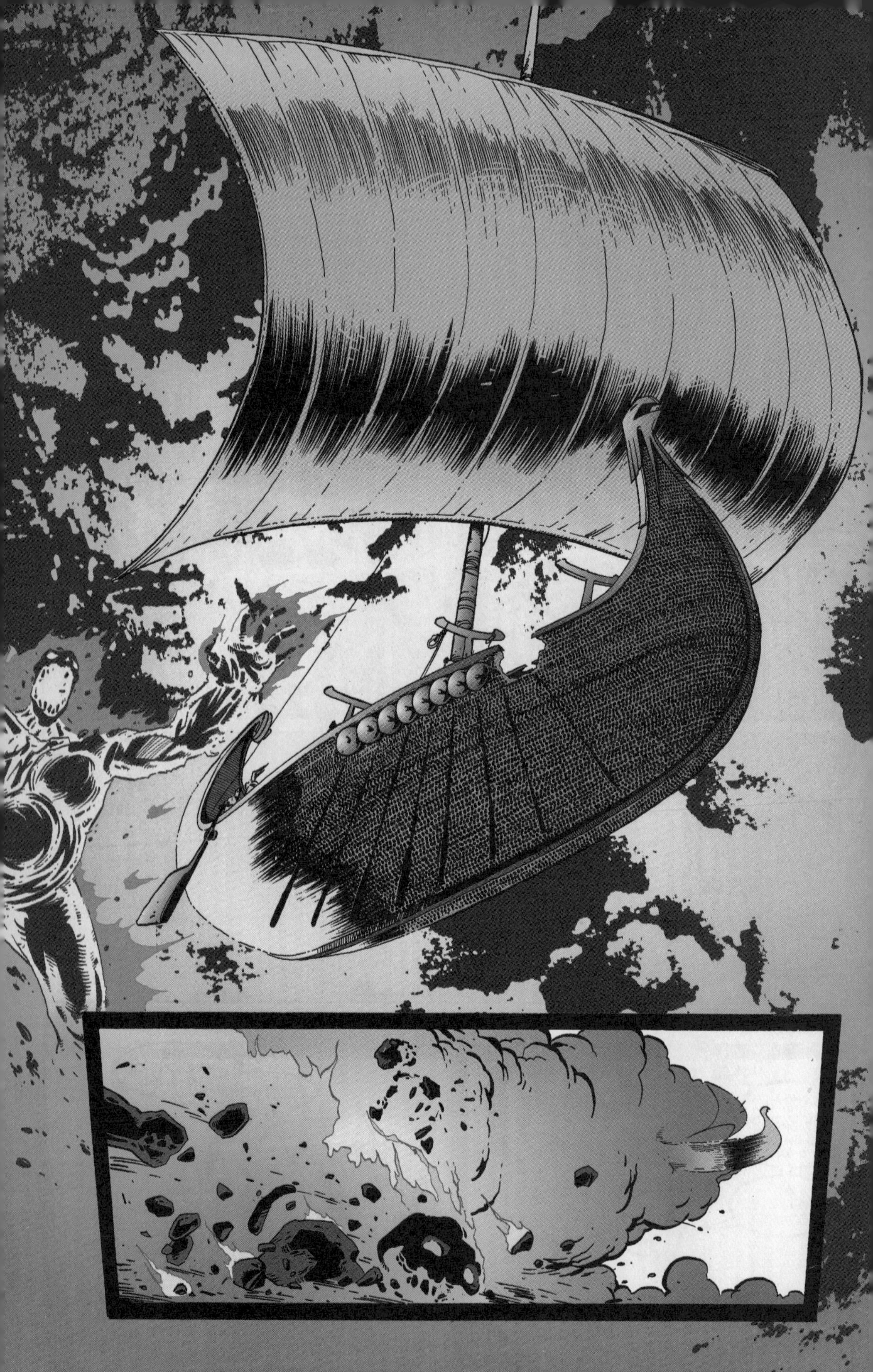

IT'S HARD TO TELL HIS ASSISTANCE FROM HIS *VENGEANCE*, ISN'T IT?

HE DID WHAT HE *NEEDED* TO.

SO, IS THERE A *NAUTICAL* TERM FOR WHAT JUST HAPPENED?

SHUT UP AND PUT THE *SAIL* OUT.

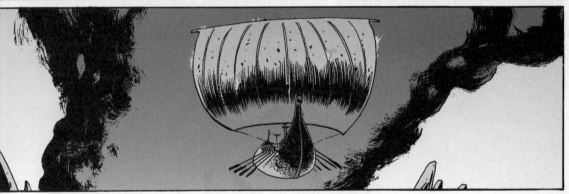

WHERE *EXACTLY* ARE WE GOING?

T...T...TO HEAVEN.

AND THEN ON B...BEYOND. FAR BEYOND.

THE MANSIONS OF THE S...S...

SILENCE.

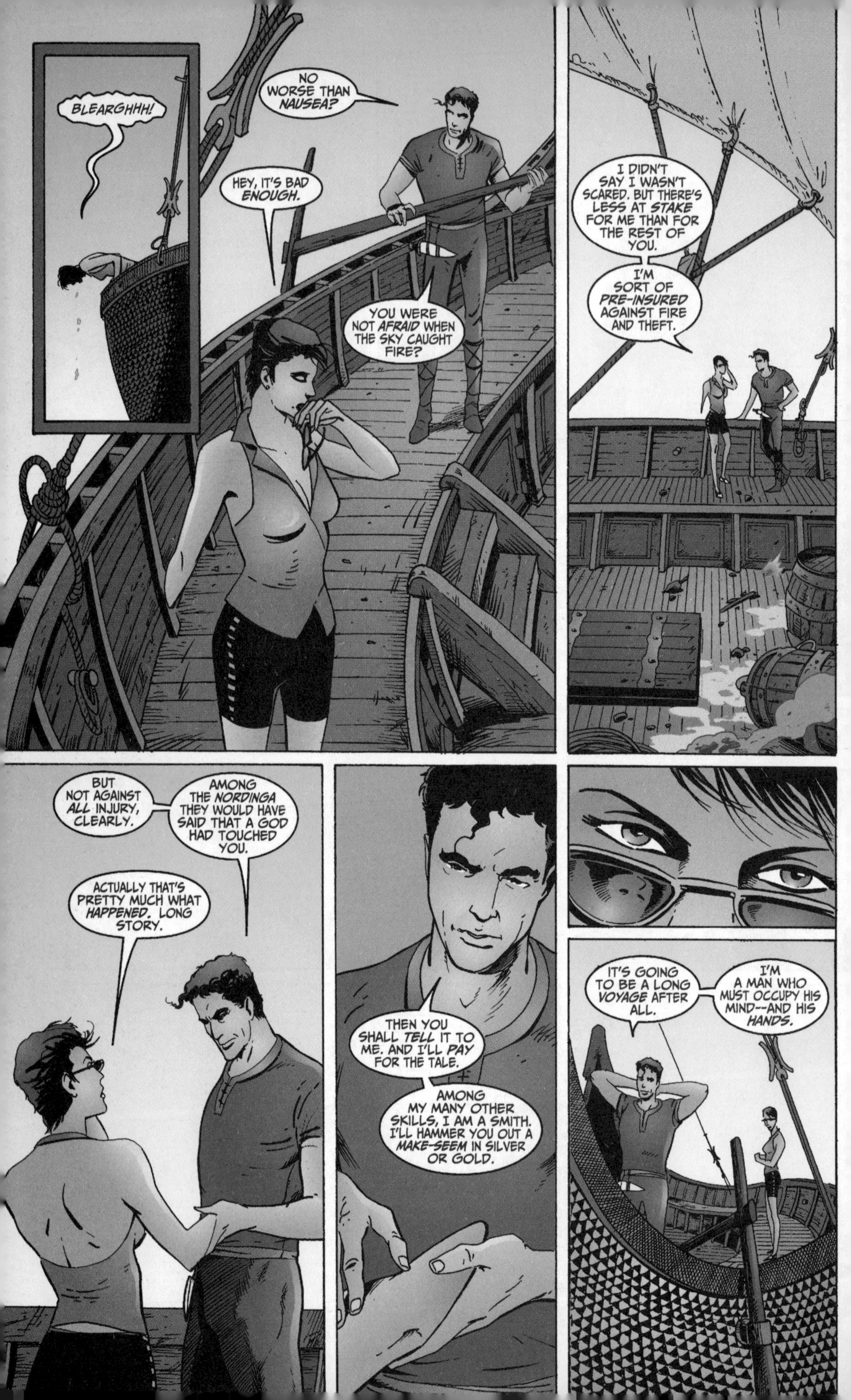
BLEARGHHH!
NO WORSE THAN NAUSEA?
HEY, IT'S BAD ENOUGH.
YOU WERE NOT AFRAID WHEN THE SKY CAUGHT FIRE?
I DIDN'T SAY I WASN'T SCARED. BUT THERE'S LESS AT STAKE FOR ME THAN FOR THE REST OF YOU.
I'M SORT OF PRE-INSURED AGAINST FIRE AND THEFT.
BUT NOT AGAINST ALL INJURY, CLEARLY.
AMONG THE NORDINGA THEY WOULD HAVE SAID THAT A GOD HAD TOUCHED YOU.
ACTUALLY THAT'S PRETTY MUCH WHAT HAPPENED. LONG STORY.
THEN YOU SHALL TELL IT TO ME. AND I'LL PAY FOR THE TALE.
AMONG MY MANY OTHER SKILLS, I AM A SMITH. I'LL HAMMER YOU OUT A MAKE-SEEM IN SILVER OR GOLD.
IT'S GOING TO BE A LONG VOYAGE AFTER ALL.
I'M A MAN WHO MUST OCCUPY HIS MIND--AND HIS HANDS.

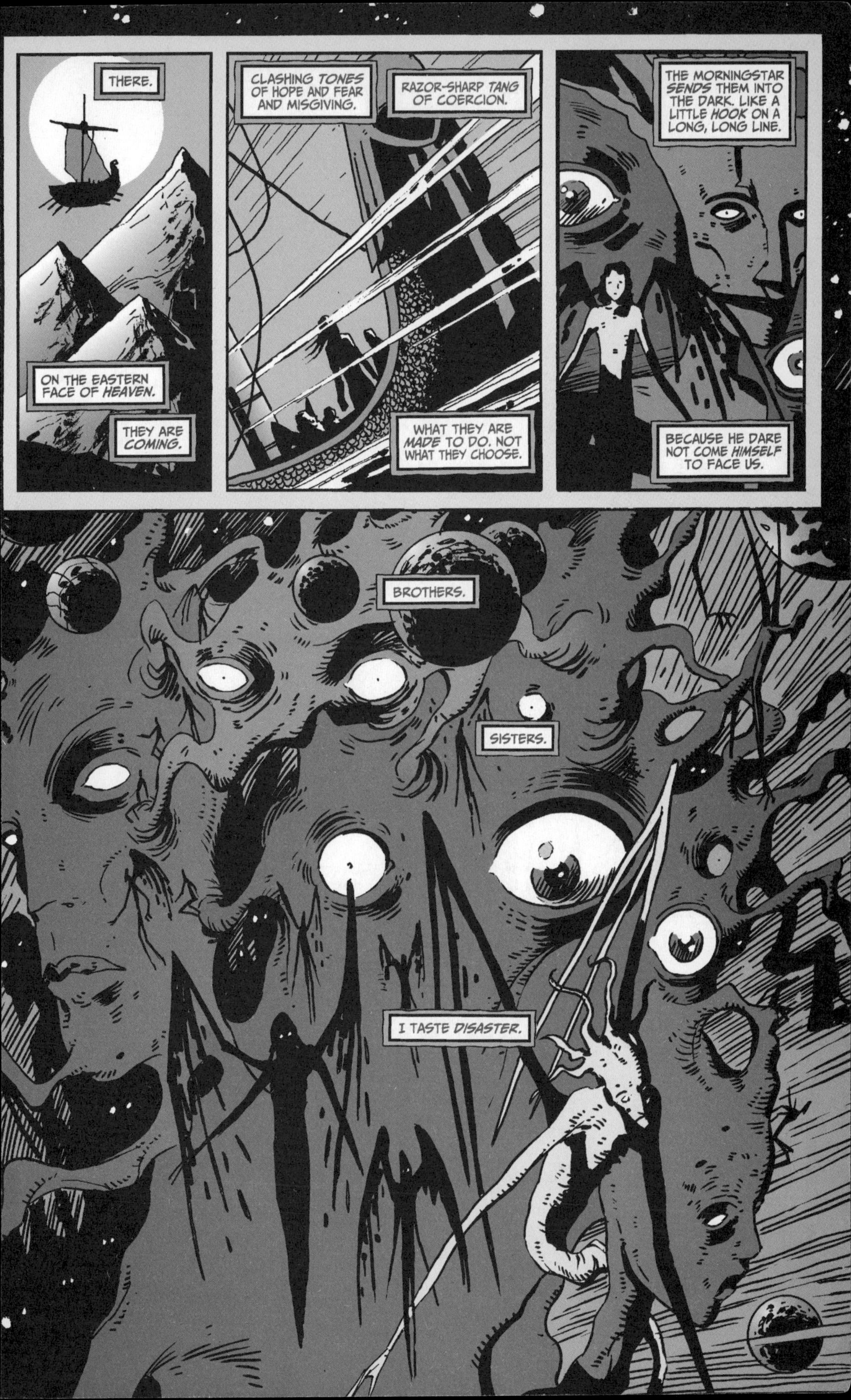
THERE.
ON THE EASTERN FACE OF HEAVEN.
THEY ARE COMING.
CLASHING TONES OF HOPE AND FEAR AND MISGIVING.
RAZOR-SHARP TANG OF COERCION.
WHAT THEY ARE MADE TO DO. NOT WHAT THEY CHOOSE.
THE MORNINGSTAR SENDS THEM INTO THE DARK. LIKE A LITTLE HOOK ON A LONG, LONG LINE.
BECAUSE HE DARE NOT COME HIMSELF TO FACE US.
BROTHERS.
SISTERS.
I TASTE DISASTER.

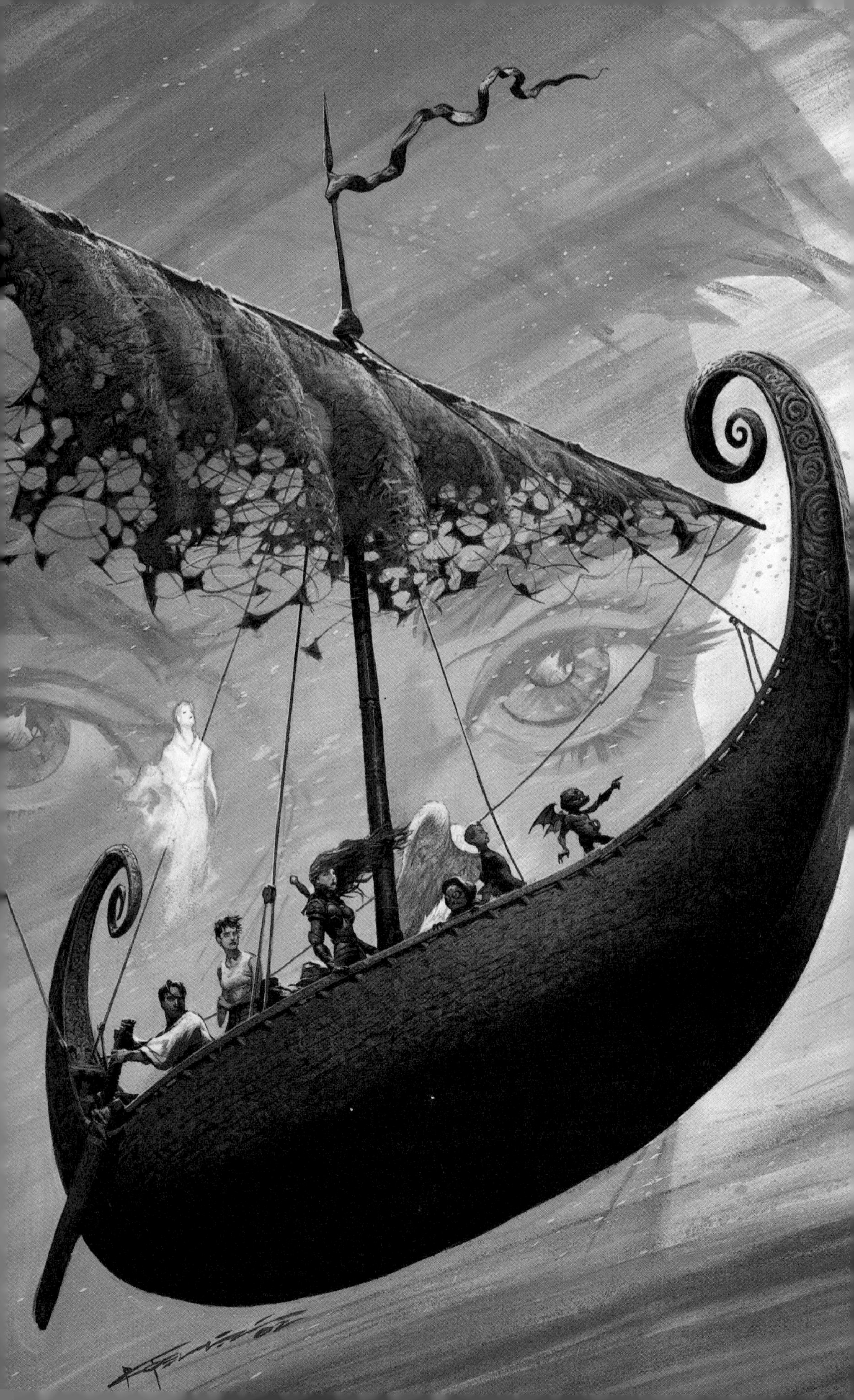

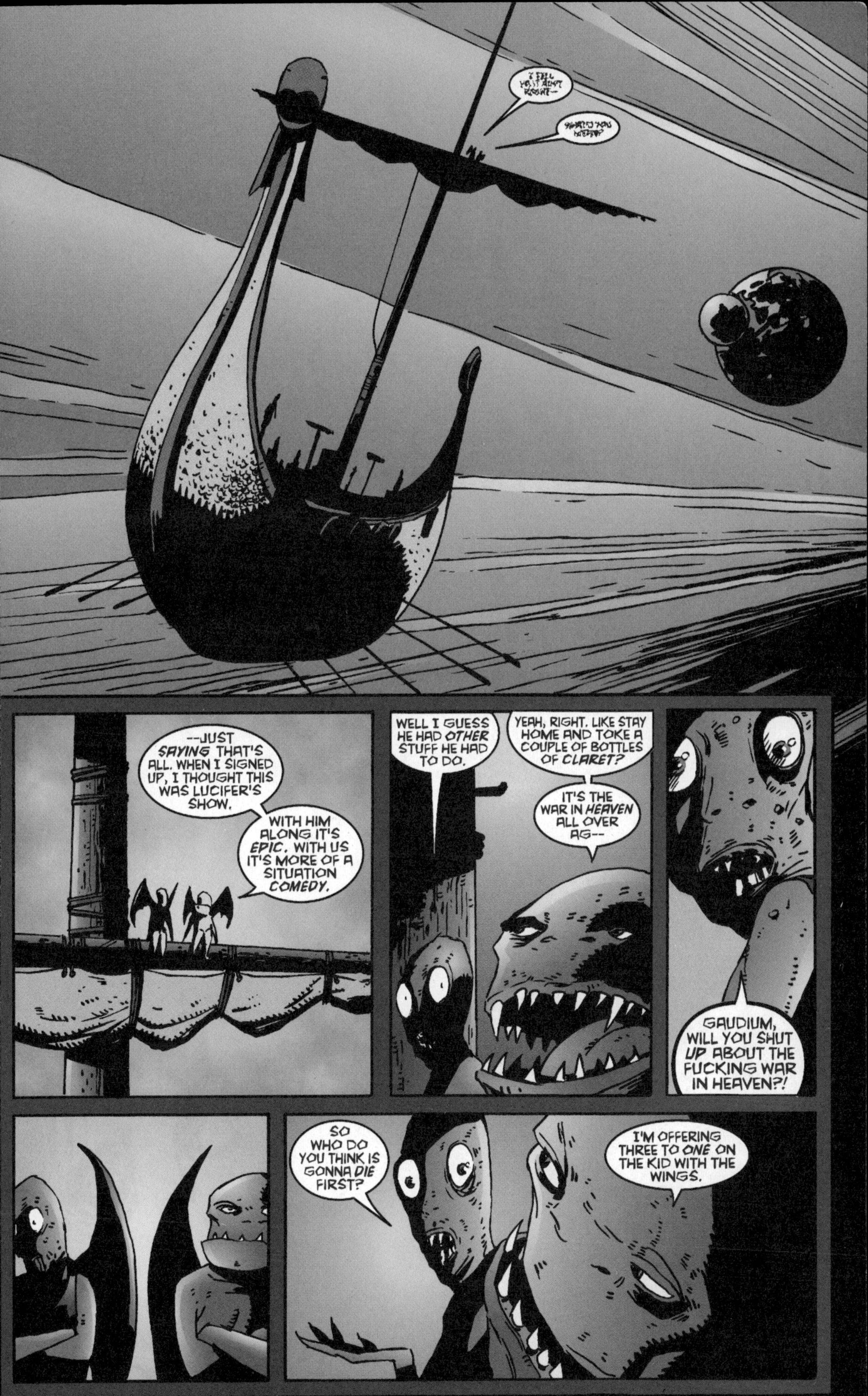
--JUST SAYING THAT'S ALL. WHEN I SIGNED UP, I THOUGHT THIS WAS LUCIFER'S SHOW.
WITH HIM ALONG IT'S EPIC. WITH US IT'S MORE OF A SITUATION COMEDY.
WELL I GUESS HE HAD OTHER STUFF HE HAD TO DO.
YEAH, RIGHT. LIKE STAY HOME AND TOKE A COUPLE OF BOTTLES OF CLARET?
IT'S THE WAR IN HEAVEN ALL OVER AG--
GAUDIUM, WILL YOU SHUT UP ABOUT THE FUCKING WAR IN HEAVEN?!
SO WHO DO YOU THINK IS GONNA DIE FIRST?
I'M OFFERING THREE TO ONE ON THE KID WITH THE WINGS.

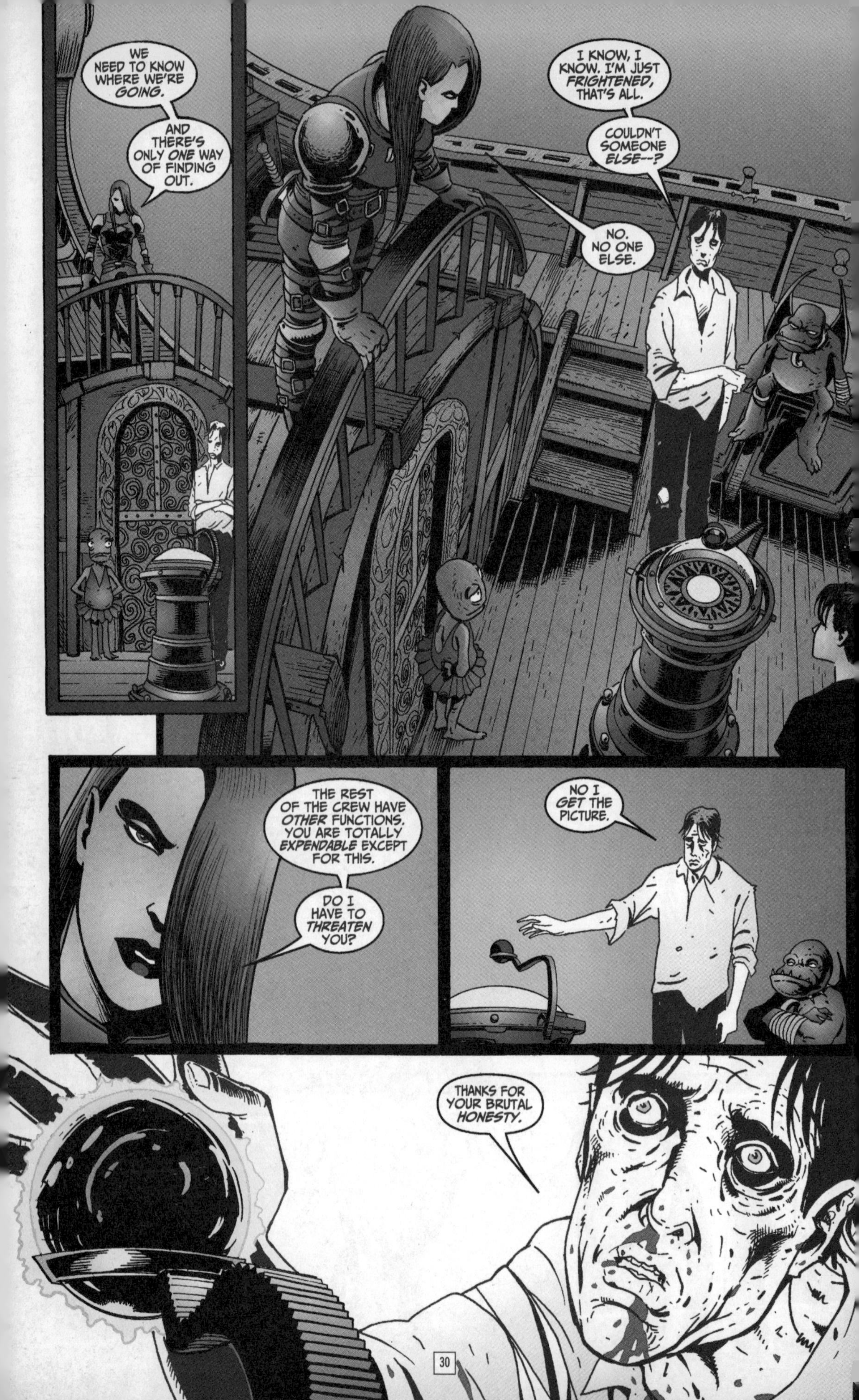

WE NEED TO KNOW WHERE WE'RE GOING.
AND THERE'S ONLY ONE WAY OF FINDING OUT.
I KNOW, I KNOW. I'M JUST FRIGHTENED, THAT'S ALL.
COULDN'T SOMEONE ELSE--?
NO. NO ONE ELSE.
THE REST OF THE CREW HAVE OTHER FUNCTIONS. YOU ARE TOTALLY EXPENDABLE EXCEPT FOR THIS.
DO I HAVE TO THREATEN YOU?
NO I GET THE PICTURE.
THANKS FOR YOUR BRUTAL HONESTY.

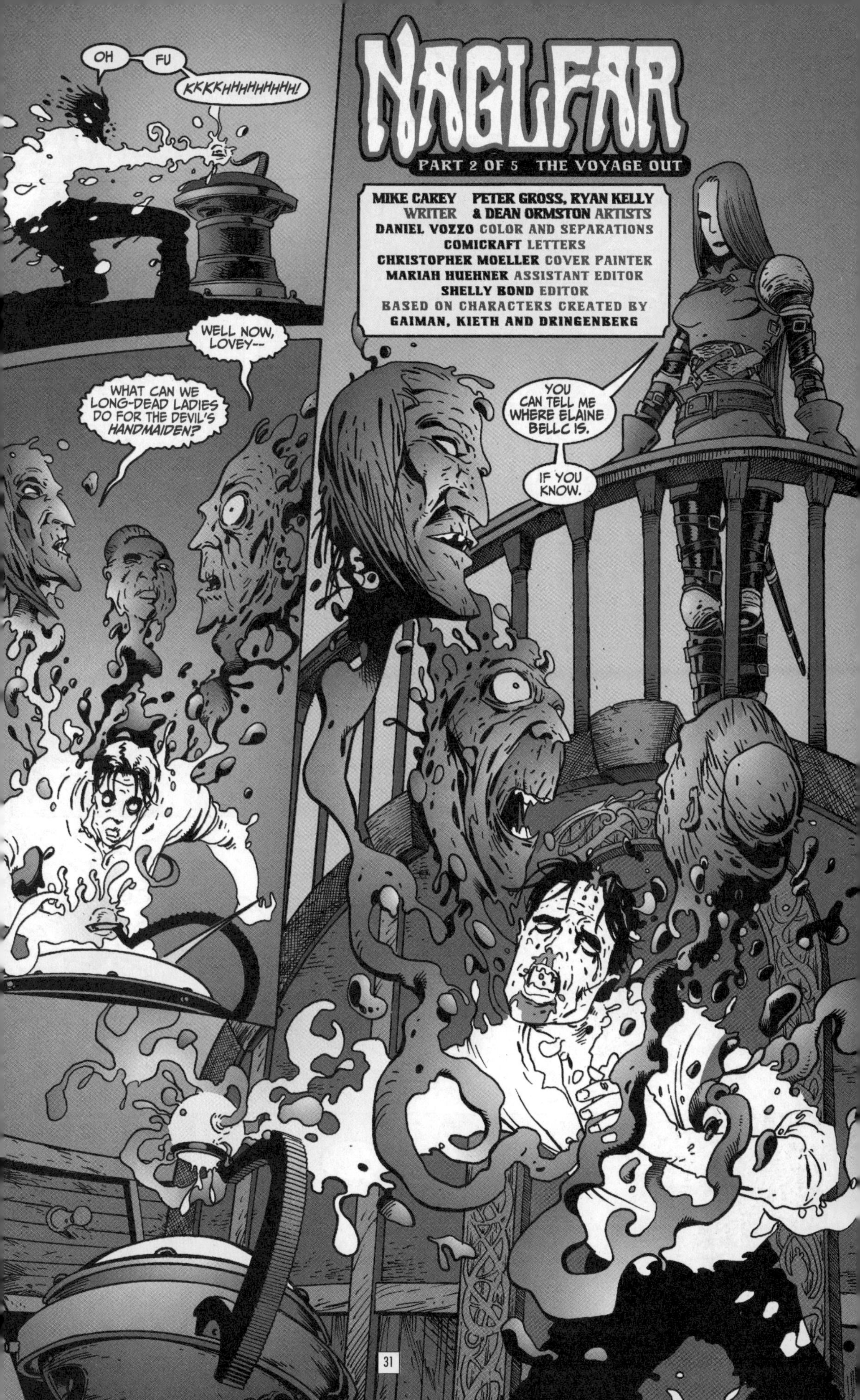

OH
FU
KKKKHHHHHHHHHH!
NAGLFAR
PART 2 OF 5 THE VOYAGE OUT
MIKE CAREY WRITER
PETER GROSS, RYAN KELLY & DEAN ORMSTON ARTISTS
DANIEL VOZZO COLOR AND SEPARATIONS
COMICRAFT LETTERS
CHRISTOPHER MOELLER COVER PAINTER
MARIAH HUEHNER ASSISTANT EDITOR
SHELLY BOND EDITOR
BASED ON CHARACTERS CREATED BY GAIMAN, KIETH AND DRINGENBERG
WELL NOW, LOVEY--
WHAT CAN WE LONG-DEAD LADIES DO FOR THE DEVIL'S HANDMAIDEN?
YOU CAN TELL ME WHERE ELAINE BELLC IS.
IF YOU KNOW.

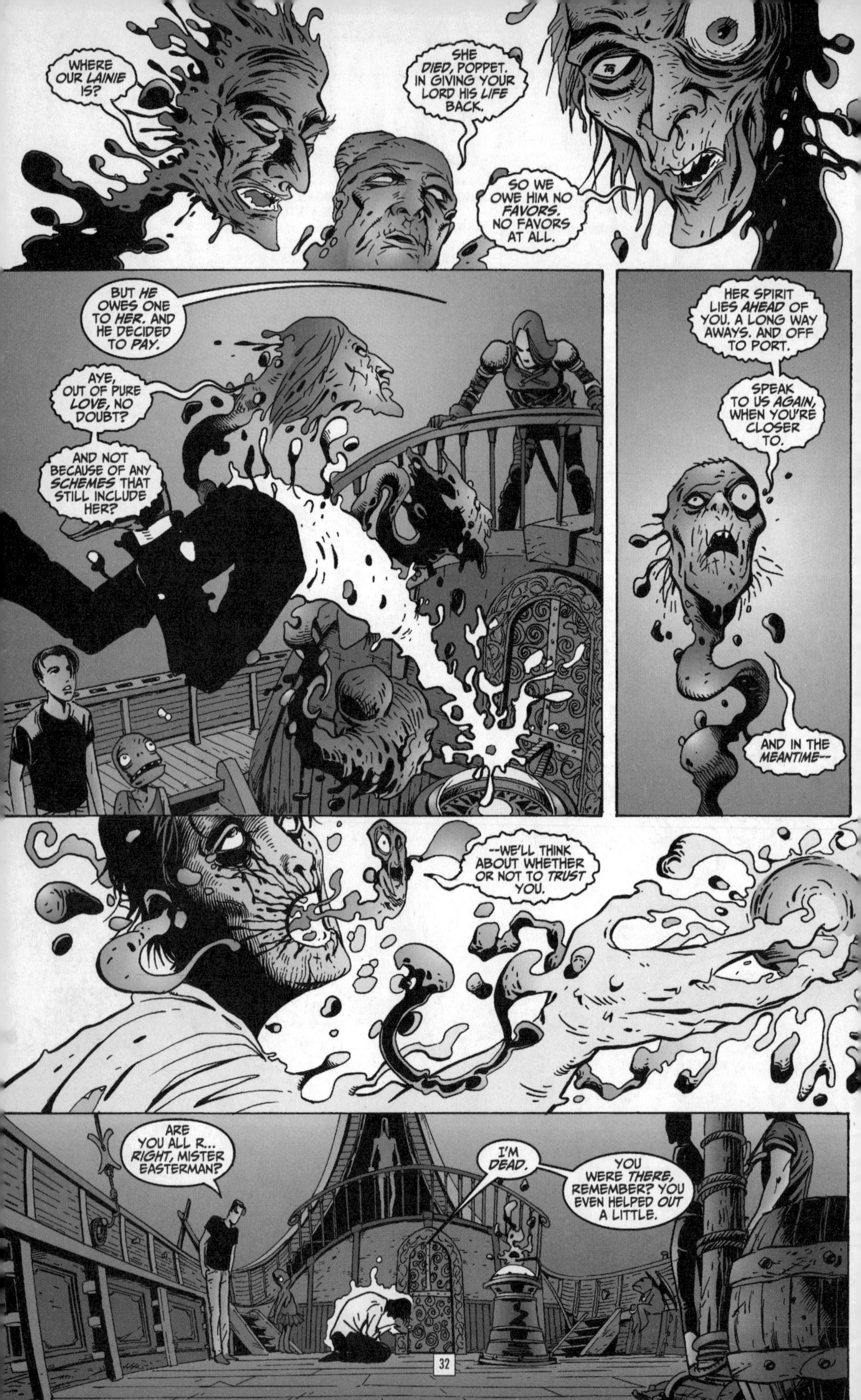
WHERE OUR LAINIE IS?
SHE DIED, POPPET. IN GIVING YOUR LORD HIS LIFE BACK.
SO WE OWE HIM NO FAVORS. NO FAVORS AT ALL.
BUT HE OWES ONE TO HER. AND HE DECIDED TO PAY.
AYE, OUT OF PURE LOVE, NO DOUBT?
AND NOT BECAUSE OF ANY SCHEMES THAT STILL INCLUDE HER?
HER SPIRIT LIES AHEAD OF YOU. A LONG WAY AWAYS. AND OFF TO PORT.
SPEAK TO US AGAIN, WHEN YOU'RE CLOSER TO.
AND IN THE MEANTIME--
--WE'LL THINK ABOUT WHETHER OR NOT TO TRUST YOU.
ARE YOU ALL R... RIGHT, MISTER EASTERMAN?
I'M DEAD.
YOU WERE THERE, REMEMBER? YOU EVEN HELPED OUT A LITTLE.

YOU'VE A TENDENCY TO *FLINCH* FROM OUR BOLD CAPTAIN, SWEETING.

I ASSUME YOU'VE CROSSED PATHS *BEFORE.*

YEAH, SHE WANTS TO KILL ME. ONLY THERE'S SOMETHING *INSIDE* ME KEEPING ME SAFE. SHE HAS TO WAIT UNTIL I *DITCH* IT.

WHICH IS WHY I'M *HERE.*

JUST WISH I KNEW WHERE THE FUCK HERE *IS.*

WELL, I'VE A *SUPERSTITION* ABOUT WOMEN'S WISHES. SO HERE NOW--

--YOU'RE FAMILIAR WITH HEAVEN AND *HELL,* ARE YOU NOT?

I'VE HEARD OF 'EM.

EXCELLENT PLACES BOTH. BUT ESSENTIALLY--IF YOU'LL PARDON THE *BANALITY* OF THE METAPHOR-- TWO FACES OF THE SAME COIN.

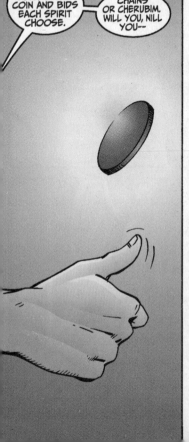

AND GOD *FLICKS* THE COIN AND BIDS EACH SPIRIT CHOOSE.

CHAINS OR CHERUBIM. WILL YOU, NILL YOU--

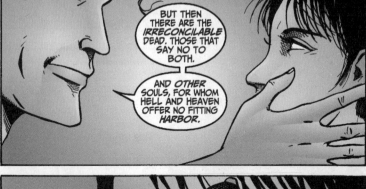

BUT THEN THERE ARE THE *IRRECONCILABLE* DEAD. THOSE THAT SAY NO TO BOTH.

AND *OTHER* SOULS, FOR WHOM HELL AND HEAVEN OFFER NO FITTING *HARBOR.*

THE *EDGE* OF THE COIN, SWEETING.

*THAT* IS WHERE WE SAIL.

33

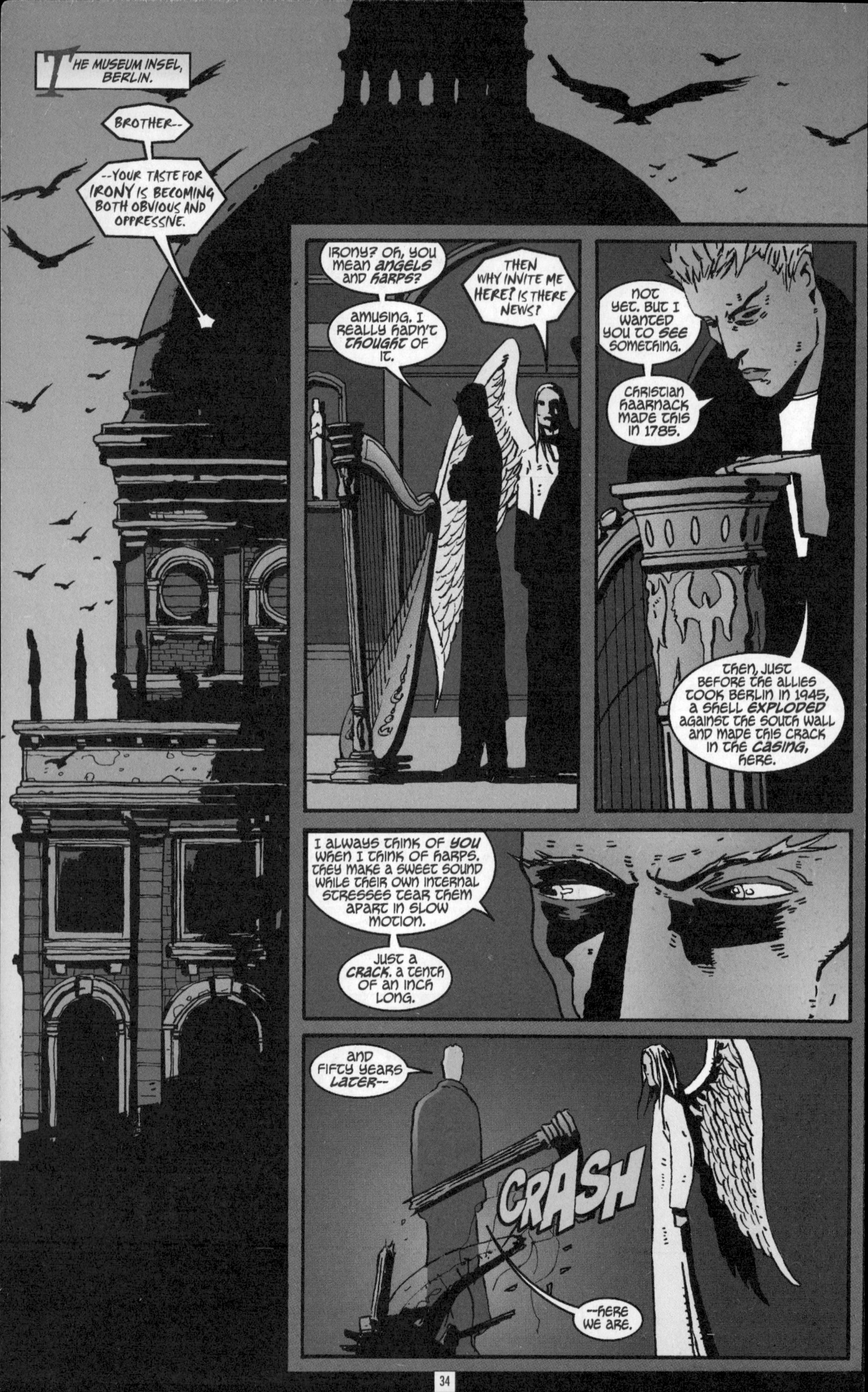
THE MUSEUM INSEL, BERLIN.
BROTHER--
--YOUR TASTE FOR IRONY IS BECOMING BOTH OBVIOUS AND OPPRESSIVE.
IRONY? OH, YOU MEAN ANGELS AND HARPS?
AMUSING. I REALLY HADN'T THOUGHT OF IT.
THEN WHY INVITE ME HERE? IS THERE NEWS?
NOT YET. BUT I WANTED YOU TO SEE SOMETHING.
CHRISTIAN HAARNACK MADE THIS IN 1785.
THEN, JUST BEFORE THE ALLIES TOOK BERLIN IN 1945, A SHELL EXPLODED AGAINST THE SOUTH WALL AND MADE THIS CRACK IN THE CASING, HERE.
I ALWAYS THINK OF YOU WHEN I THINK OF HARPS. THEY MAKE A SWEET SOUND WHILE THEIR OWN INTERNAL STRESSES TEAR THEM APART IN SLOW MOTION.
JUST A CRACK, A TENTH OF AN INCH LONG.
AND FIFTY YEARS LATER--
CRASH
--HERE WE ARE.

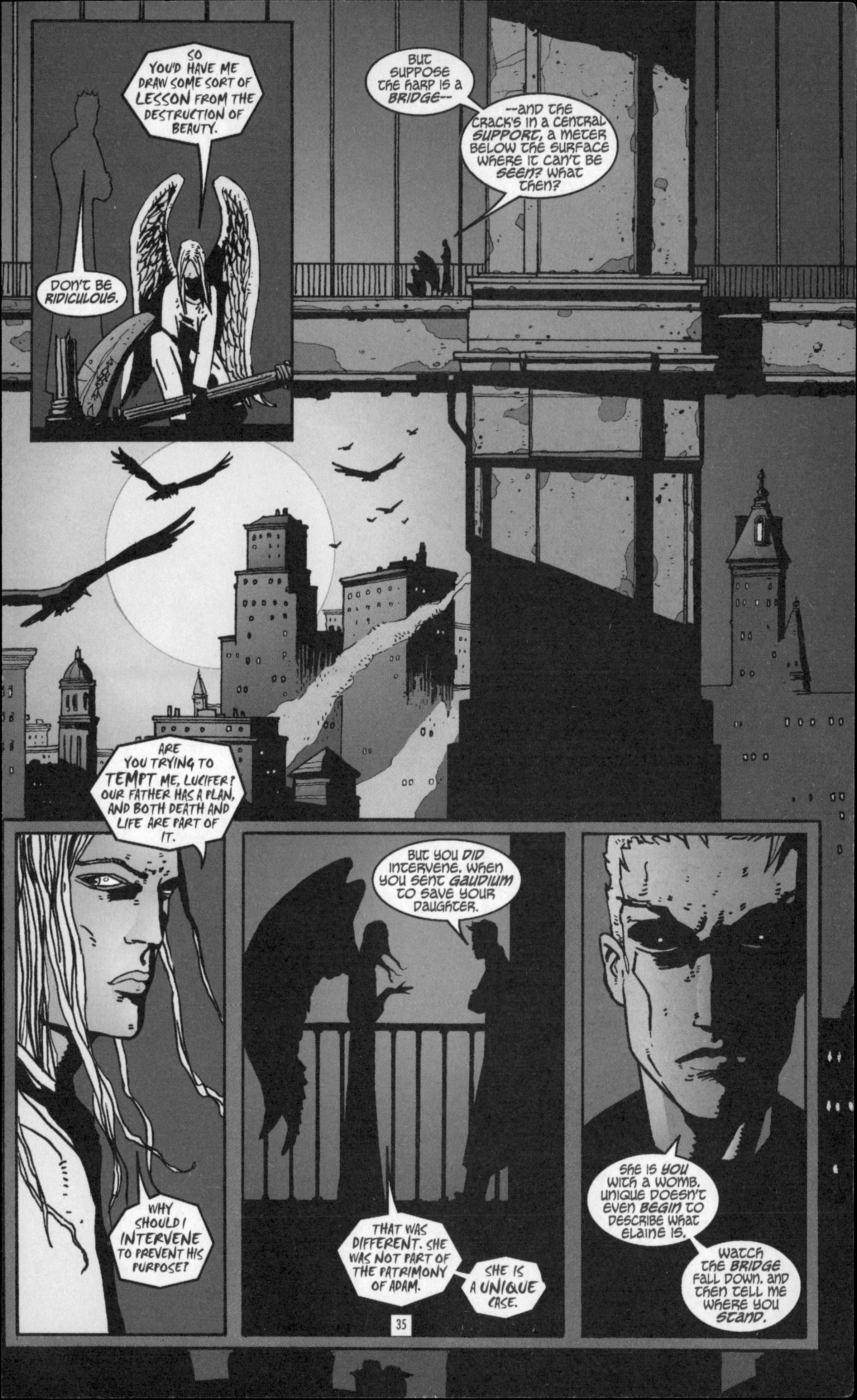
SO YOU'D HAVE ME DRAW SOME SORT OF LESSON FROM THE DESTRUCTION OF BEAUTY.
DON'T BE RIDICULOUS.
BUT SUPPOSE THE HARP IS A BRIDGE--
--AND THE CRACK'S IN A CENTRAL SUPPORT, A METER BELOW THE SURFACE WHERE IT CAN'T BE SEEN? WHAT THEN?
ARE YOU TRYING TO TEMPT ME, LUCIFER? OUR FATHER HAS A PLAN, AND BOTH DEATH AND LIFE ARE PART OF IT.
WHY SHOULD I INTERVENE TO PREVENT HIS PURPOSE?
BUT YOU DID INTERVENE. WHEN YOU SENT GAUDIUM TO SAVE YOUR DAUGHTER.
THAT WAS DIFFERENT. SHE WAS NOT PART OF THE PATRIMONY OF ADAM.
SHE IS A UNIQUE CASE.
SHE IS YOU WITH A WOMB. UNIQUE DOESN'T EVEN BEGIN TO DESCRIBE WHAT ELAINE IS.
WATCH THE BRIDGE FALL DOWN, AND THEN TELL ME WHERE YOU STAND.

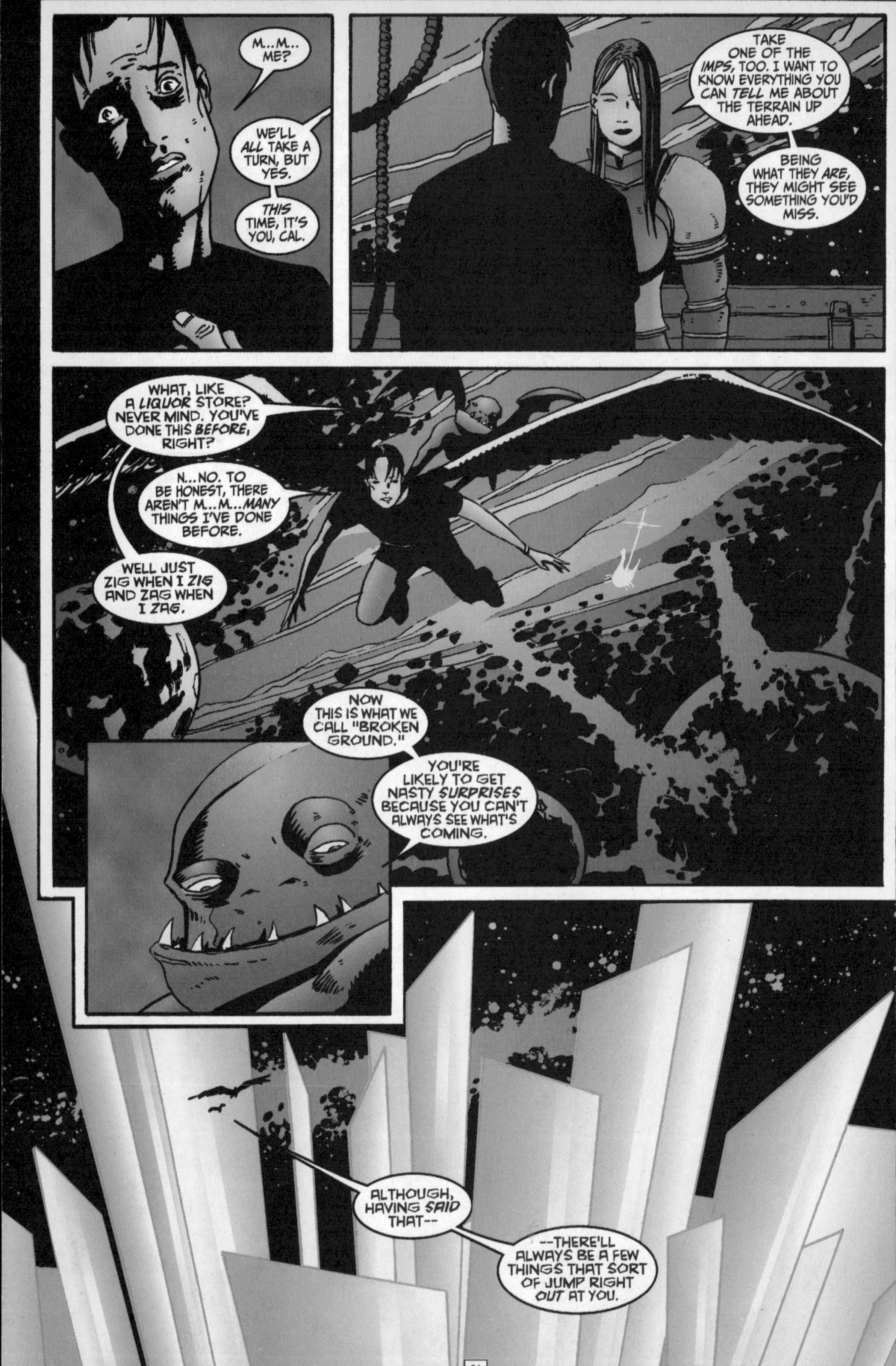
M...M... ME?
WE'LL ALL TAKE A TURN, BUT YES.
THIS TIME, IT'S YOU, CAL.
TAKE ONE OF THE IMPS, TOO. I WANT TO KNOW EVERYTHING YOU CAN TELL ME ABOUT THE TERRAIN UP AHEAD.
BEING WHAT THEY ARE, THEY MIGHT SEE SOMETHING YOU'D MISS.
WHAT, LIKE A LIQUOR STORE? NEVER MIND. YOU'VE DONE THIS BEFORE, RIGHT?
N...NO. TO BE HONEST, THERE AREN'T M...M...MANY THINGS I'VE DONE BEFORE.
WELL JUST ZIG WHEN I ZIG AND ZAG WHEN I ZAG.
NOW THIS IS WHAT WE CALL "BROKEN GROUND."
YOU'RE LIKELY TO GET NASTY SURPRISES BECAUSE YOU CAN'T ALWAYS SEE WHAT'S COMING.
ALTHOUGH, HAVING SAID THAT--
--THERE'LL ALWAYS BE A FEW THINGS THAT SORT OF JUMP RIGHT OUT AT YOU.

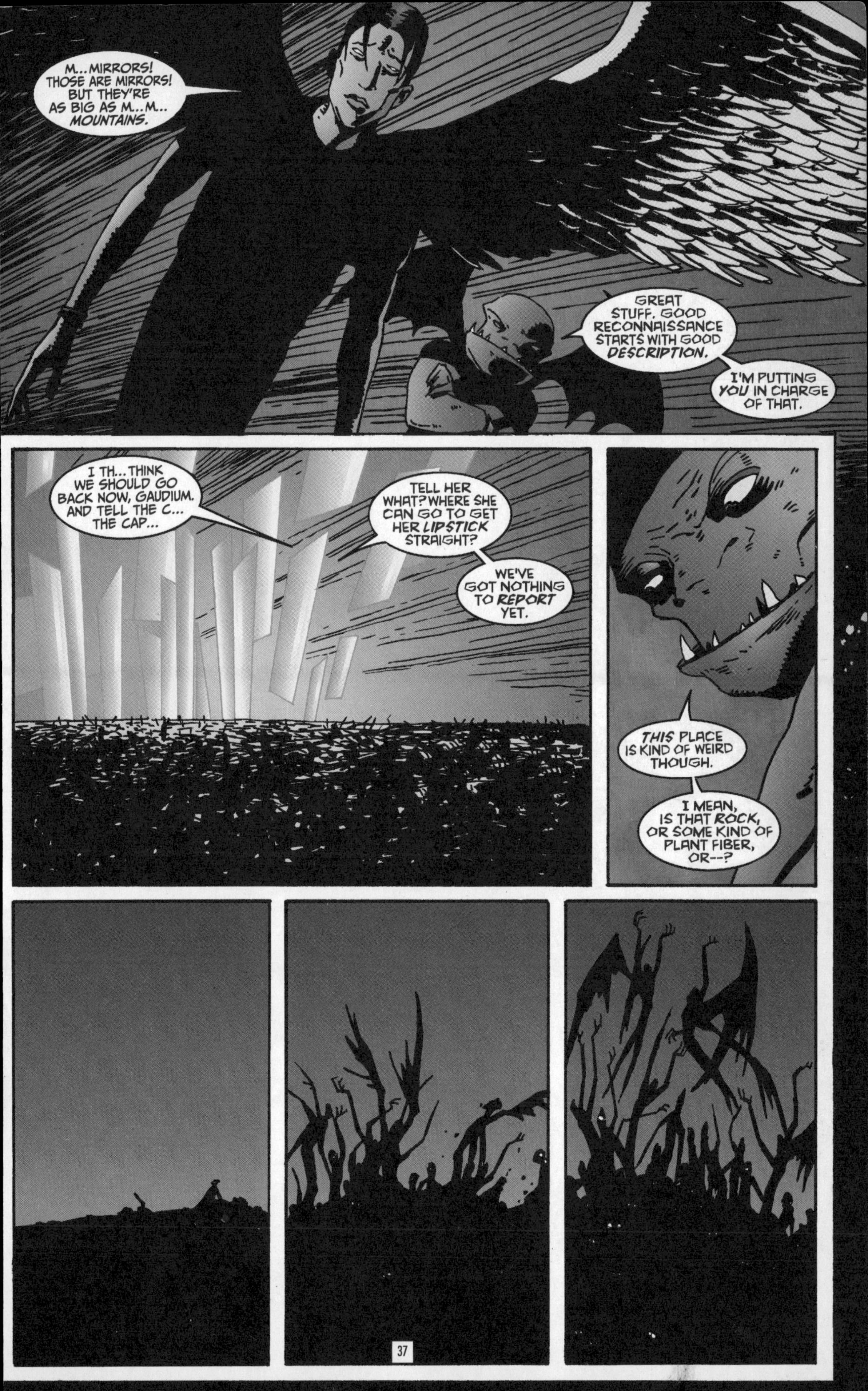

M...MIRRORS! THOSE ARE MIRRORS! BUT THEY'RE AS BIG AS M...M... MOUNTAINS.
GREAT STUFF. GOOD RECONNAISSANCE STARTS WITH GOOD DESCRIPTION.
I'M PUTTING YOU IN CHARGE OF THAT.
I TH...THINK WE SHOULD GO BACK NOW, GAUDIUM. AND TELL THE C... THE CAP...
TELL HER WHAT? WHERE SHE CAN GO TO GET HER LIPSTICK STRAIGHT?
WE'VE GOT NOTHING TO REPORT YET.
THIS PLACE IS KIND OF WEIRD THOUGH.
I MEAN, IS THAT ROCK, OR SOME KIND OF PLANT FIBER, OR--?

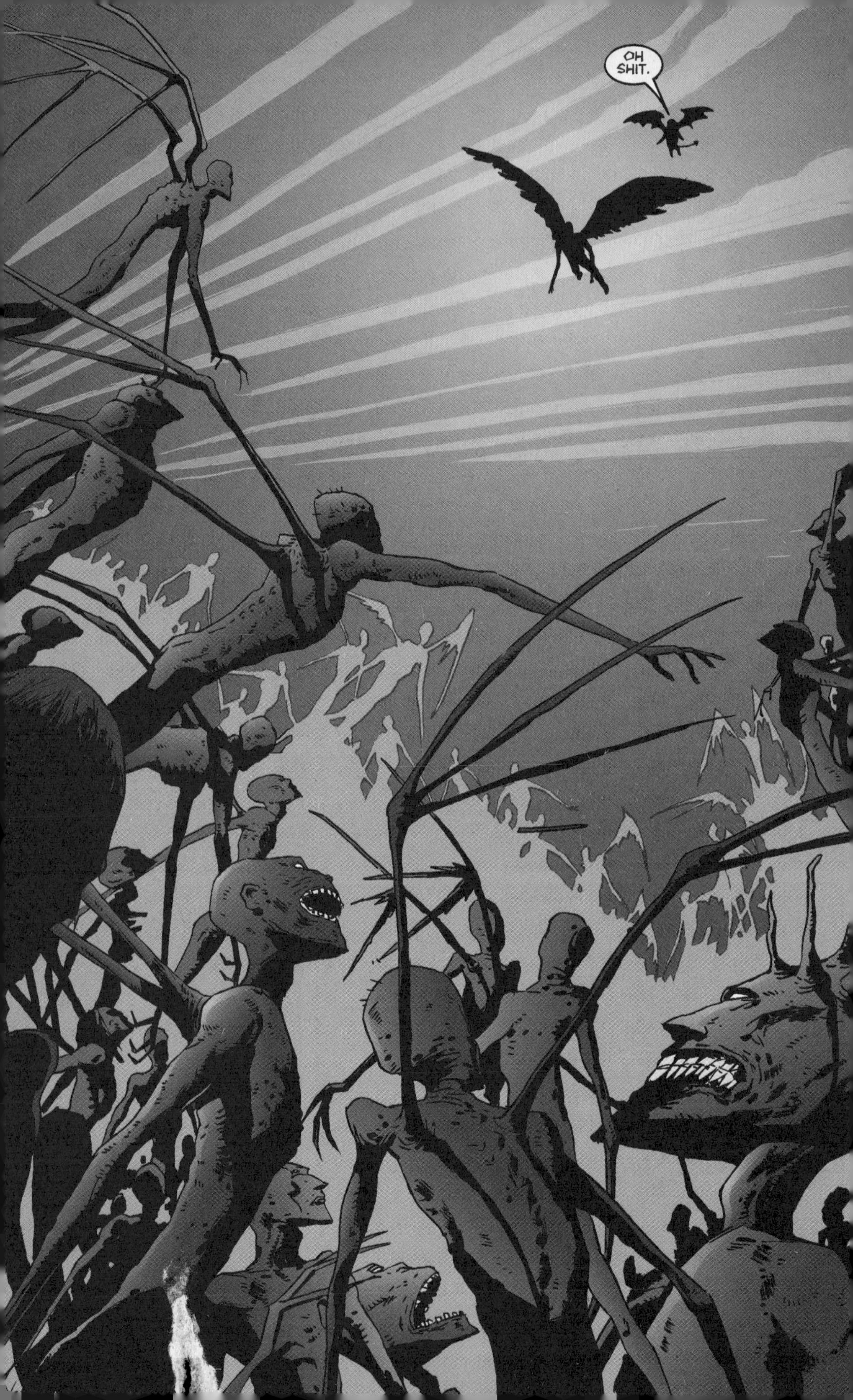
OH SHIT.

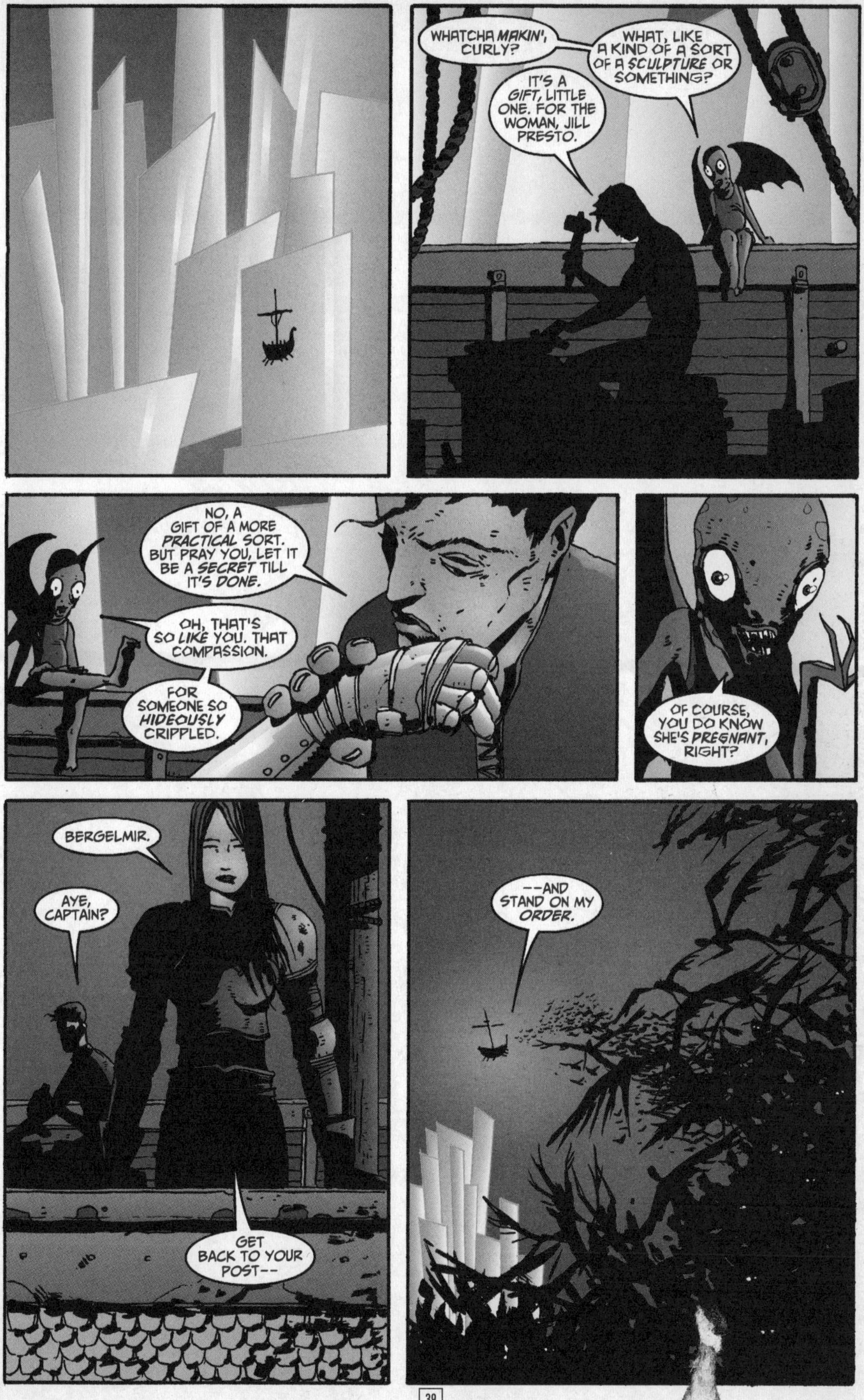

WHATCHA MAKIN', CURLY?
WHAT, LIKE A KIND OF A SORT OF A SCULPTURE OR SOMETHING?
IT'S A GIFT, LITTLE ONE. FOR THE WOMAN, JILL PRESTO.
NO, A GIFT OF A MORE PRACTICAL SORT. BUT PRAY YOU, LET IT BE A SECRET TILL IT'S DONE.
OH, THAT'S SO LIKE YOU. THAT COMPASSION.
FOR SOMEONE SO HIDEOUSLY CRIPPLED.
OF COURSE, YOU DO KNOW SHE'S PREGNANT, RIGHT?
BERGELMIR.
AYE, CAPTAIN?
GET BACK TO YOUR POST--
--AND STAND ON MY ORDER.

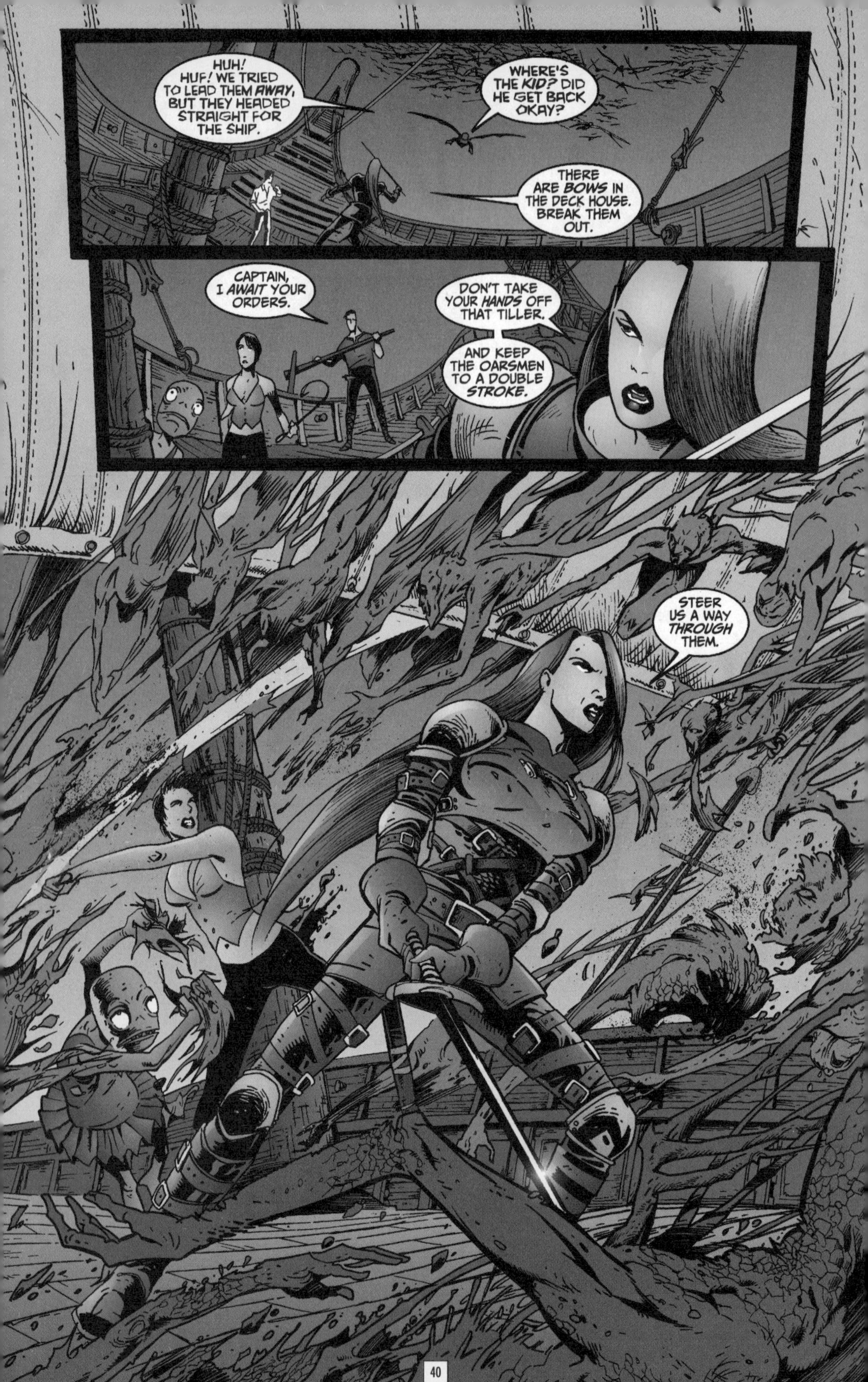
HUH! HUF! WE TRIED TO LEAD THEM *AWAY*, BUT THEY HEADED STRAIGHT FOR THE SHIP.
WHERE'S THE *KID?* DID HE GET BACK OKAY?
THERE ARE *BOWS* IN THE DECK HOUSE. BREAK THEM OUT.
CAPTAIN, I *AWAIT* YOUR ORDERS.
DON'T TAKE YOUR *HANDS* OFF THAT TILLER.
AND KEEP THE OARSMEN TO A DOUBLE *STROKE*.
STEER US A WAY *THROUGH* THEM.

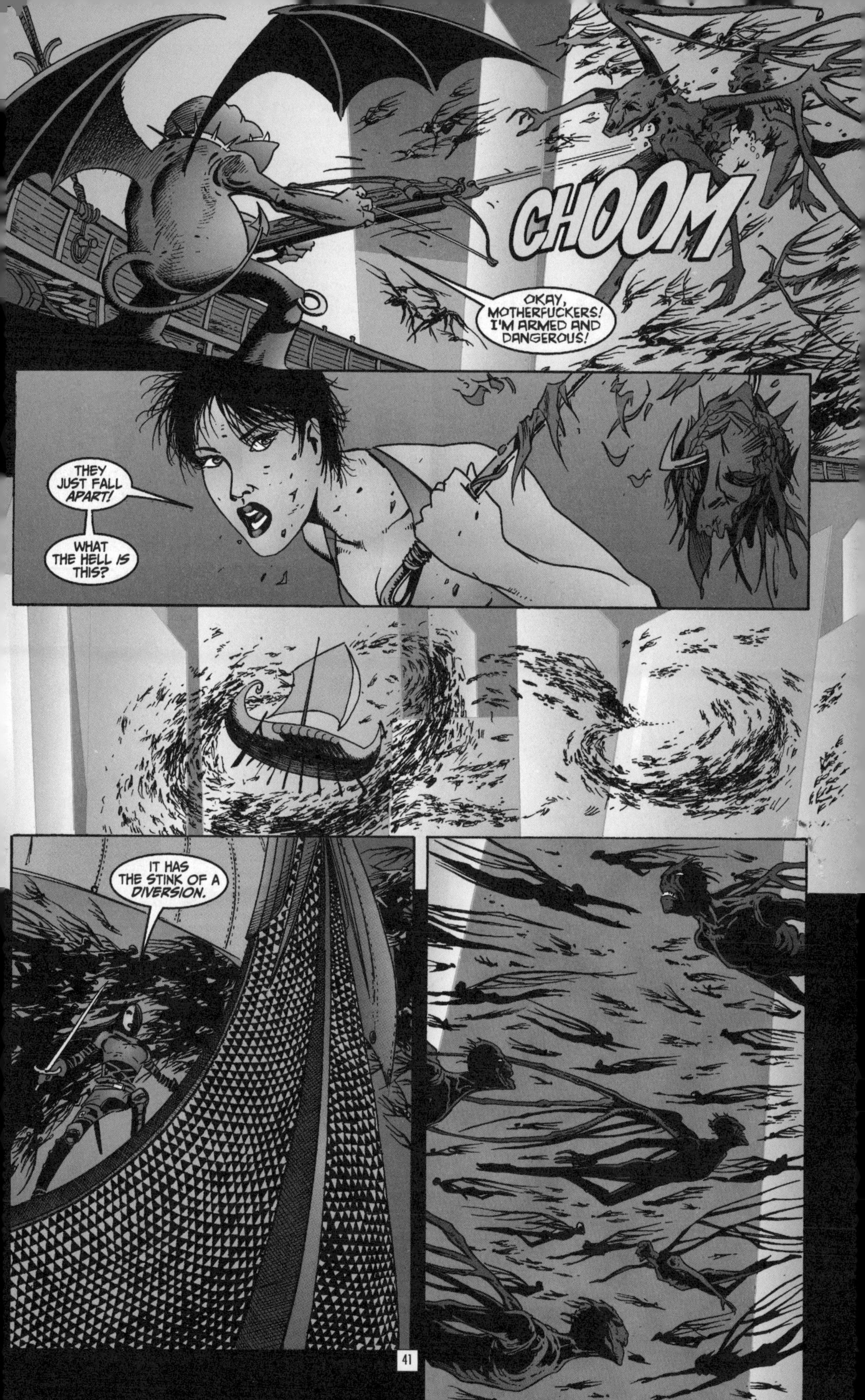
CHOOM
OKAY, MOTHERFUCKERS! I'M ARMED AND DANGEROUS!
THEY JUST FALL APART!
WHAT THE HELL IS THIS?
IT HAS THE STINK OF A DIVERSION.

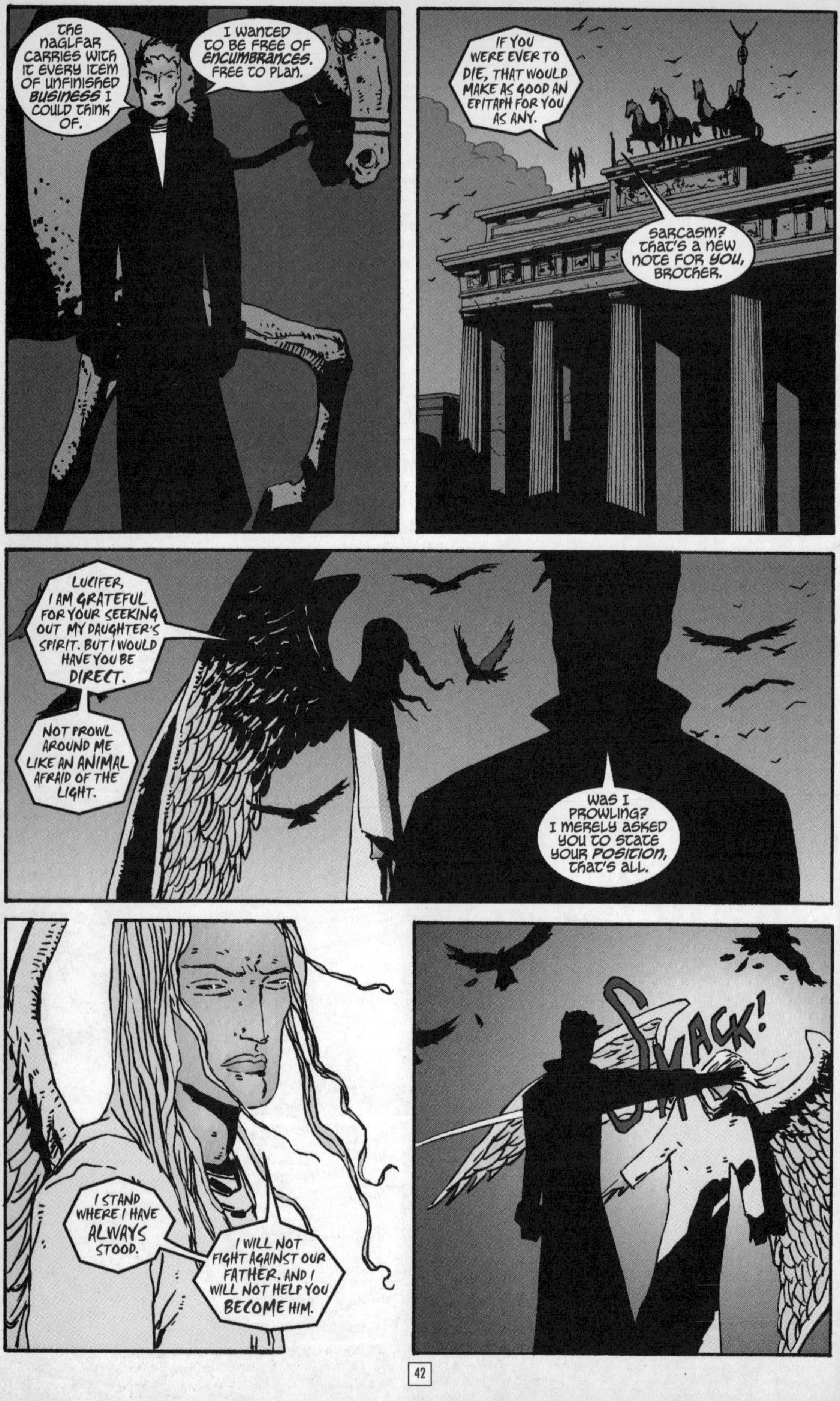
THE NAGLFAR CARRIES WITH IT EVERY ITEM OF UNFINISHED BUSINESS I COULD THINK OF.
I WANTED TO BE FREE OF ENCUMBRANCES. FREE TO PLAN.
IF YOU WERE EVER TO DIE, THAT WOULD MAKE AS GOOD AN EPITAPH FOR YOU AS ANY.
SARCASM? THAT'S A NEW NOTE FOR YOU, BROTHER.
LUCIFER, I AM GRATEFUL FOR YOUR SEEKING OUT MY DAUGHTER'S SPIRIT. BUT I WOULD HAVE YOU BE DIRECT.
NOT PROWL AROUND ME LIKE AN ANIMAL AFRAID OF THE LIGHT.
WAS I PROWLING? I MERELY ASKED YOU TO STATE YOUR POSITION, THAT'S ALL.
I STAND WHERE I HAVE ALWAYS STOOD.
I WILL NOT FIGHT AGAINST OUR FATHER. AND I WILL NOT HELP YOU BECOME HIM.
SMACK!

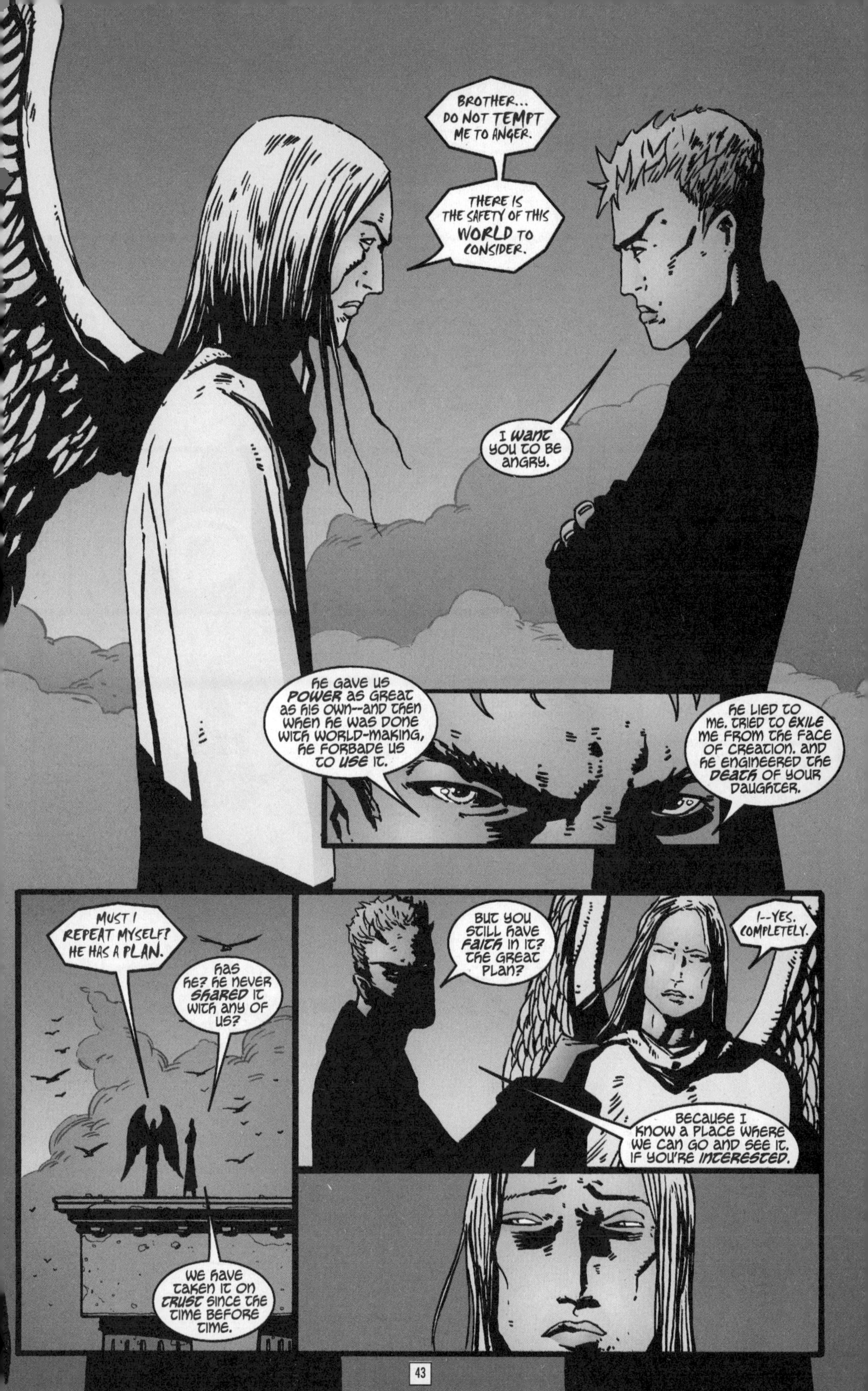
BROTHER... DO NOT TEMPT ME TO ANGER.
THERE IS THE SAFETY OF THIS WORLD TO CONSIDER.
I WANT YOU TO BE ANGRY.
HE GAVE US POWER AS GREAT AS HIS OWN--AND THEN WHEN HE WAS DONE WITH WORLD-MAKING, HE FORBADE US TO USE IT.
HE LIED TO ME. TRIED TO EXILE ME FROM THE FACE OF CREATION. AND HE ENGINEERED THE DEATH OF YOUR DAUGHTER.
MUST I REPEAT MYSELF? HE HAS A PLAN.
HAS HE? HE NEVER SHARED IT WITH ANY OF US?
WE HAVE TAKEN IT ON TRUST SINCE THE TIME BEFORE TIME.
BUT YOU STILL HAVE FAITH IN IT? THE GREAT PLAN?
I--YES. COMPLETELY.
BECAUSE I KNOW A PLACE WHERE WE CAN GO AND SEE IT. IF YOU'RE INTERESTED.

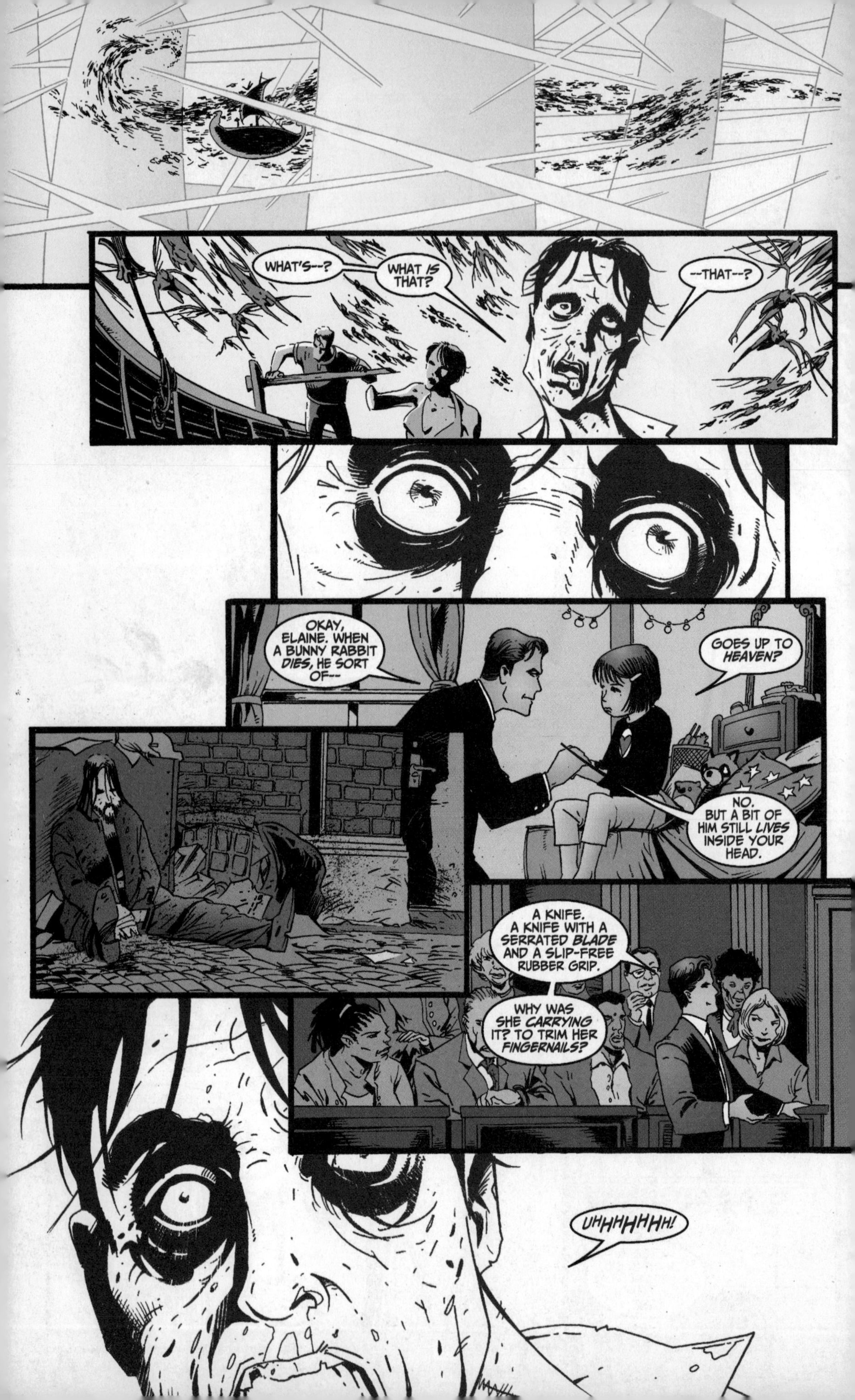
WHAT'S--?
WHAT *IS* THAT?
--THAT--?
OKAY, ELAINE. WHEN A BUNNY RABBIT *DIES,* HE SORT OF--
GOES UP TO *HEAVEN?*
NO. BUT A BIT OF HIM STILL *LIVES* INSIDE YOUR HEAD.
A KNIFE. A KNIFE WITH A SERRATED *BLADE* AND A SLIP-FREE RUBBER GRIP.
WHY WAS SHE *CARRYING* IT? TO TRIM HER *FINGERNAILS?*
UHHHHHHH!

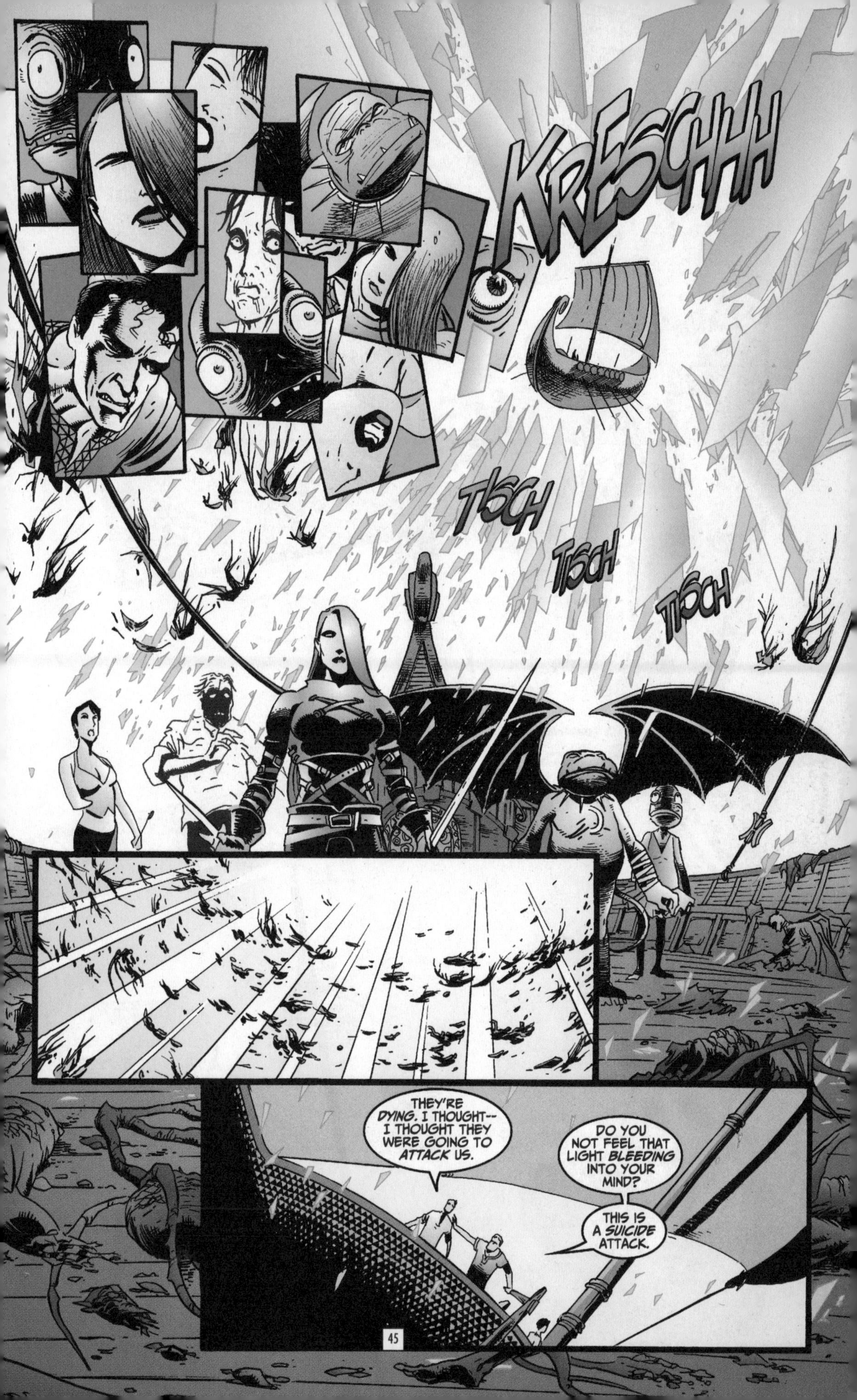
KRESCHH
TISCH
TISCH
TISCH
THEY'RE DYING. I THOUGHT-- I THOUGHT THEY WERE GOING TO ATTACK US.
DO YOU NOT FEEL THAT LIGHT BLEEDING INTO YOUR MIND?
THIS IS A SUICIDE ATTACK.

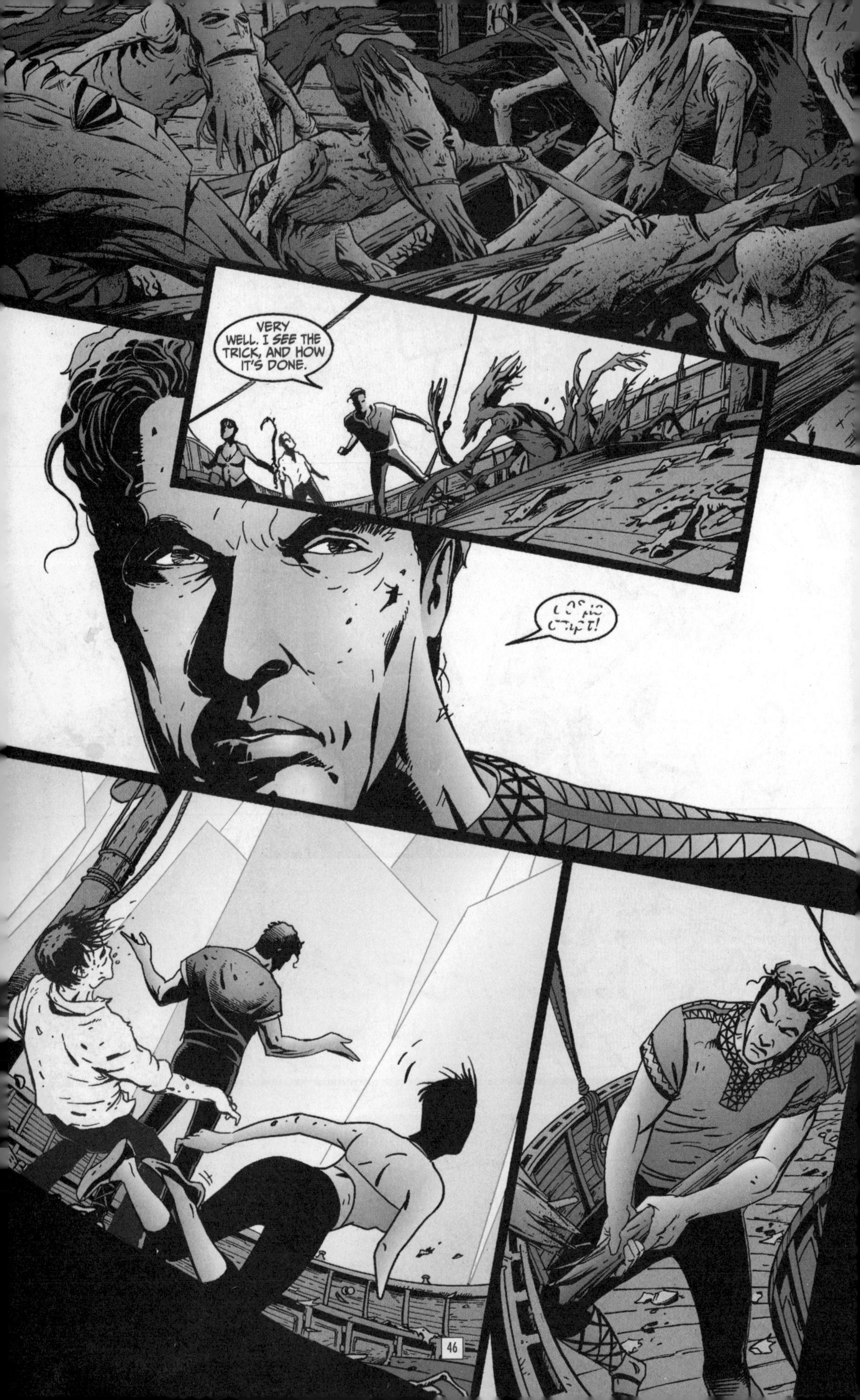
VERY WELL. I SEE THE TRICK, AND HOW IT'S DONE.

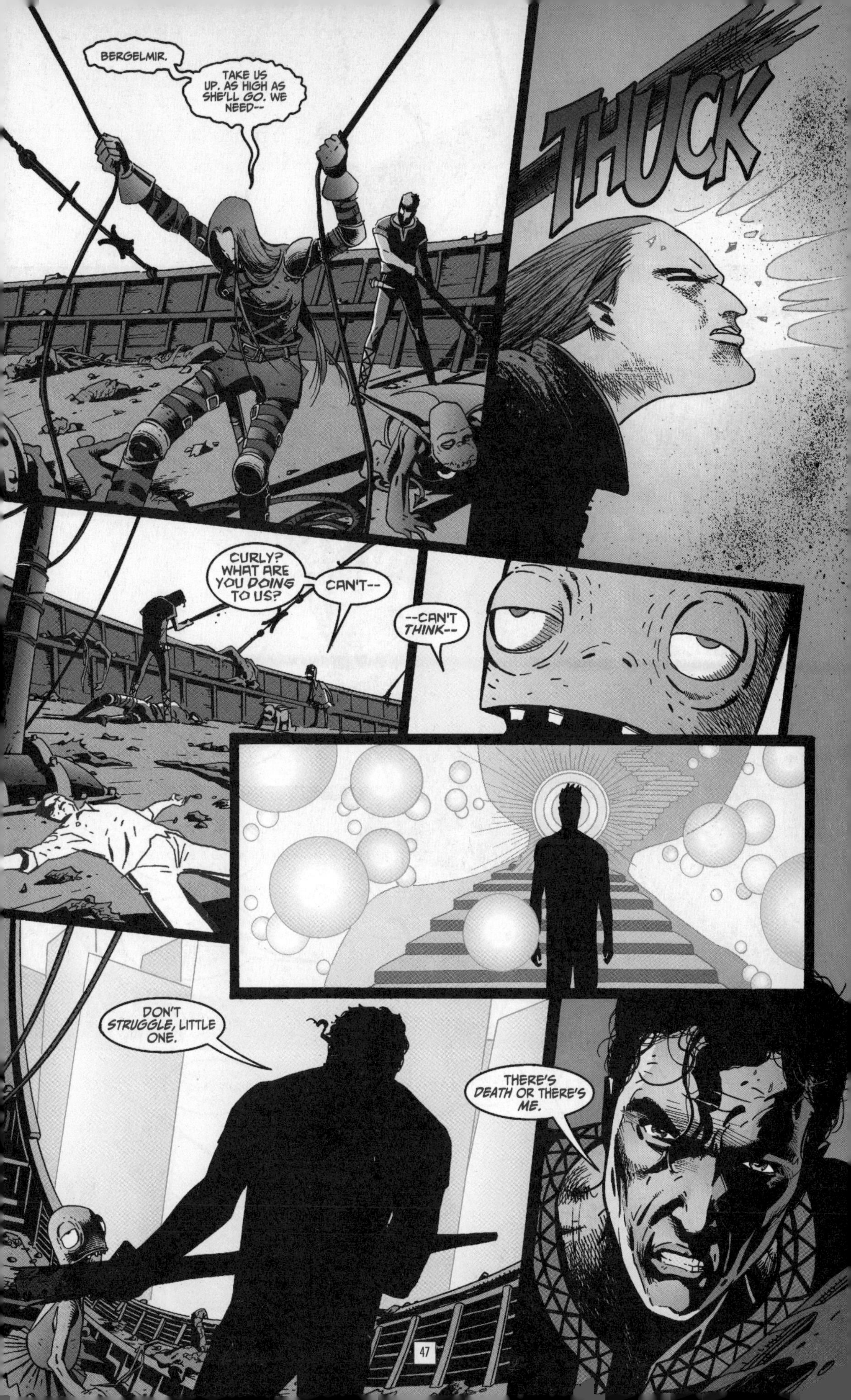
BERGELMIR.
TAKE US UP. AS HIGH AS SHE'LL GO. WE NEED--
THUCK
CURLY? WHAT ARE YOU DOING TO US?
CAN'T--
--CAN'T THINK--
DON'T STRUGGLE, LITTLE ONE.
THERE'S DEATH OR THERE'S ME.

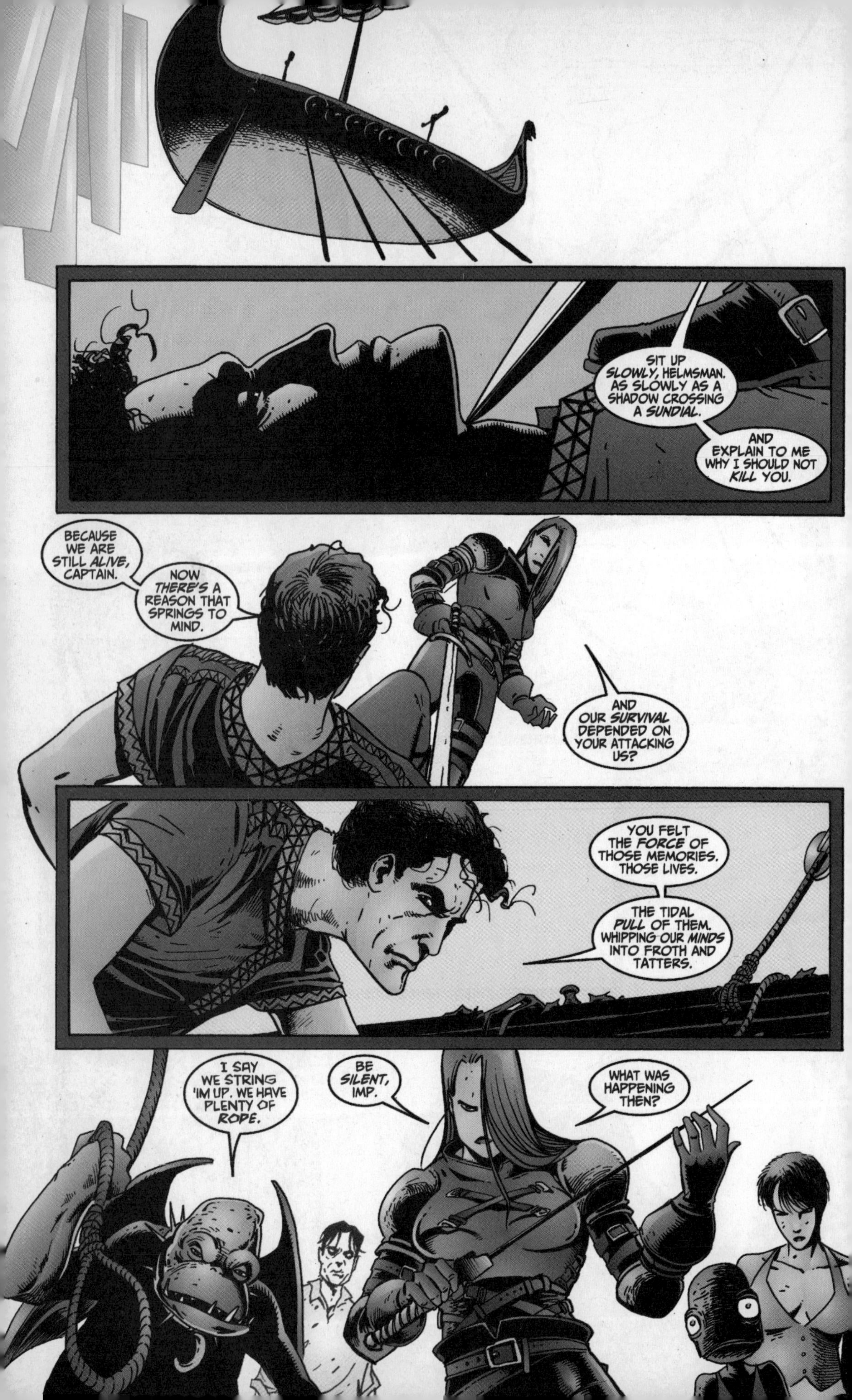
SIT UP SLOWLY, HELMSMAN. AS SLOWLY AS A SHADOW CROSSING A SUNDIAL.
AND EXPLAIN TO ME WHY I SHOULD NOT KILL YOU.
BECAUSE WE ARE STILL ALIVE, CAPTAIN.
NOW THERE'S A REASON THAT SPRINGS TO MIND.
AND OUR SURVIVAL DEPENDED ON YOUR ATTACKING US?
YOU FELT THE FORCE OF THOSE MEMORIES. THOSE LIVES.
THE TIDAL PULL OF THEM. WHIPPING OUR MINDS INTO FROTH AND TATTERS.
I SAY WE STRING 'IM UP. WE HAVE PLENTY OF ROPE.
BE SILENT, IMP.
WHAT WAS HAPPENING THEN?

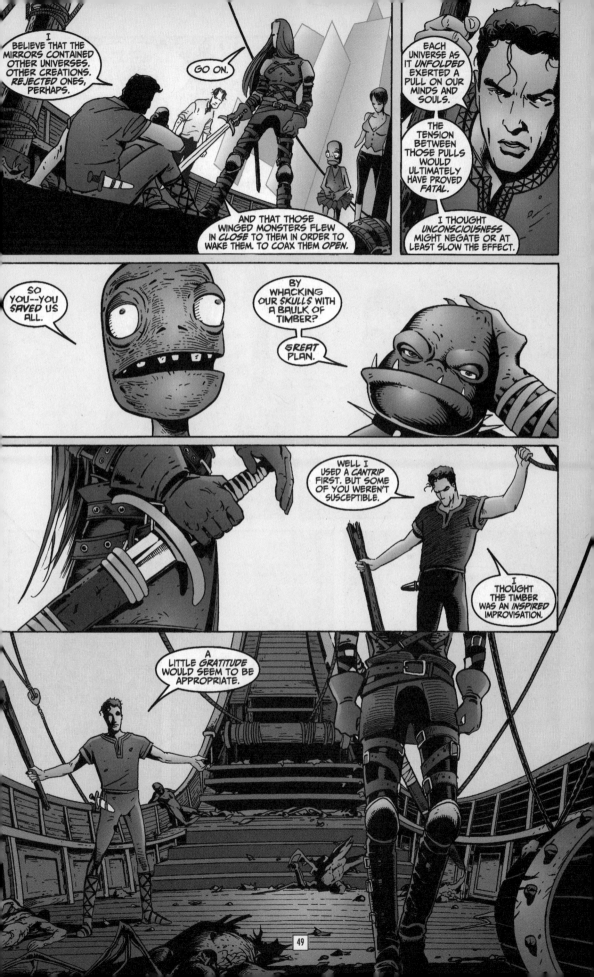

I BELIEVE THAT THE MIRRORS CONTAINED OTHER UNIVERSES. OTHER CREATIONS. *REJECTED* ONES, PERHAPS.

GO ON.

AND THAT THOSE WINGED MONSTERS FLEW IN *CLOSE* TO THEM IN ORDER TO WAKE THEM. TO COAX THEM *OPEN*.

EACH UNIVERSE AS IT *UNFOLDED* EXERTED A PULL ON OUR MINDS AND SOULS.

THE TENSION BETWEEN THOSE PULLS WOULD ULTIMATELY HAVE PROVED *FATAL*.

I THOUGHT UNCONSCIOUSNESS MIGHT NEGATE OR AT LEAST SLOW THE EFFECT.

SO--YOU *SAVED* US ALL.

BY *WHACKING* OUR *SKULLS* WITH A BAULK OF *TIMBER?*

*GREAT* PLAN.

WELL I USED A *CANTRIP* FIRST. BUT SOME OF YOU WEREN'T SUSCEPTIBLE.

I THOUGHT THE TIMBER WAS AN *INSPIRED* IMPROVISATION.

A LITTLE *GRATITUDE* WOULD SEEM TO BE APPROPRIATE.

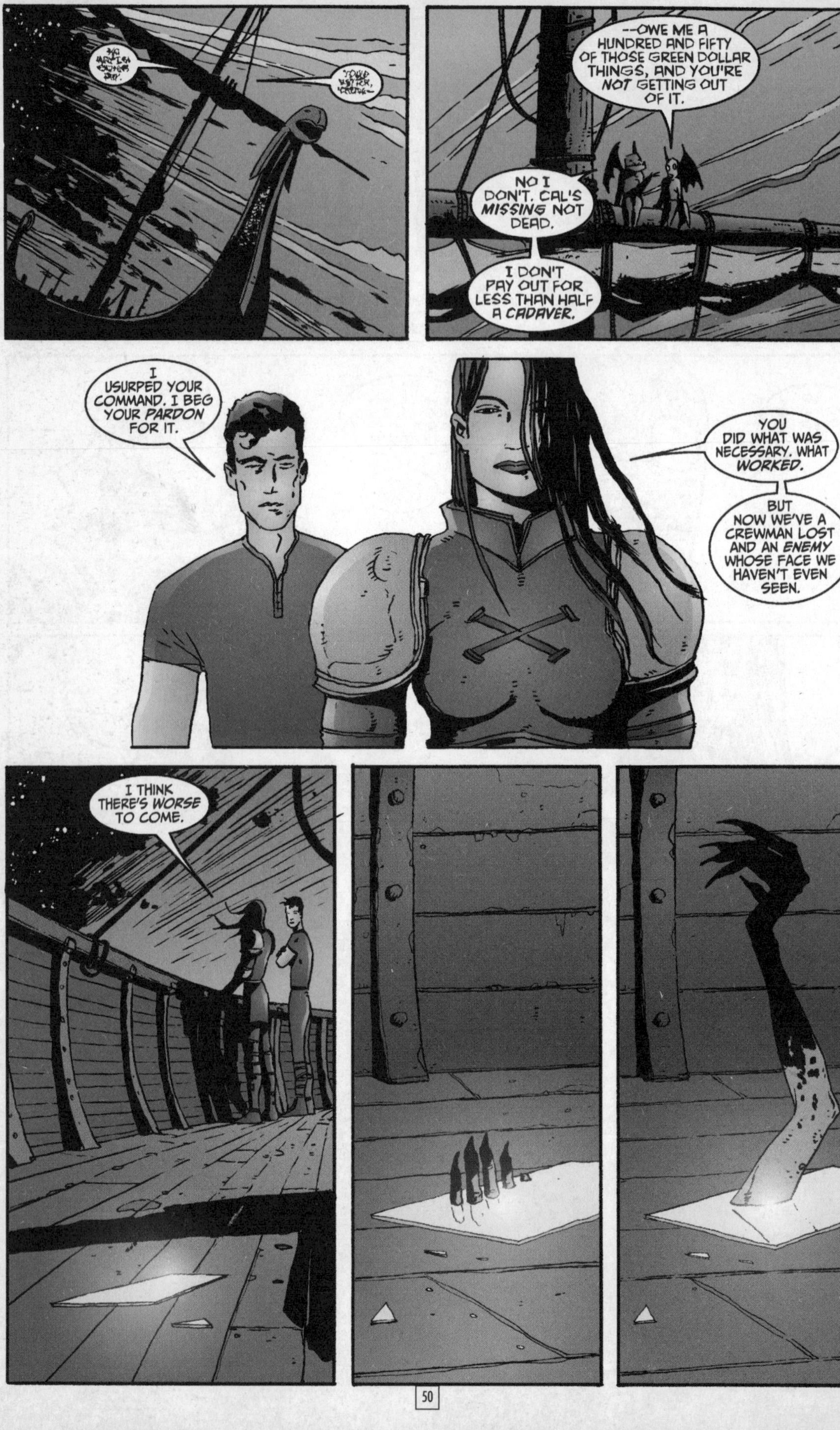
--OWE ME A HUNDRED AND FIFTY OF THOSE GREEN DOLLAR THINGS, AND YOU'RE *NOT* GETTING OUT OF IT.
NO I DON'T. CAL'S *MISSING* NOT DEAD.
I DON'T PAY OUT FOR LESS THAN HALF A *CADAVER*.
I USURPED YOUR COMMAND. I BEG YOUR *PARDON* FOR IT.
YOU DID WHAT WAS NECESSARY. WHAT *WORKED*.
BUT NOW WE'VE A CREWMAN LOST AND AN *ENEMY* WHOSE FACE WE HAVEN'T EVEN SEEN.
I THINK THERE'S *WORSE* TO COME.

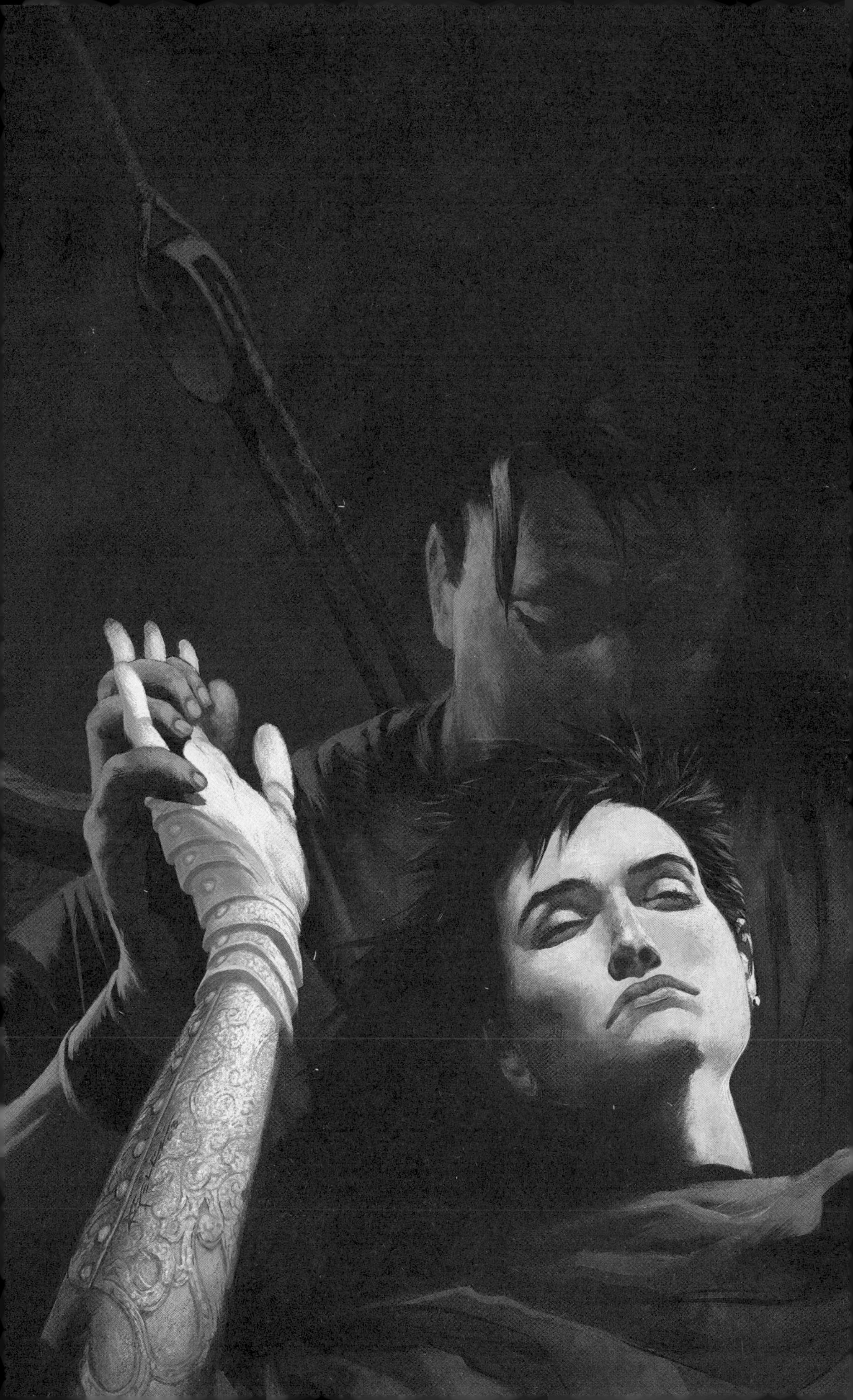

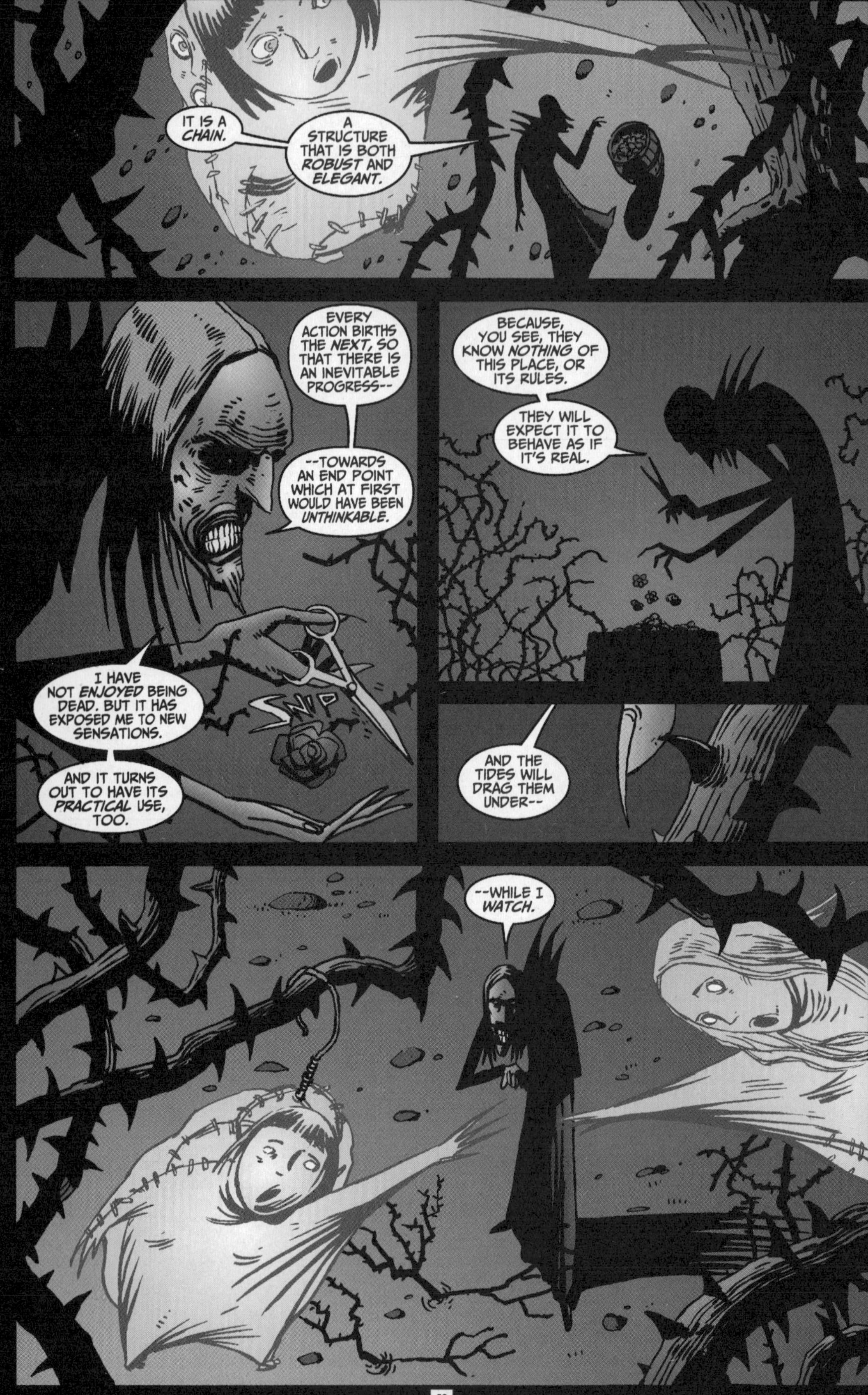
IT IS A CHAIN.
A STRUCTURE THAT IS BOTH ROBUST AND ELEGANT.
EVERY ACTION BIRTHS THE NEXT, SO THAT THERE IS AN INEVITABLE PROGRESS--
--TOWARDS AN END POINT WHICH AT FIRST WOULD HAVE BEEN UNTHINKABLE.
I HAVE NOT ENJOYED BEING DEAD. BUT IT HAS EXPOSED ME TO NEW SENSATIONS.
SNIP
AND IT TURNS OUT TO HAVE ITS PRACTICAL USE, TOO.
BECAUSE, YOU SEE, THEY KNOW NOTHING OF THIS PLACE, OR ITS RULES.
THEY WILL EXPECT IT TO BEHAVE AS IF IT'S REAL.
AND THE TIDES WILL DRAG THEM UNDER--
--WHILE I WATCH.

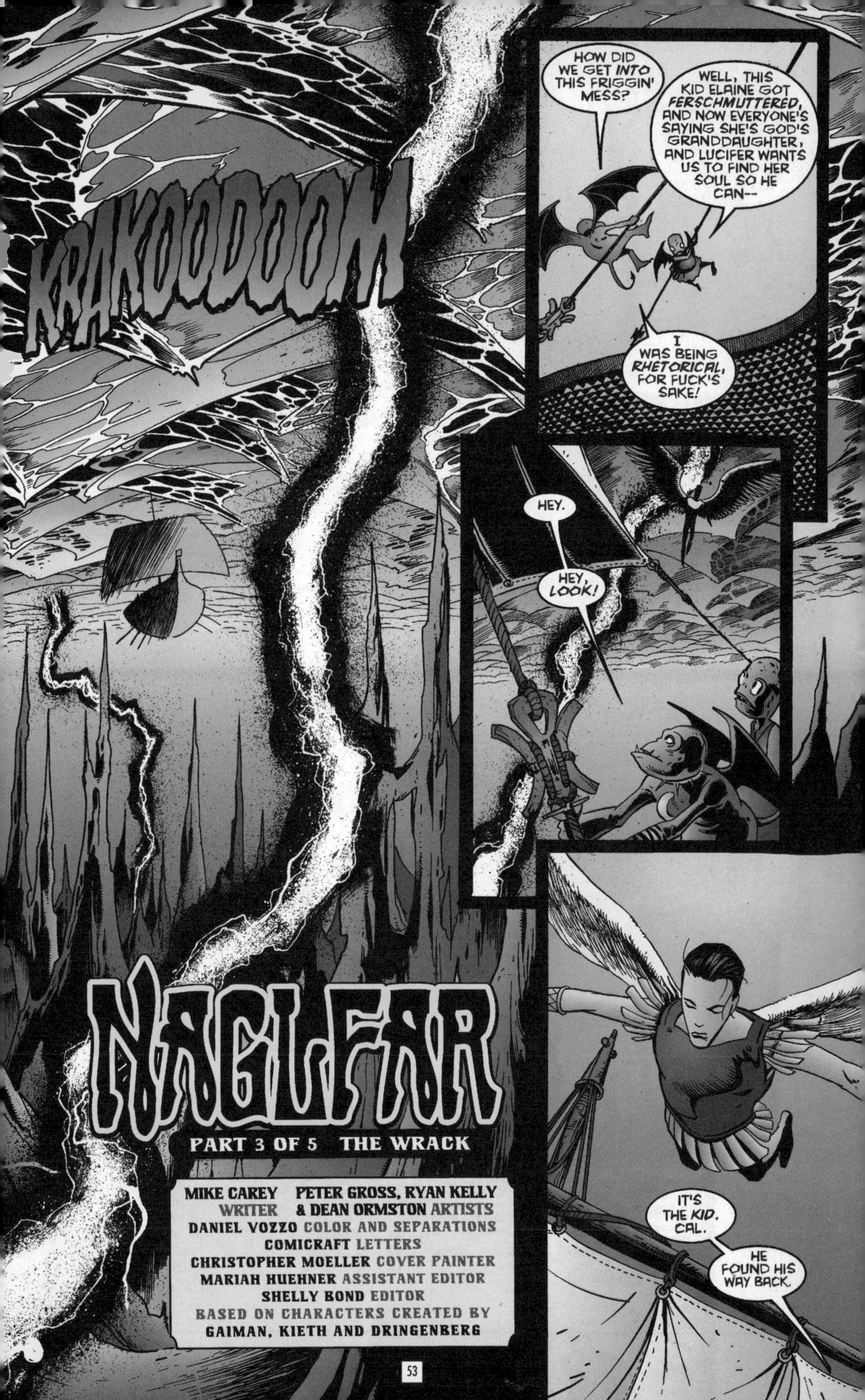
KRAKOODOOM
HOW DID WE GET INTO THIS FRIGGIN' MESS?
WELL, THIS KID ELAINE GOT FERSCHMUTTERED, AND NOW EVERYONE'S SAYING SHE'S GOD'S GRANDDAUGHTER, AND LUCIFER WANTS US TO FIND HER SOUL SO HE CAN--
I WAS BEING RHETORICAL, FOR FUCK'S SAKE!
HEY.
HEY, LOOK!
NAGLFAR
PART 3 OF 5 THE WRACK
MIKE CAREY WRITER
PETER GROSS, RYAN KELLY & DEAN ORMSTON ARTISTS
DANIEL VOZZO COLOR AND SEPARATIONS
COMICRAFT LETTERS
CHRISTOPHER MOELLER COVER PAINTER
MARIAH HUEHNER ASSISTANT EDITOR
SHELLY BOND EDITOR
BASED ON CHARACTERS CREATED BY GAIMAN, KIETH AND DRINGENBERG
IT'S THE KID, CAL.
HE FOUND HIS WAY BACK.

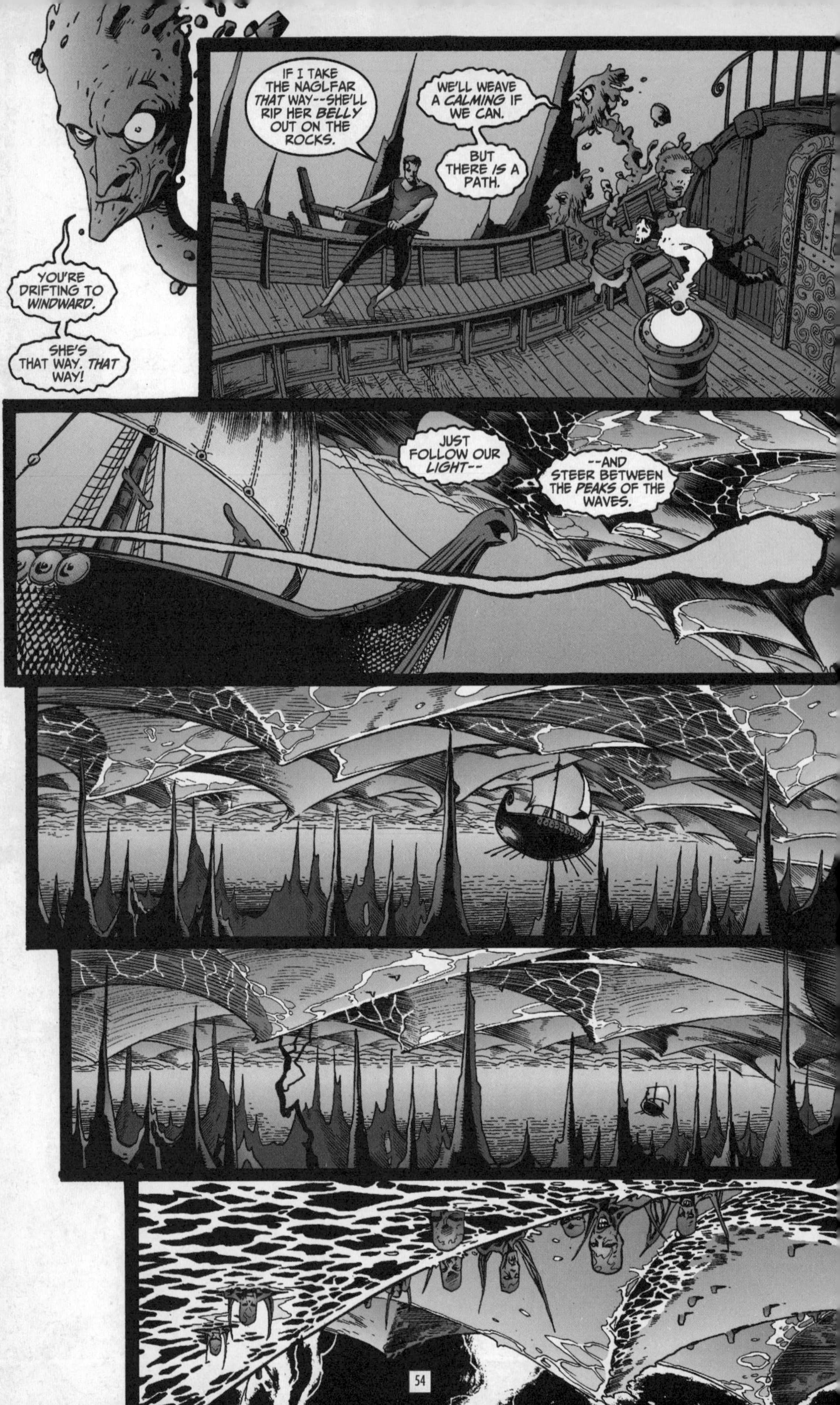
IF I TAKE THE NAGLFAR THAT WAY--SHE'LL RIP HER BELLY OUT ON THE ROCKS.
WE'LL WEAVE A CALMING IF WE CAN.
BUT THERE IS A PATH.
YOU'RE DRIFTING TO WINDWARD.
SHE'S THAT WAY. THAT WAY!
JUST FOLLOW OUR LIGHT--
--AND STEER BETWEEN THE PEAKS OF THE WAVES.

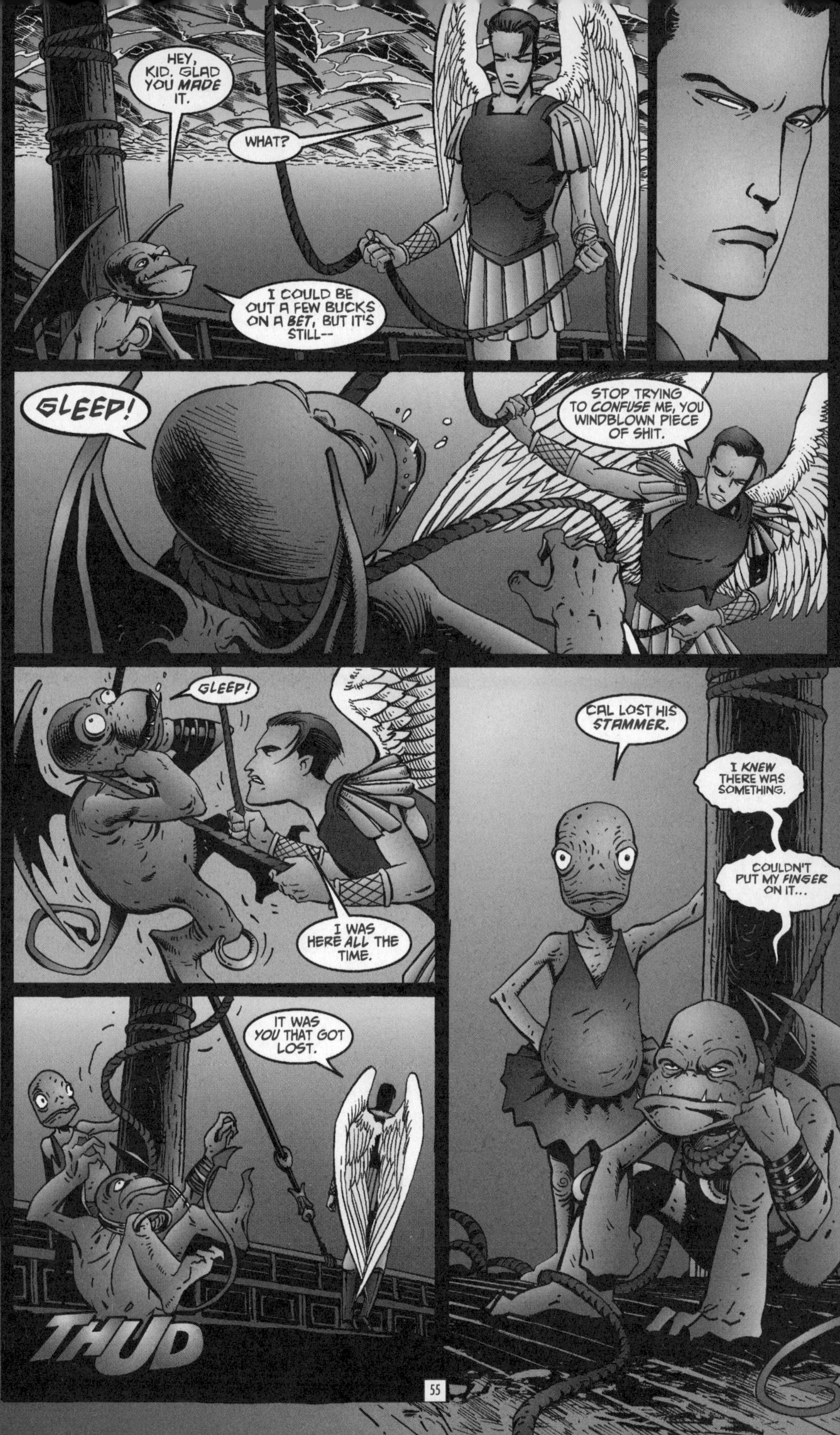
HEY, KID, GLAD YOU MADE IT.
WHAT?
I COULD BE OUT A FEW BUCKS ON A BET, BUT IT'S STILL--
GLEEP!
STOP TRYING TO CONFUSE ME, YOU WINDBLOWN PIECE OF SHIT.
GLEEP!
I WAS HERE ALL THE TIME.
IT WAS YOU THAT GOT LOST.
THUD
CAL LOST HIS STAMMER.
I KNEW THERE WAS SOMETHING.
COULDN'T PUT MY FINGER ON IT...

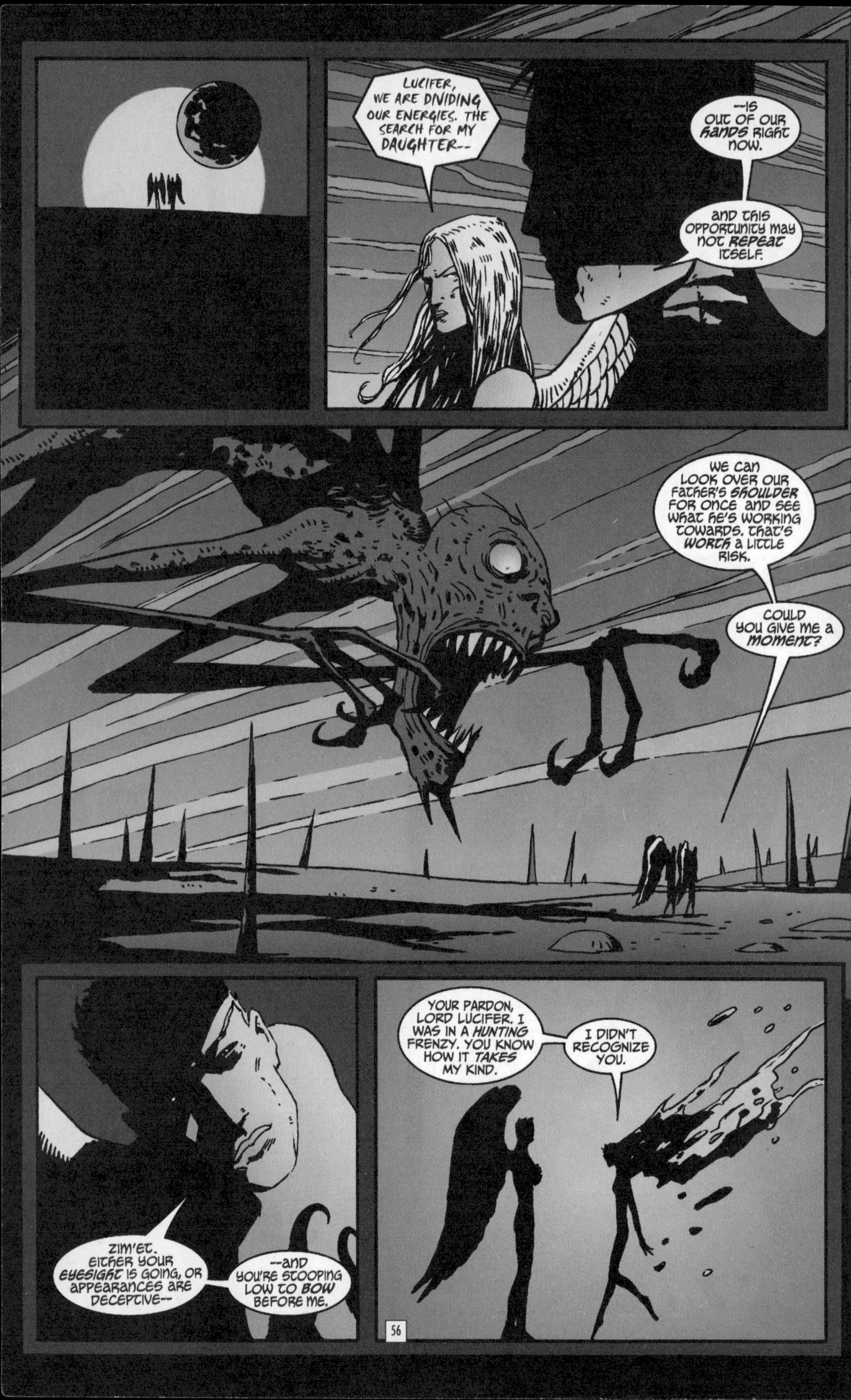
LUCIFER, WE ARE DIVIDING OUR ENERGIES. THE SEARCH FOR MY DAUGHTER--
--IS OUT OF OUR HANDS RIGHT NOW.
AND THIS OPPORTUNITY MAY NOT REPEAT ITSELF.
WE CAN LOOK OVER OUR FATHER'S SHOULDER FOR ONCE AND SEE WHAT HE'S WORKING TOWARDS. THAT'S WORTH A LITTLE RISK.
COULD YOU GIVE ME A MOMENT?
ZIM'ET. EITHER YOUR EYESIGHT IS GOING, OR APPEARANCES ARE DECEPTIVE--
--AND YOU'RE STOOPING LOW TO BOW BEFORE ME.
YOUR PARDON, LORD LUCIFER. I WAS IN A HUNTING FRENZY. YOU KNOW HOW IT TAKES MY KIND.
I DIDN'T RECOGNIZE YOU.

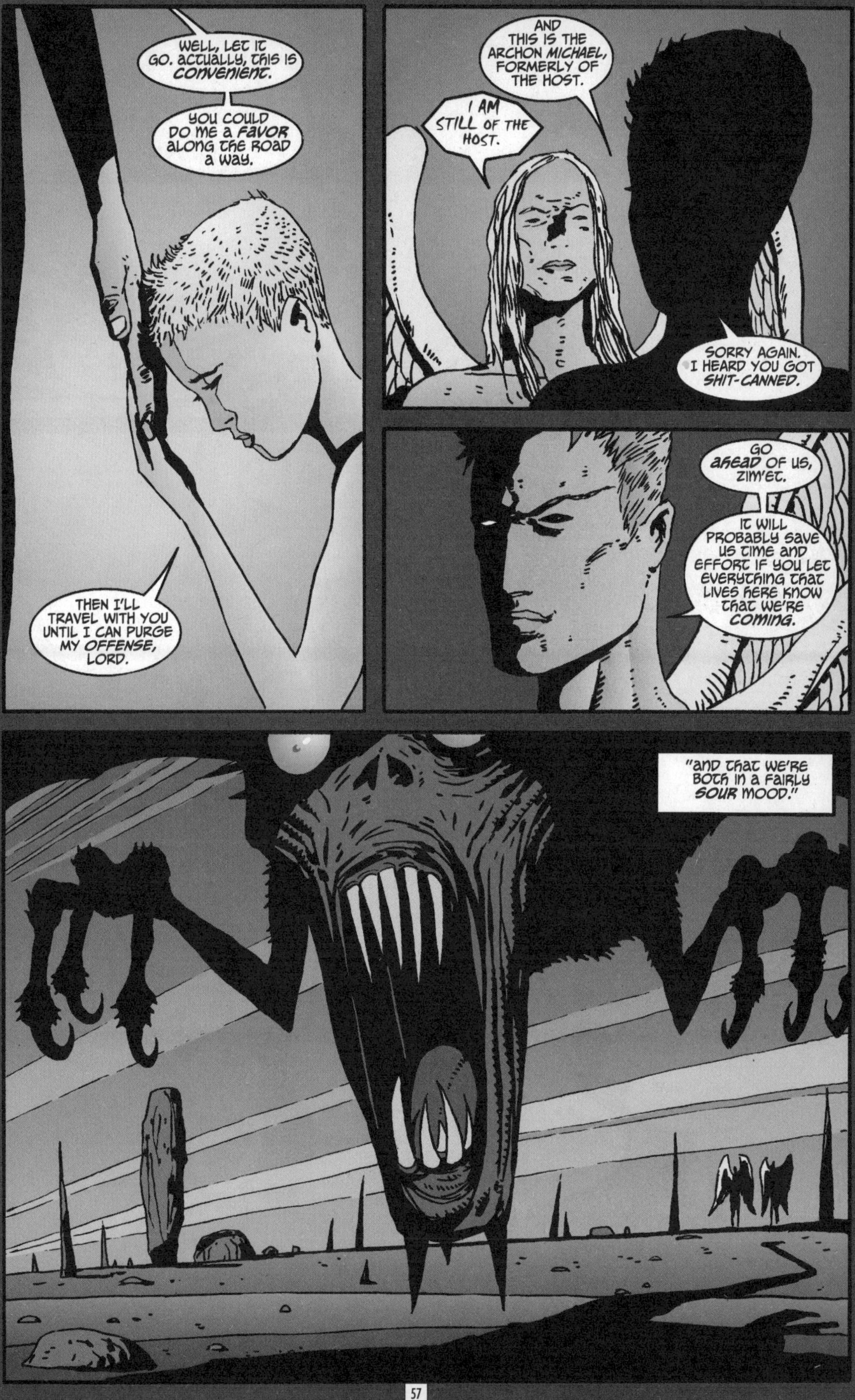
WELL, LET IT GO. ACTUALLY, THIS IS CONVENIENT.
YOU COULD DO ME A FAVOR ALONG THE ROAD A WAY.
THEN I'LL TRAVEL WITH YOU UNTIL I CAN PURGE MY OFFENSE, LORD.
AND THIS IS THE ARCHON MICHAEL, FORMERLY OF THE HOST.
I AM STILL OF THE HOST.
SORRY AGAIN. I HEARD YOU GOT SHIT-CANNED.
GO AHEAD OF US, ZIM'ET.
IT WILL PROBABLY SAVE US TIME AND EFFORT IF YOU LET EVERYTHING THAT LIVES HERE KNOW THAT WE'RE COMING.
"AND THAT WE'RE BOTH IN A FAIRLY SOUR MOOD."

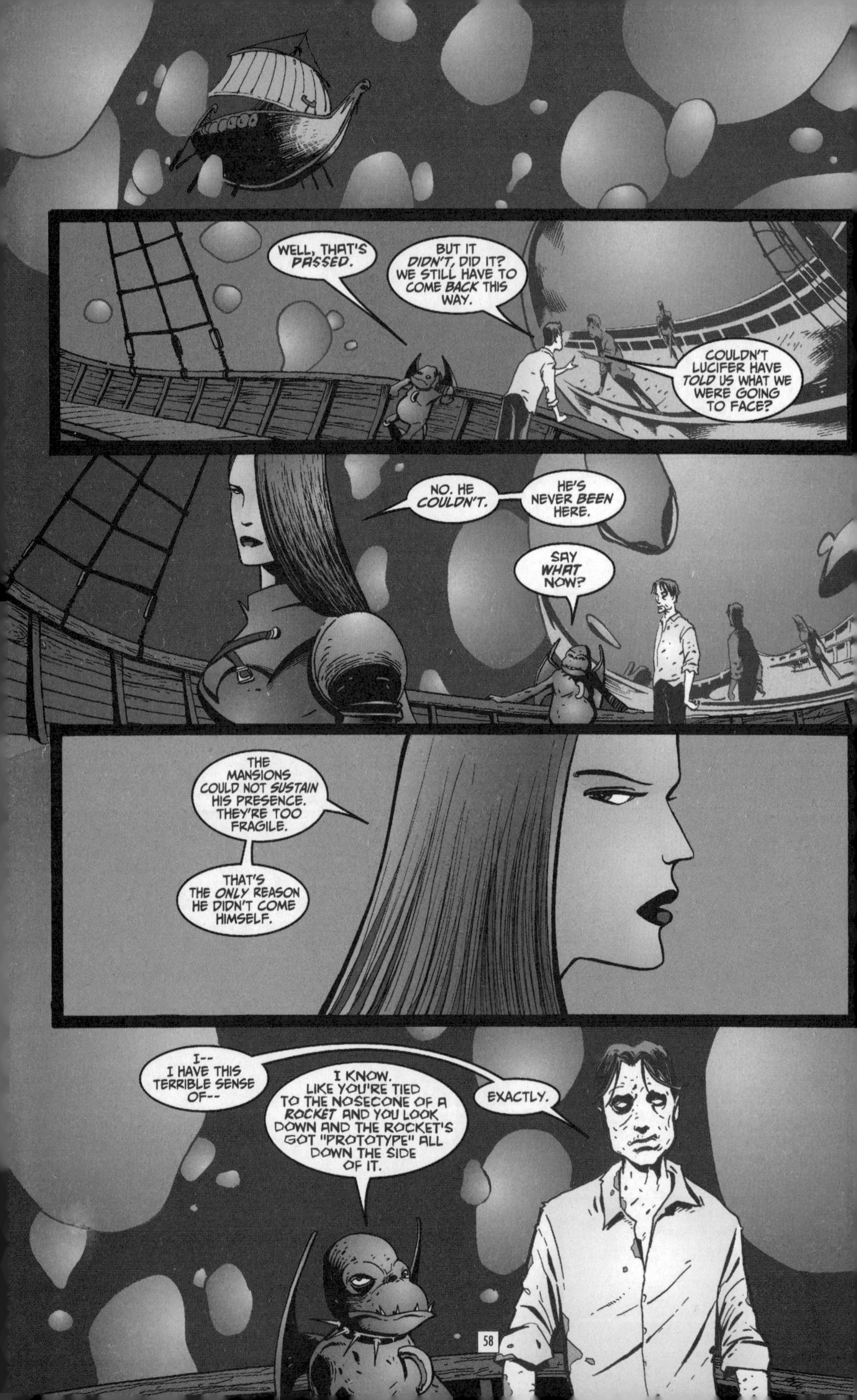

WELL, THAT'S PASSED.
BUT IT DIDN'T, DID IT? WE STILL HAVE TO COME BACK THIS WAY.
COULDN'T LUCIFER HAVE TOLD US WHAT WE WERE GOING TO FACE?
NO. HE COULDN'T.
HE'S NEVER BEEN HERE.
SAY WHAT NOW?
THE MANSIONS COULD NOT SUSTAIN HIS PRESENCE. THEY'RE TOO FRAGILE.
THAT'S THE ONLY REASON HE DIDN'T COME HIMSELF.
I-- I HAVE THIS TERRIBLE SENSE OF--
I KNOW. LIKE YOU'RE TIED TO THE NOSECONE OF A ROCKET AND YOU LOOK DOWN AND THE ROCKET'S GOT "PROTOTYPE" ALL DOWN THE SIDE OF IT.
EXACTLY.

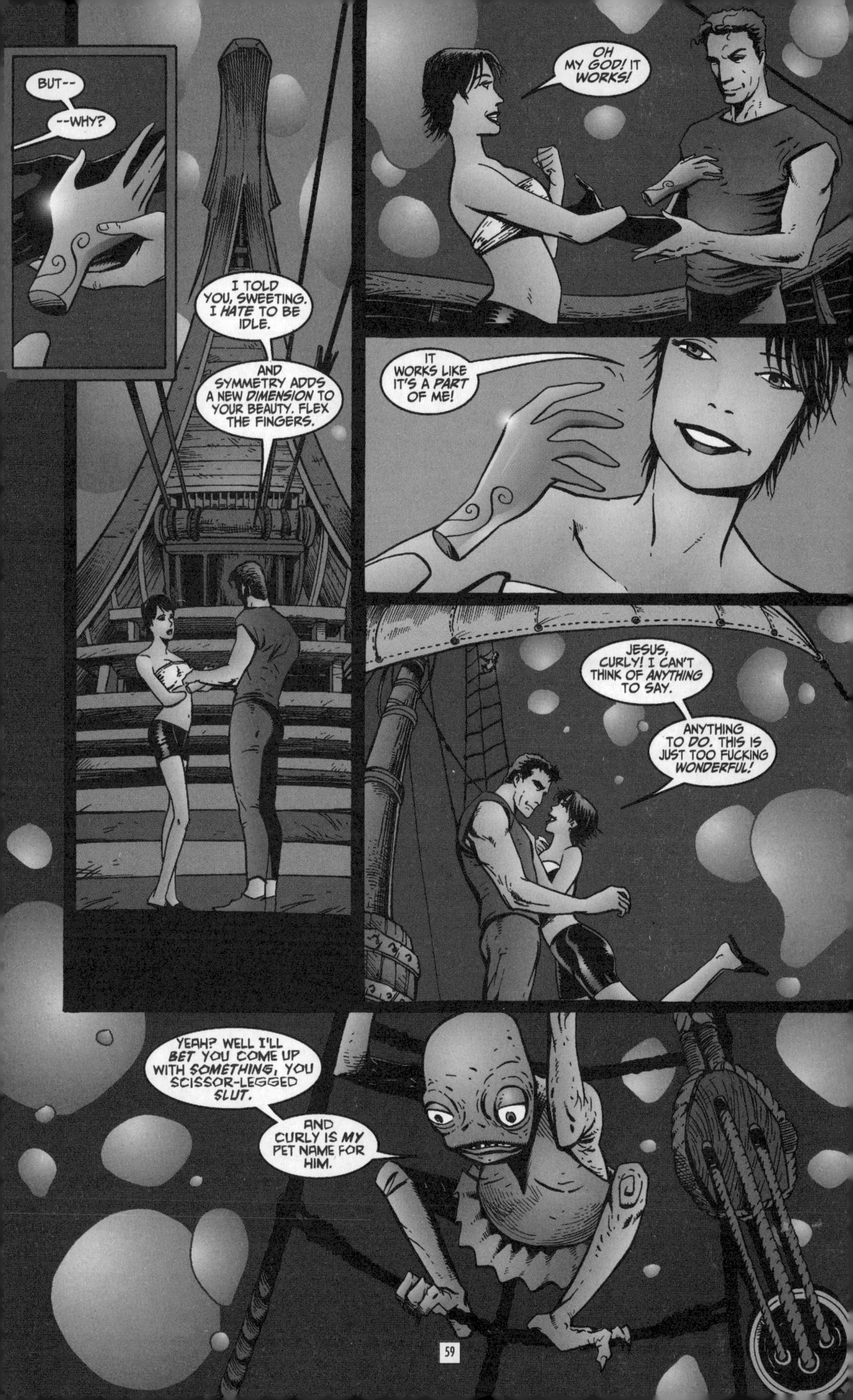
BUT--
--WHY?
I TOLD YOU, SWEETING. I HATE TO BE IDLE.
AND SYMMETRY ADDS A NEW DIMENSION TO YOUR BEAUTY. FLEX THE FINGERS.
OH MY GOD! IT WORKS!
IT WORKS LIKE IT'S A PART OF ME!
JESUS, CURLY! I CAN'T THINK OF ANYTHING TO SAY.
ANYTHING TO DO. THIS IS JUST TOO FUCKING WONDERFUL!
YEAH? WELL I'LL BET YOU COME UP WITH SOMETHING, YOU SCISSOR-LEGGED SLUT.
AND CURLY IS MY PET NAME FOR HIM.

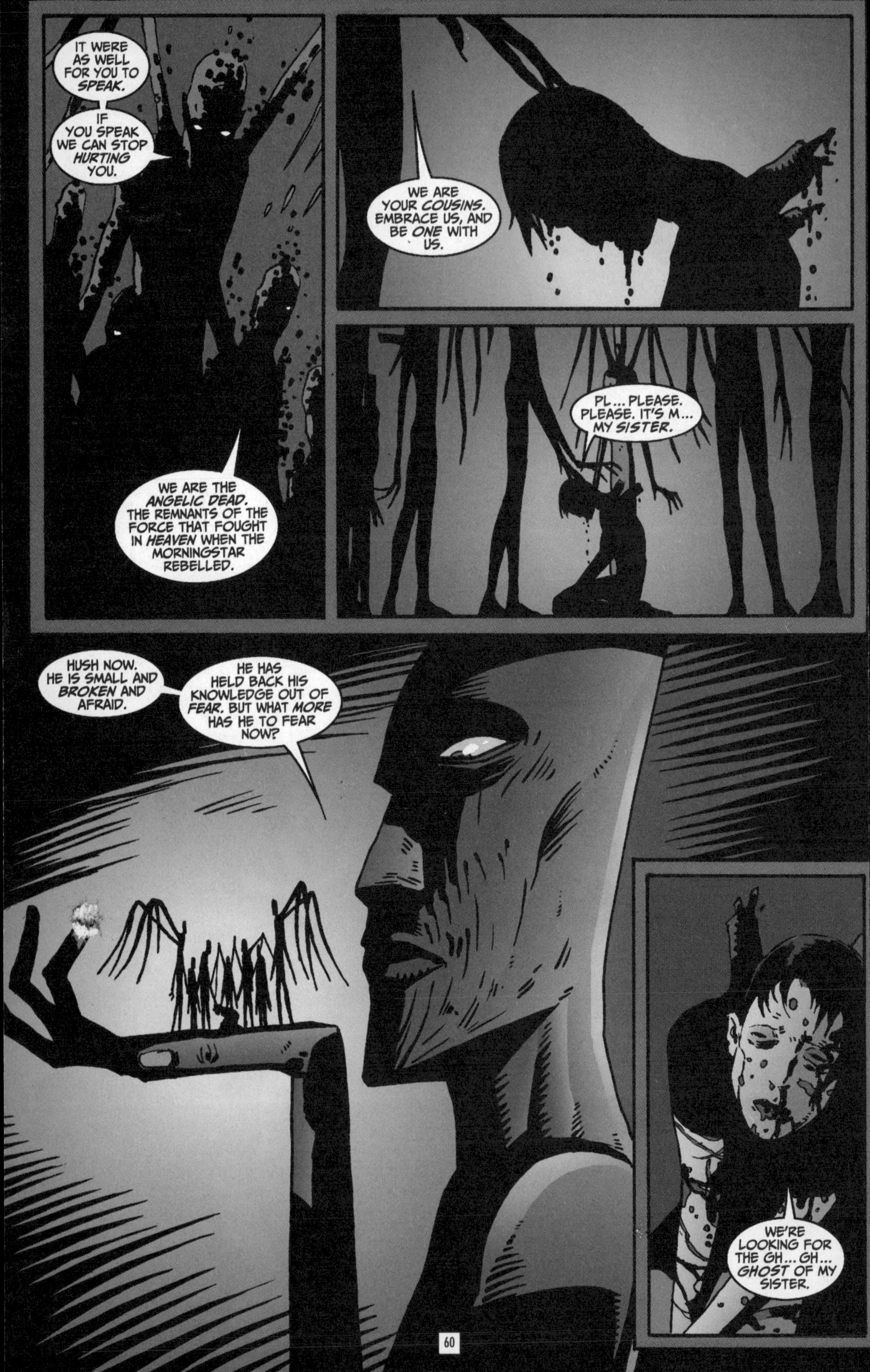
IT WERE AS WELL FOR YOU TO *SPEAK.*
IF YOU SPEAK WE CAN STOP *HURTING* YOU.
WE ARE THE *ANGELIC DEAD.* THE REMNANTS OF THE FORCE THAT FOUGHT IN *HEAVEN* WHEN THE MORNINGSTAR REBELLED.
WE ARE YOUR *COUSINS.* EMBRACE US, AND BE *ONE* WITH US.
PL... PLEASE. PLEASE. IT'S M... MY *SISTER.*
HUSH NOW. HE IS SMALL AND *BROKEN* AND AFRAID.
HE HAS HELD BACK HIS KNOWLEDGE OUT OF *FEAR.* BUT WHAT *MORE* HAS HE TO FEAR NOW?
WE'RE LOOKING FOR THE GH... GH... *GHOST* OF MY SISTER.

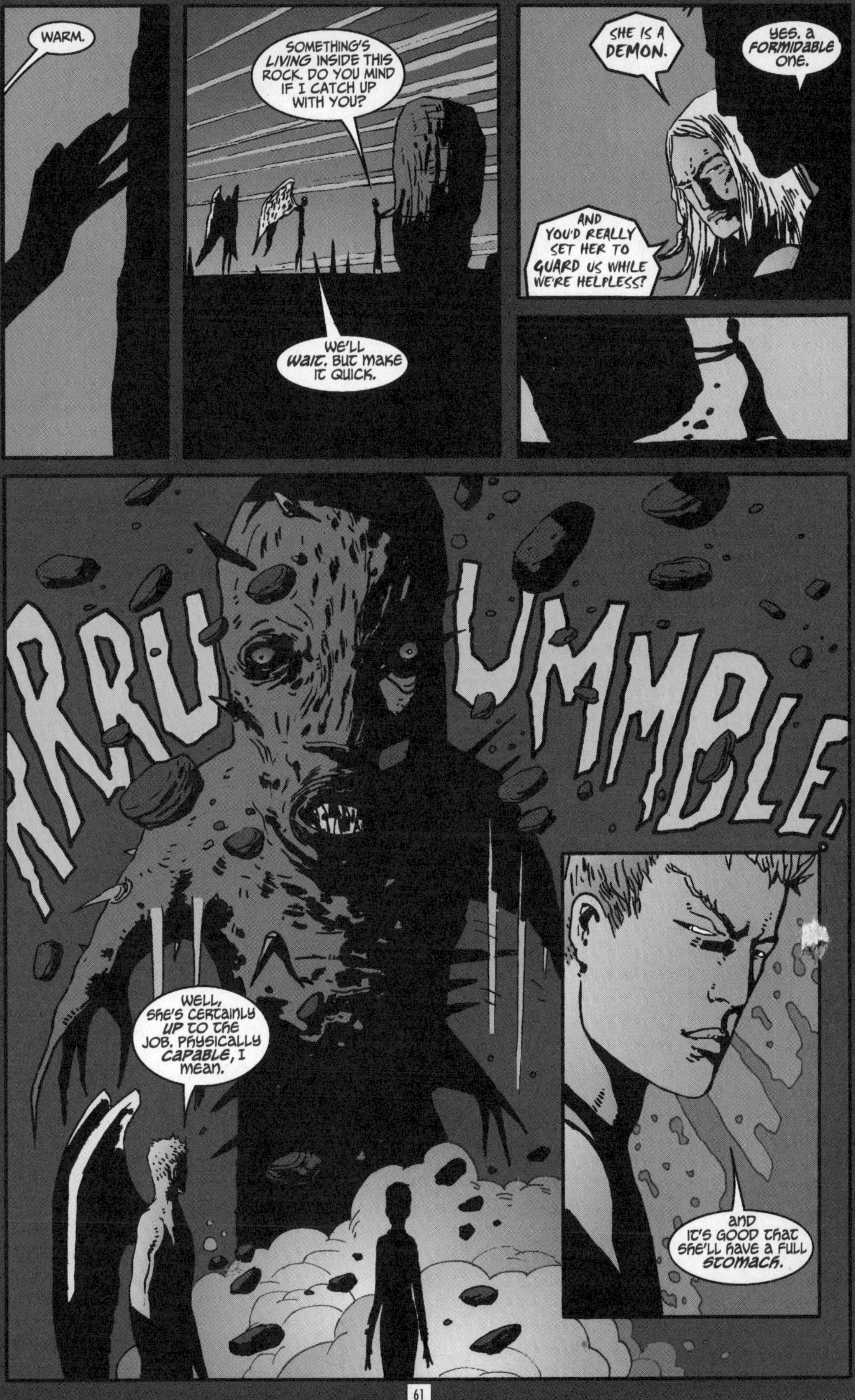
WARM.
SOMETHING'S LIVING INSIDE THIS ROCK. DO YOU MIND IF I CATCH UP WITH YOU?
WE'LL WAIT. BUT MAKE IT QUICK.
SHE IS A DEMON.
YES, A FORMIDABLE ONE.
AND YOU'D REALLY SET HER TO GUARD US WHILE WE'RE HELPLESS?
RRRUUMMBLE
WELL, SHE'S CERTAINLY UP TO THE JOB. PHYSICALLY CAPABLE, I MEAN.
AND IT'S GOOD THAT SHE'LL HAVE A FULL STOMACH.

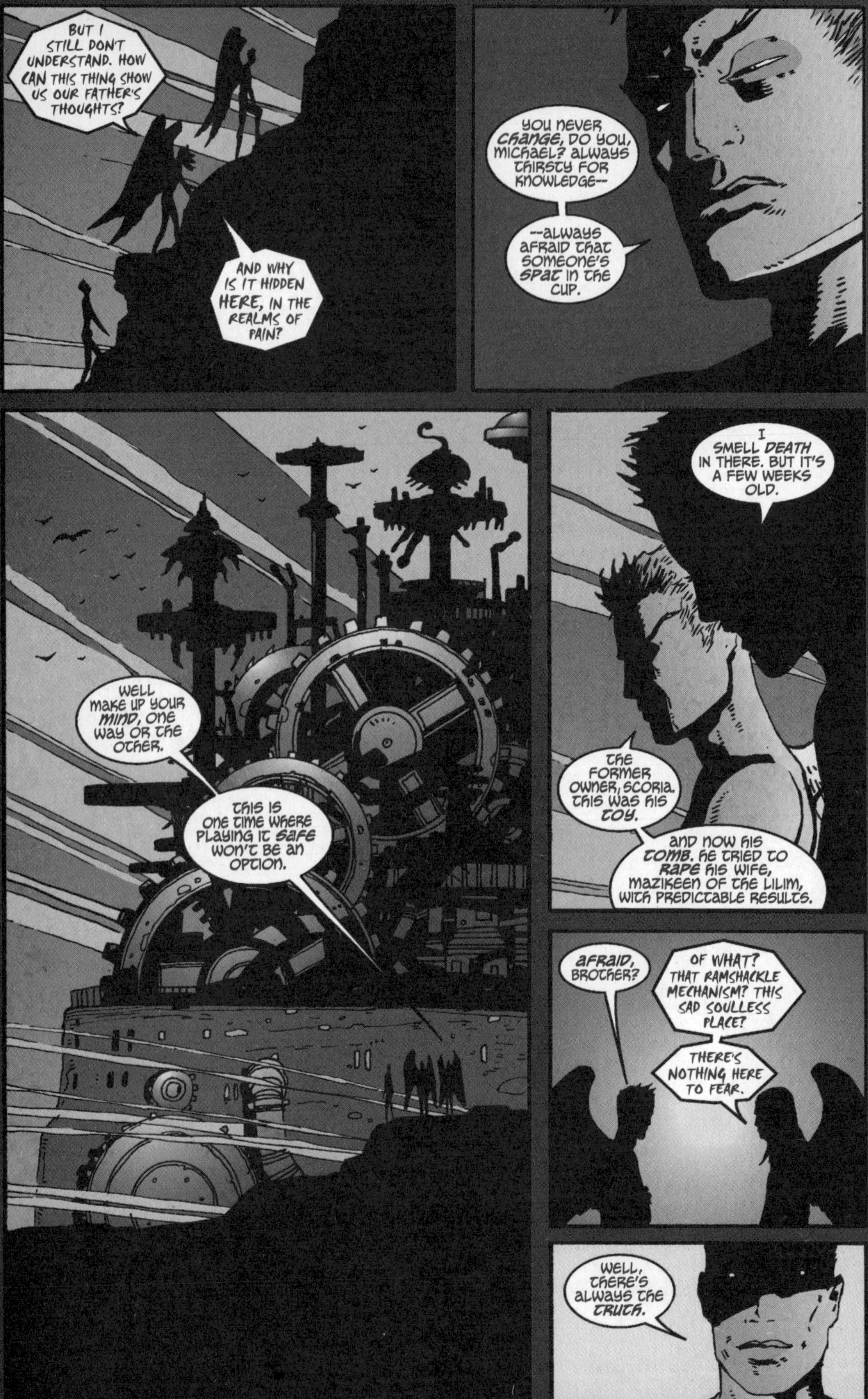

BUT I STILL DON'T UNDERSTAND. HOW CAN THIS THING SHOW US OUR FATHER'S THOUGHTS?
AND WHY IS IT HIDDEN HERE, IN THE REALMS OF PAIN?
YOU NEVER CHANGE, DO YOU, MICHAEL? ALWAYS THIRSTY FOR KNOWLEDGE--
--ALWAYS AFRAID THAT SOMEONE'S SPAT IN THE CUP.
WELL MAKE UP YOUR MIND, ONE WAY OR THE OTHER.
THIS IS ONE TIME WHERE PLAYING IT SAFE WON'T BE AN OPTION.
I SMELL DEATH IN THERE. BUT IT'S A FEW WEEKS OLD.
THE FORMER OWNER, SCORIA. THIS WAS HIS TOY.
AND NOW HIS TOMB. HE TRIED TO RAPE HIS WIFE, MAZIKEEN OF THE LILIM, WITH PREDICTABLE RESULTS.
AFRAID, BROTHER?
OF WHAT? THAT RAMSHACKLE MECHANISM? THIS SAD SOULLESS PLACE?
THERE'S NOTHING HERE TO FEAR.
WELL, THERE'S ALWAYS THE TRUTH.

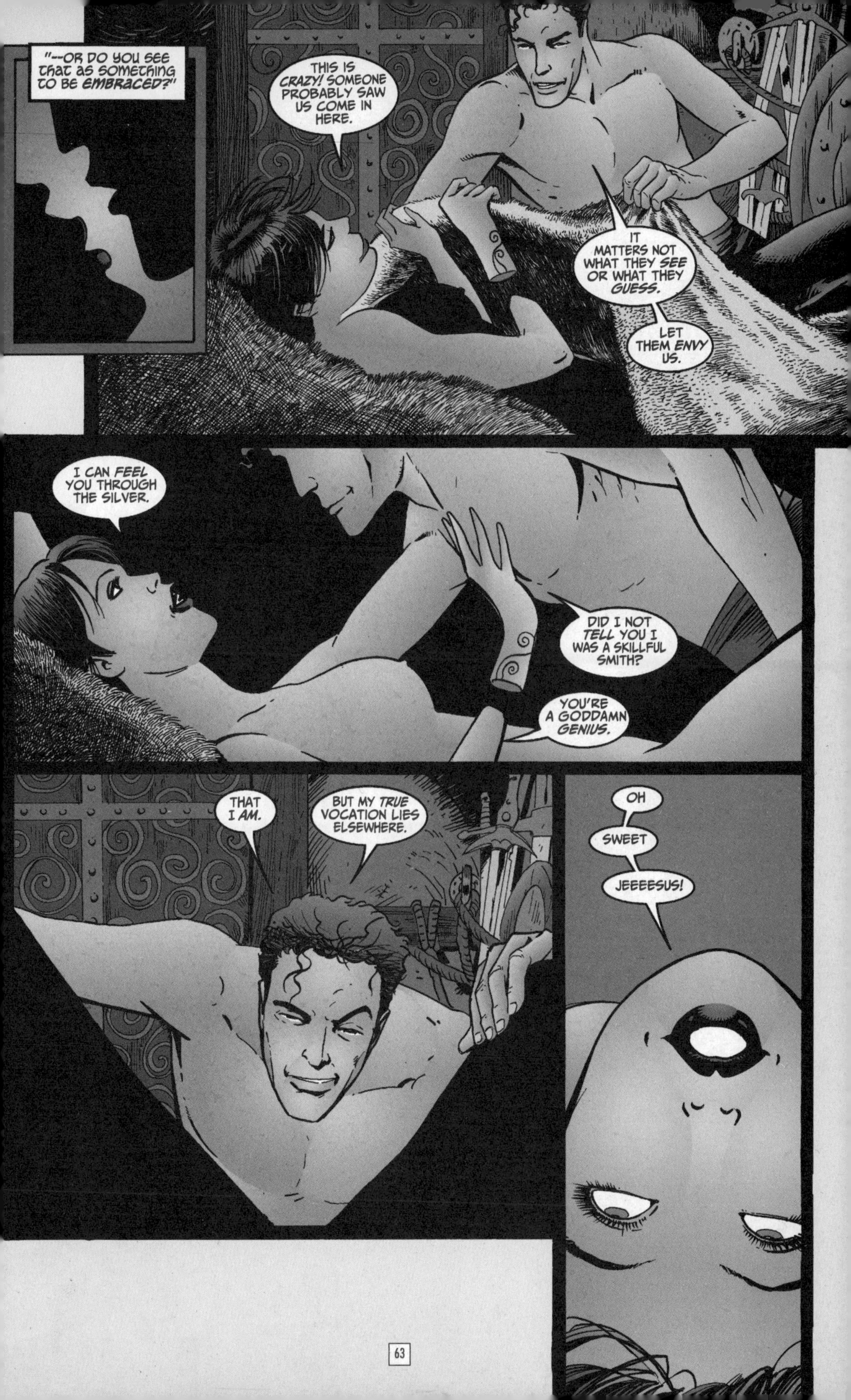
"--OR DO YOU SEE THAT AS SOMETHING TO BE EMBRACED?"
THIS IS CRAZY! SOMEONE PROBABLY SAW US COME IN HERE.
IT MATTERS NOT WHAT THEY SEE OR WHAT THEY GUESS.
LET THEM ENVY US.
I CAN FEEL YOU THROUGH THE SILVER.
DID I NOT TELL YOU I WAS A SKILLFUL SMITH?
YOU'RE A GODDAMN GENIUS.
THAT I AM.
BUT MY TRUE VOCATION LIES ELSEWHERE.
OH
SWEET
JEEEESUS!

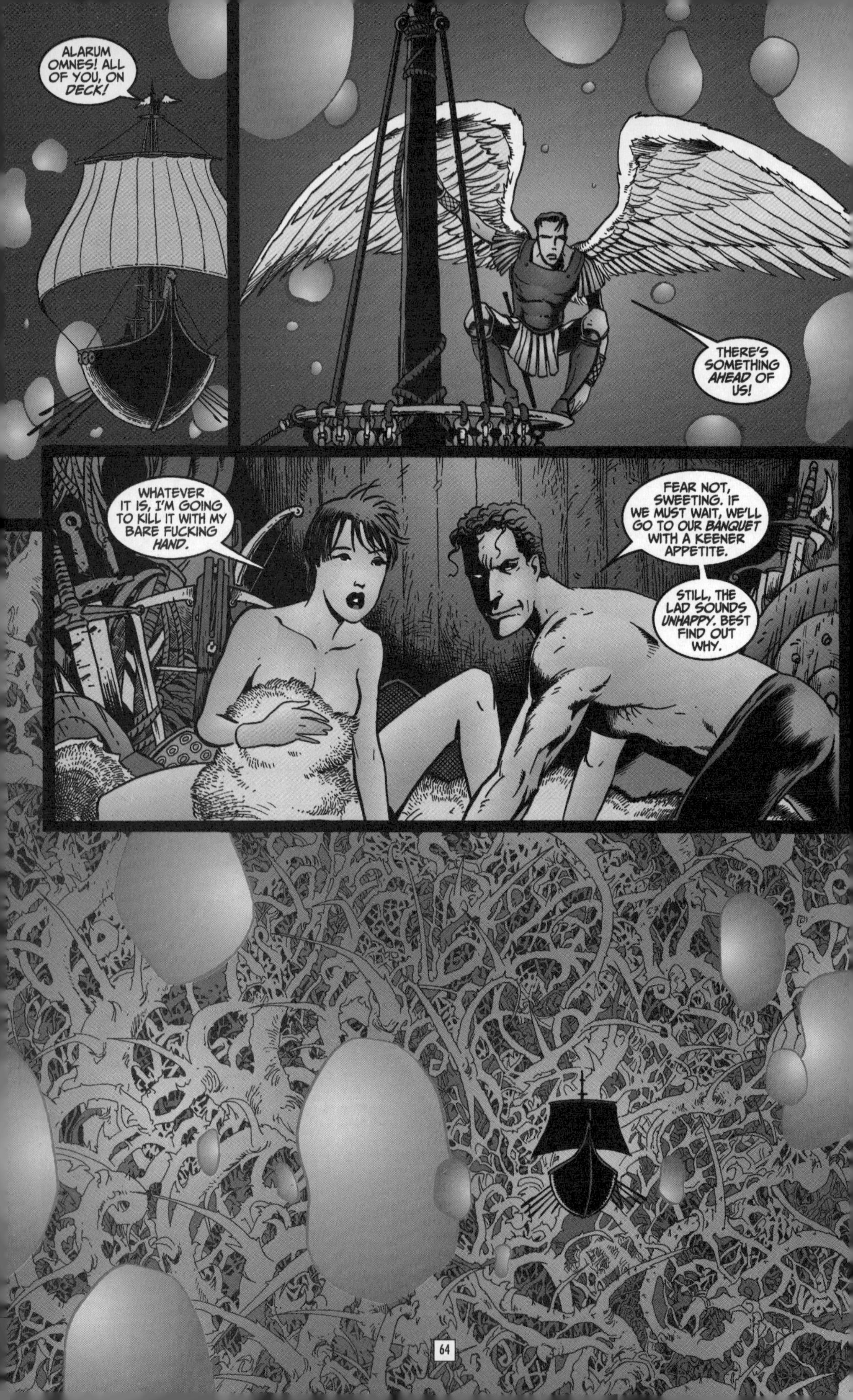
ALARUM OMNES! ALL OF YOU, ON DECK!
THERE'S SOMETHING AHEAD OF US!
WHATEVER IT IS, I'M GOING TO KILL IT WITH MY BARE FUCKING HAND.
FEAR NOT, SWEETING. IF WE MUST WAIT, WE'LL GO TO OUR BANQUET WITH A KEENER APPETITE.
STILL, THE LAD SOUNDS UNHAPPY. BEST FIND OUT WHY.

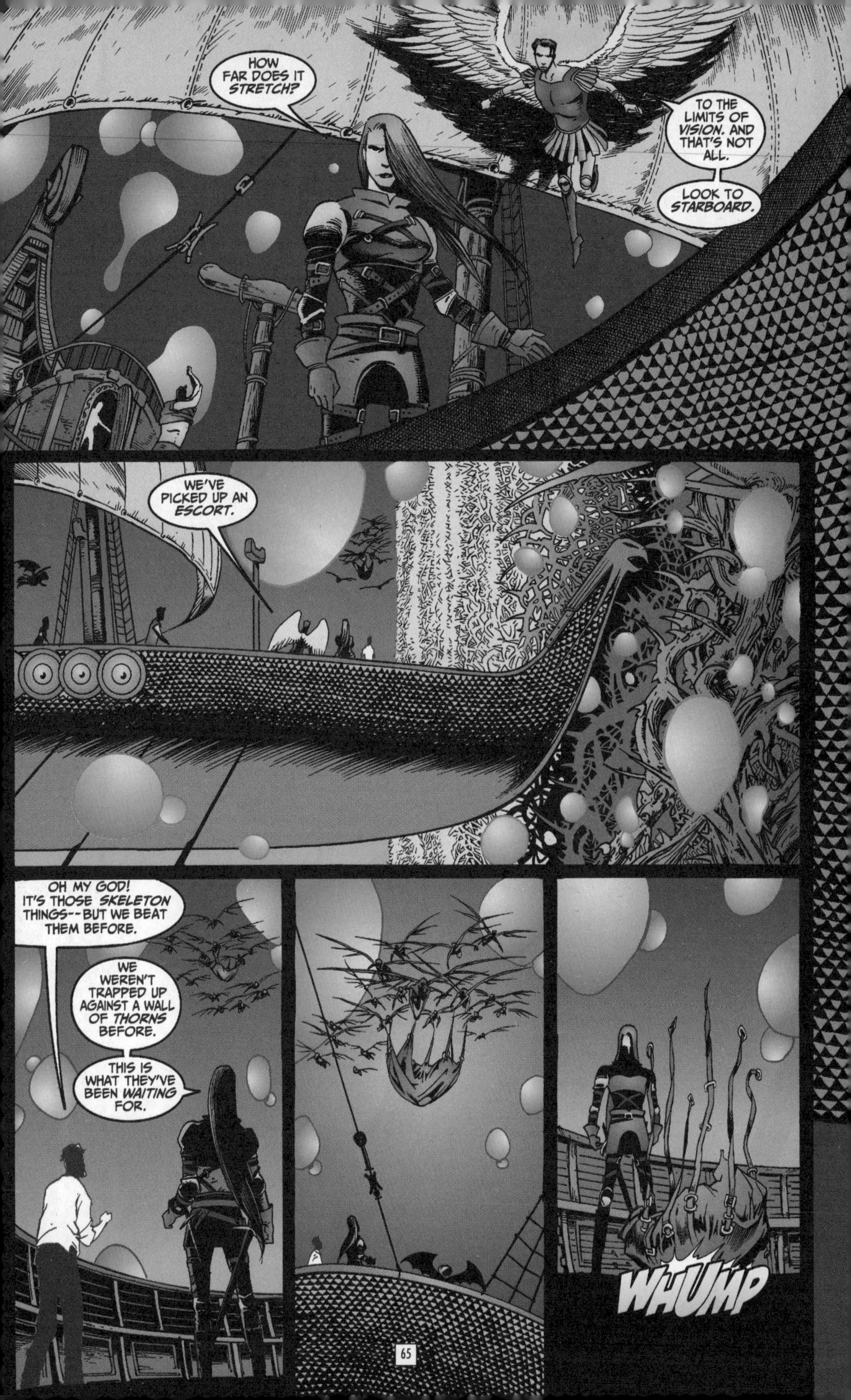
HOW FAR DOES IT STRETCH?
TO THE LIMITS OF VISION. AND THAT'S NOT ALL.
LOOK TO STARBOARD.
WE'VE PICKED UP AN ESCORT.
OH MY GOD! IT'S THOSE SKELETON THINGS--BUT WE BEAT THEM BEFORE.
WE WEREN'T TRAPPED UP AGAINST A WALL OF THORNS BEFORE.
THIS IS WHAT THEY'VE BEEN WAITING FOR.
WHUMP

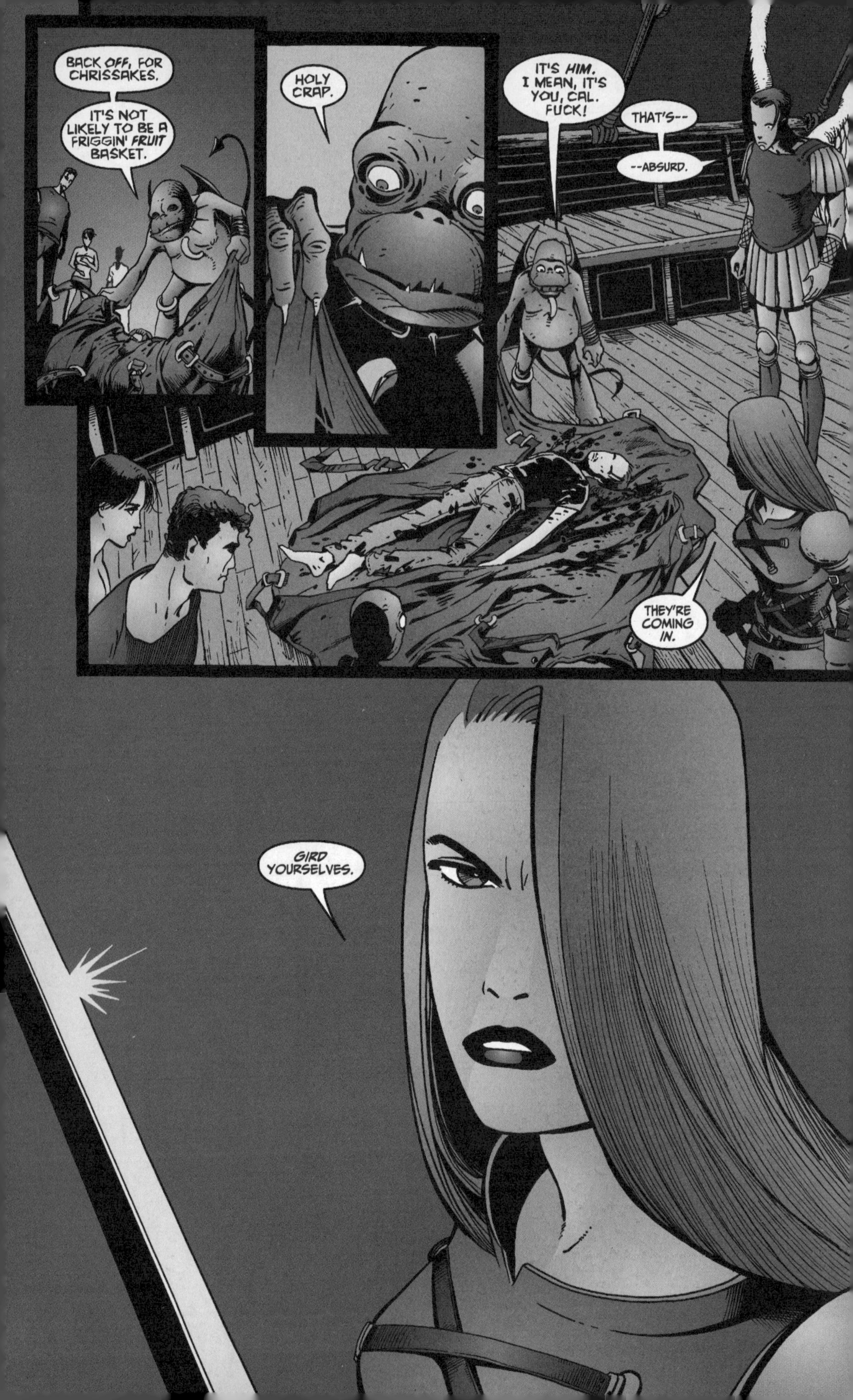
BACK OFF, FOR CHRISSAKES.
IT'S NOT LIKELY TO BE A FRIGGIN' FRUIT BASKET.
HOLY CRAP.
IT'S HIM. I MEAN, IT'S YOU, CAL. FUCK!
THAT'S--
--ABSURD.
THEY'RE COMING IN.
GIRD YOURSELVES.

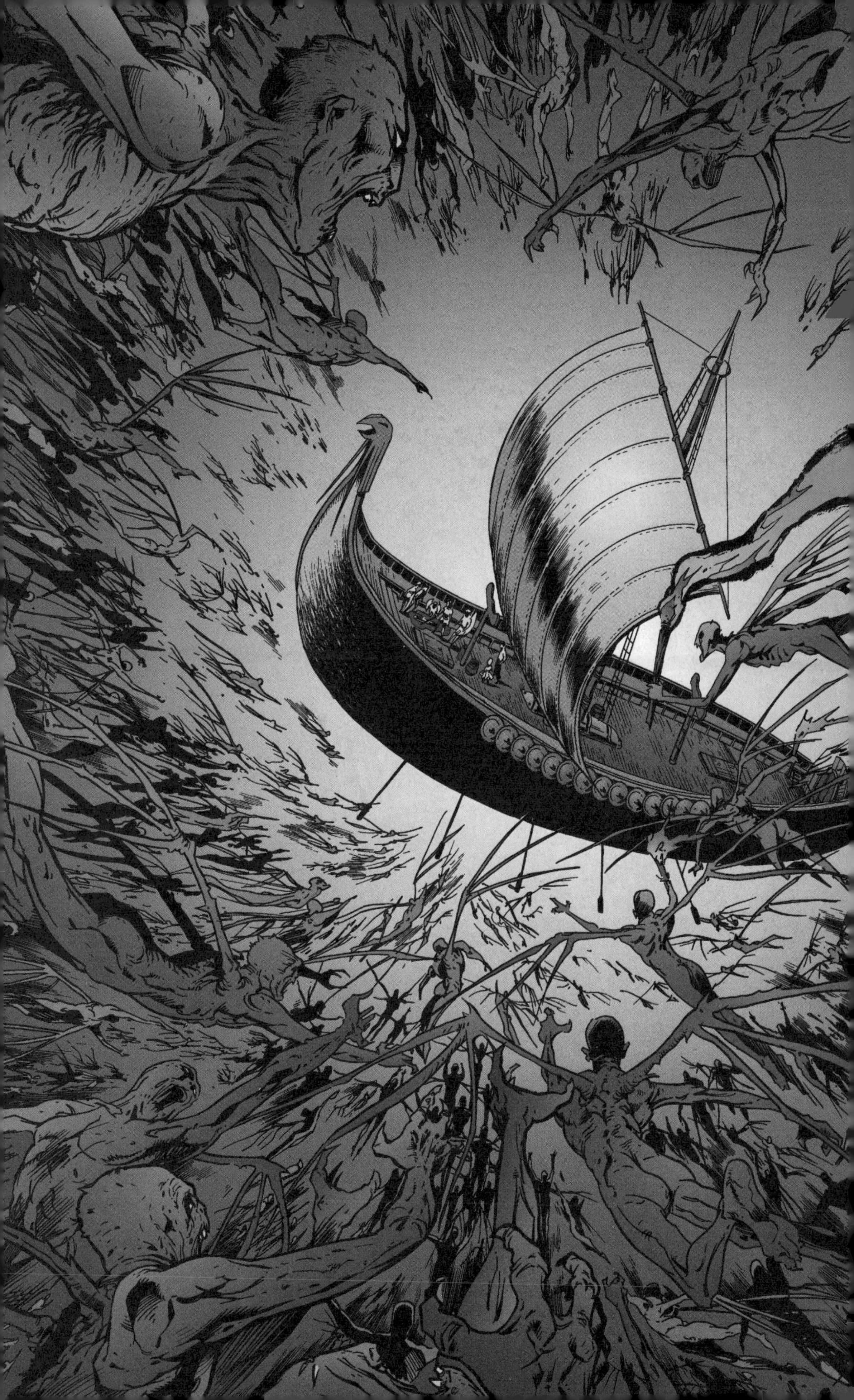

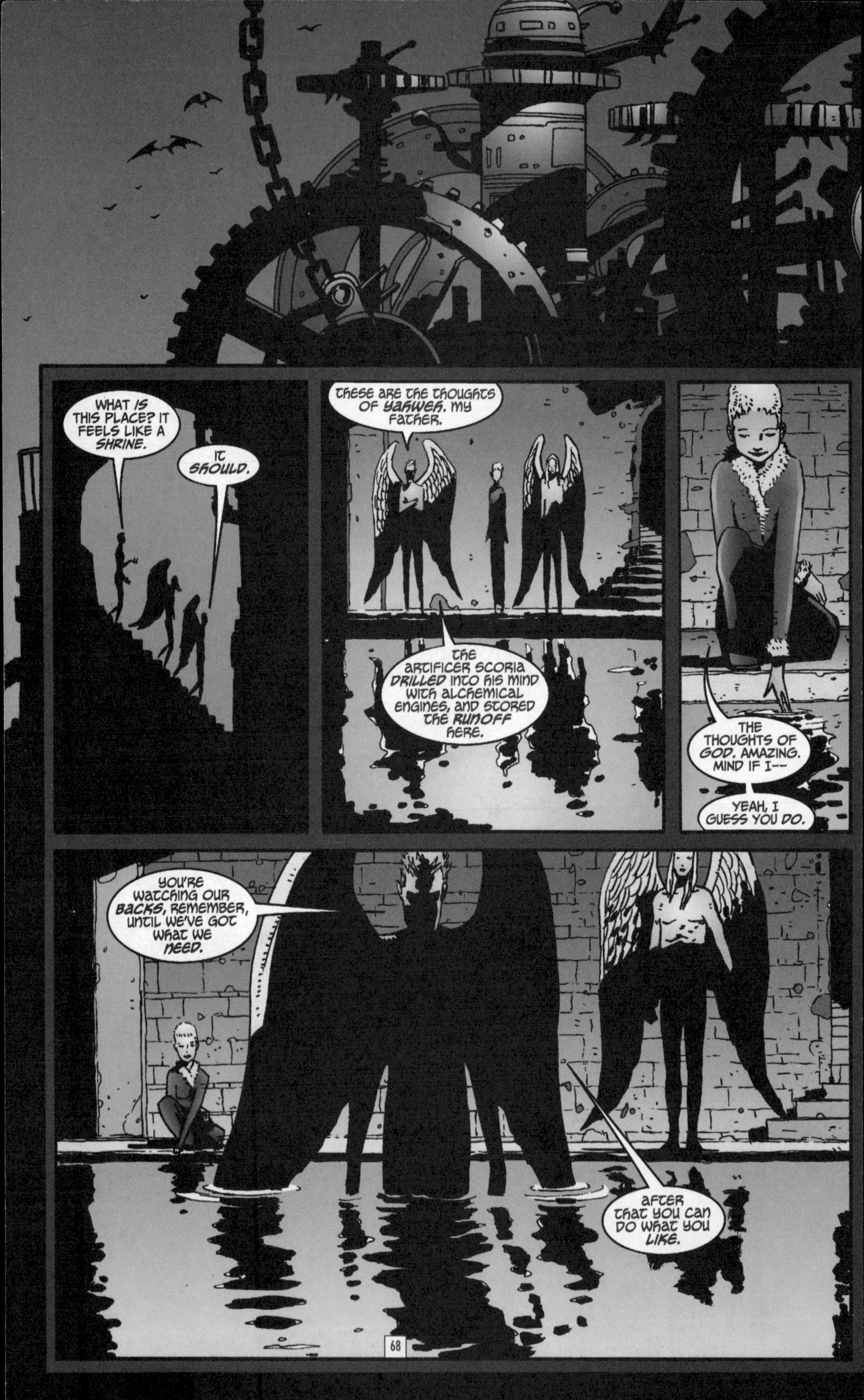

WHAT IS THIS PLACE? IT FEELS LIKE A SHRINE.
IT SHOULD.
THESE ARE THE THOUGHTS OF YAHWEH. MY FATHER.
THE ARTIFICER SCORIA DRILLED INTO HIS MIND WITH ALCHEMICAL ENGINES, AND STORED THE RUNOFF HERE.
THE THOUGHTS OF GOD. AMAZING. MIND IF I--
YEAH, I GUESS YOU DO.
YOU'RE WATCHING OUR BACKS, REMEMBER, UNTIL WE'VE GOT WHAT WE NEED.
AFTER THAT YOU CAN DO WHAT YOU LIKE.

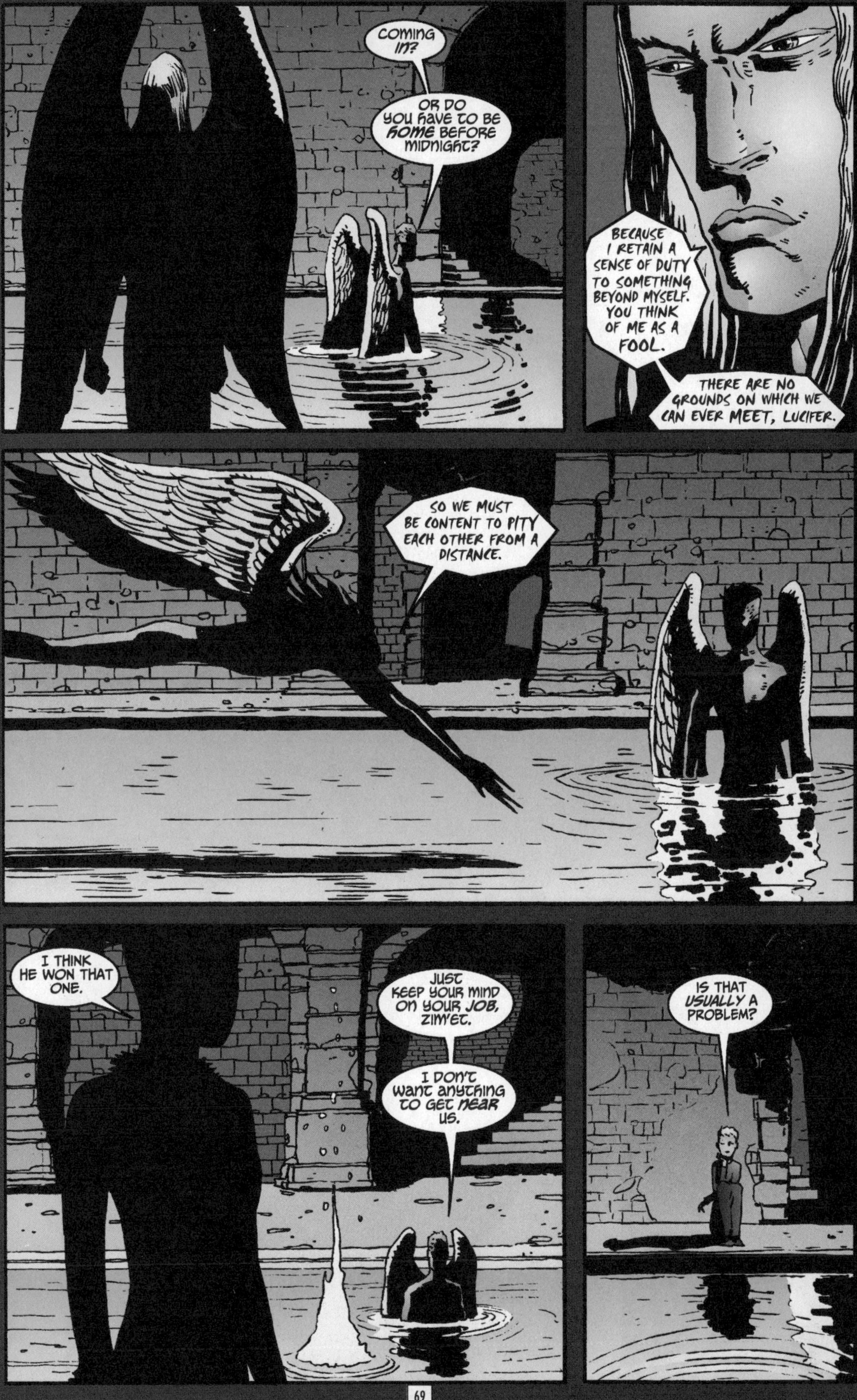
COMING IN?
OR DO YOU HAVE TO BE HOME BEFORE MIDNIGHT?
BECAUSE I RETAIN A SENSE OF DUTY TO SOMETHING BEYOND MYSELF. YOU THINK OF ME AS A FOOL.
THERE ARE NO GROUNDS ON WHICH WE CAN EVER MEET, LUCIFER.
SO WE MUST BE CONTENT TO PITY EACH OTHER FROM A DISTANCE.
I THINK HE WON THAT ONE.
JUST KEEP YOUR MIND ON YOUR JOB, ZIM'ET.
I DON'T WANT ANYTHING TO GET NEAR US.
IS THAT USUALLY A PROBLEM?

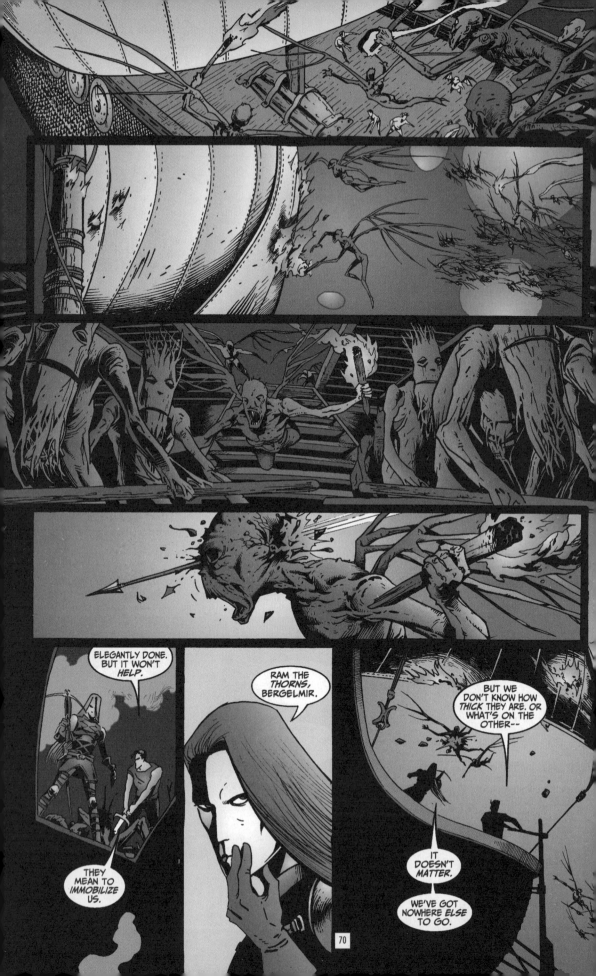

ELEGANTLY DONE. BUT IT WON'T *HELP*.

THEY MEAN TO *IMMOBILIZE* US.

RAM THE *THORNS*, BERGELMIR.

BUT WE DON'T KNOW HOW *THICK* THEY ARE. OR WHAT'S ON THE *OTHER*--

IT DOESN'T *MATTER*.

WE'VE GOT NOWHERE *ELSE* TO GO.

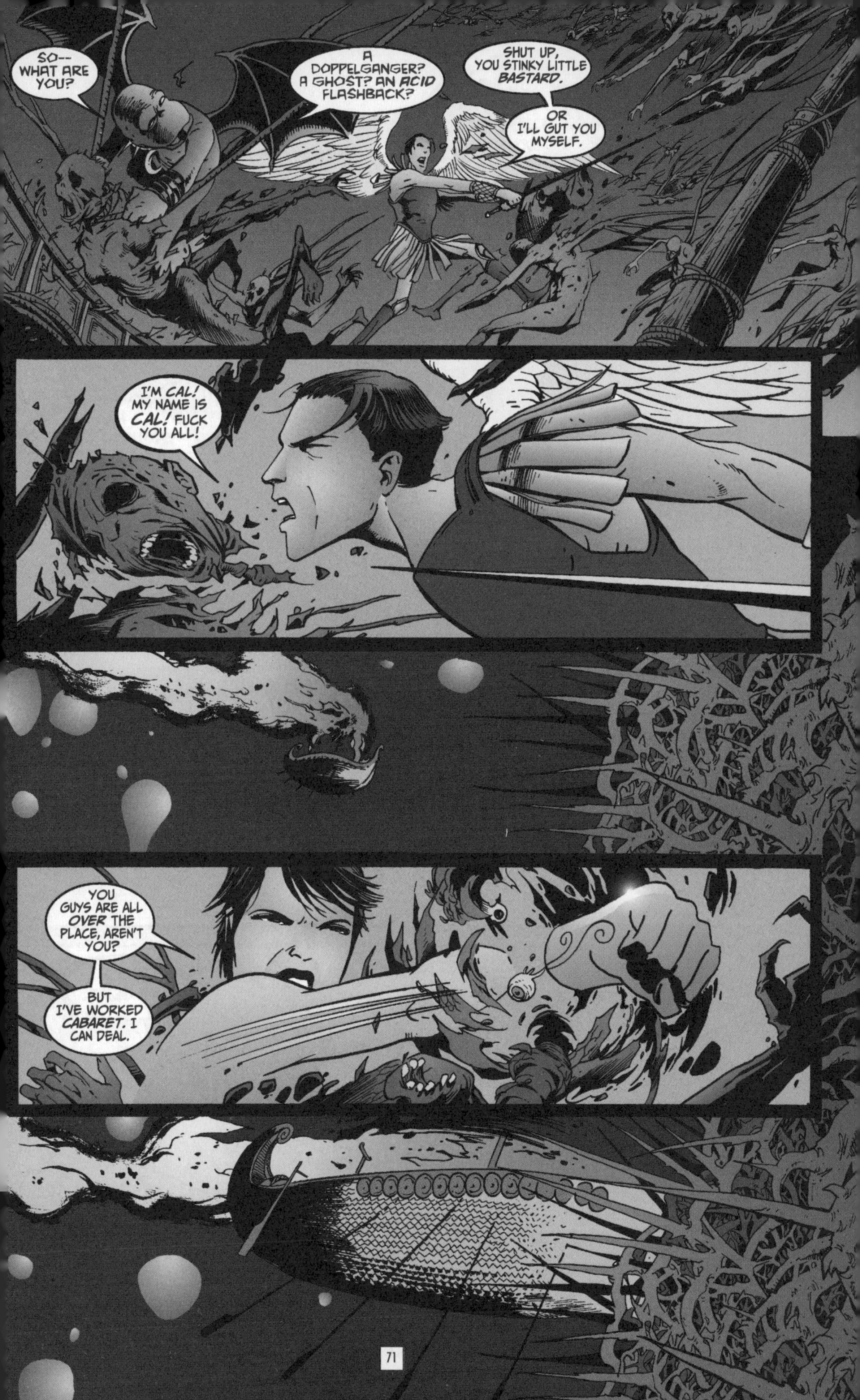
SO-- WHAT ARE YOU?
A DOPPELGANGER? A GHOST? AN ACID FLASHBACK?
SHUT UP, YOU STINKY LITTLE BASTARD.
OR I'LL GUT YOU MYSELF.
I'M CAL! MY NAME IS CAL! FUCK YOU ALL!
YOU GUYS ARE ALL OVER THE PLACE, AREN'T YOU?
BUT I'VE WORKED CABARET. I CAN DEAL.

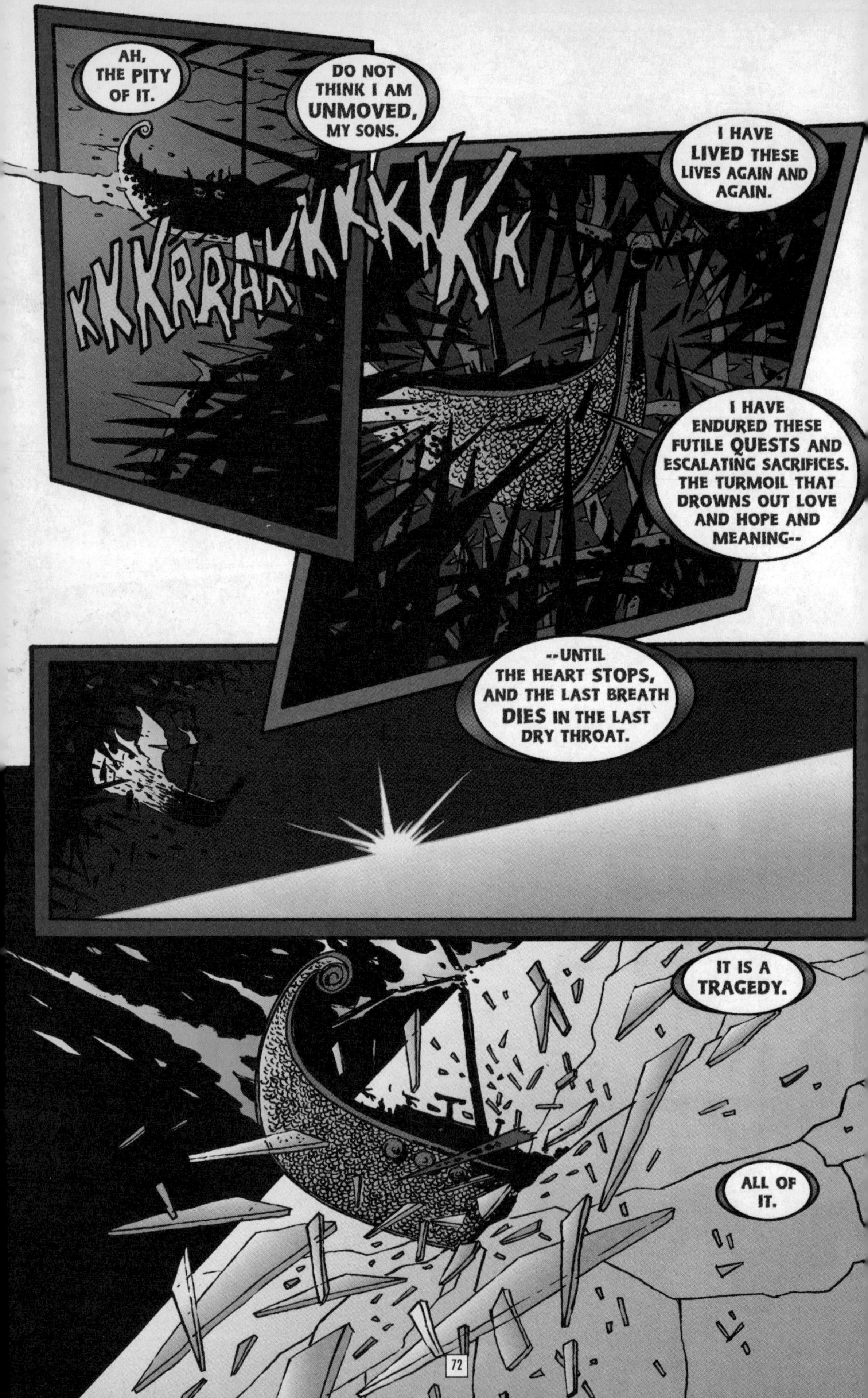
AH, THE PITY OF IT.
DO NOT THINK I AM UNMOVED, MY SONS.
I HAVE LIVED THESE LIVES AGAIN AND AGAIN.
KKKRRAKKKKKKKK
I HAVE ENDURED THESE FUTILE QUESTS AND ESCALATING SACRIFICES. THE TURMOIL THAT DROWNS OUT LOVE AND HOPE AND MEANING--
--UNTIL THE HEART STOPS, AND THE LAST BREATH DIES IN THE LAST DRY THROAT.
IT IS A TRAGEDY.
ALL OF IT.

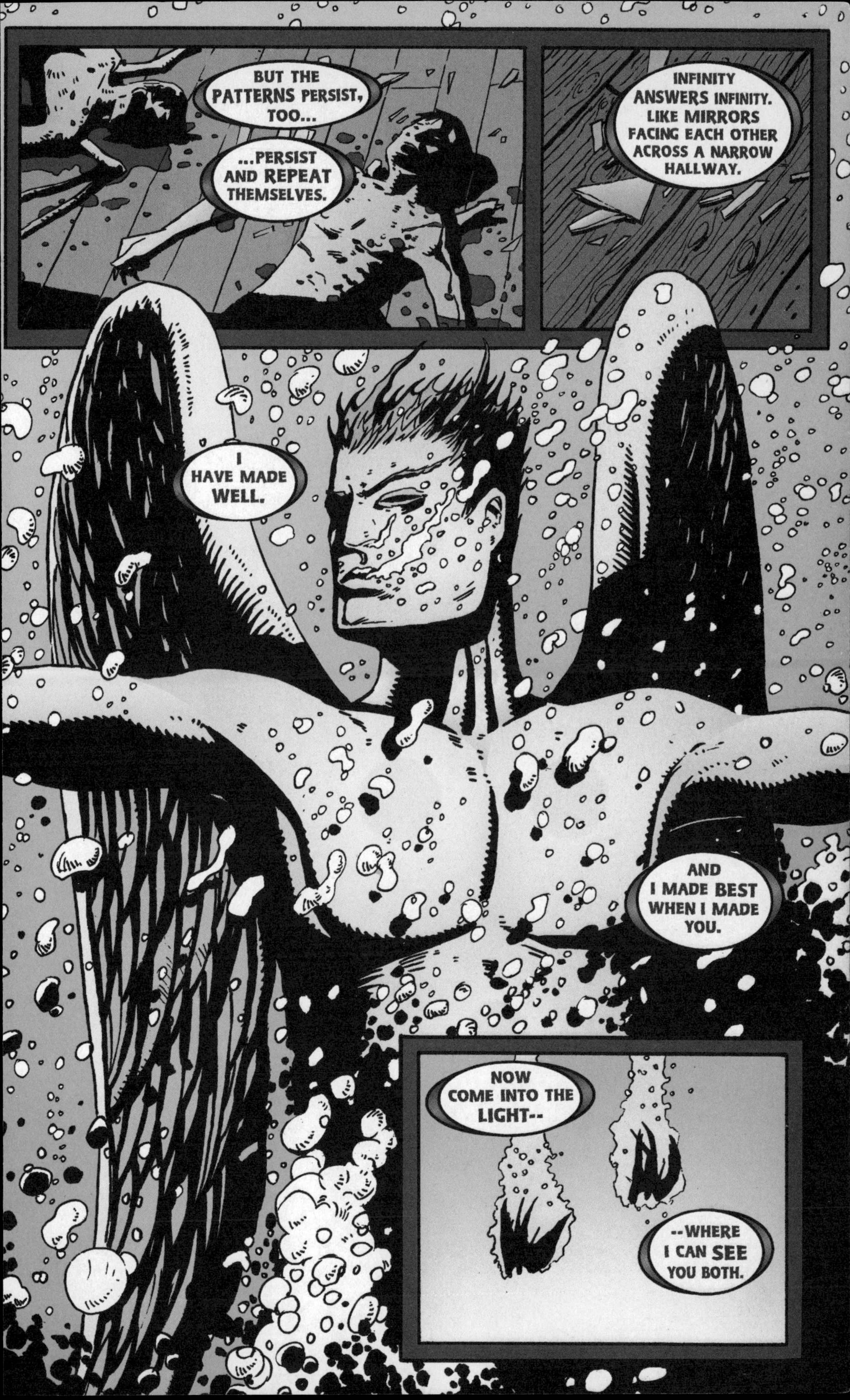
BUT THE PATTERNS PERSIST, TOO...
...PERSIST AND REPEAT THEMSELVES.
INFINITY ANSWERS INFINITY. LIKE MIRRORS FACING EACH OTHER ACROSS A NARROW HALLWAY.
I HAVE MADE WELL.
AND I MADE BEST WHEN I MADE YOU.
NOW COME INTO THE LIGHT--
--WHERE I CAN SEE YOU BOTH.

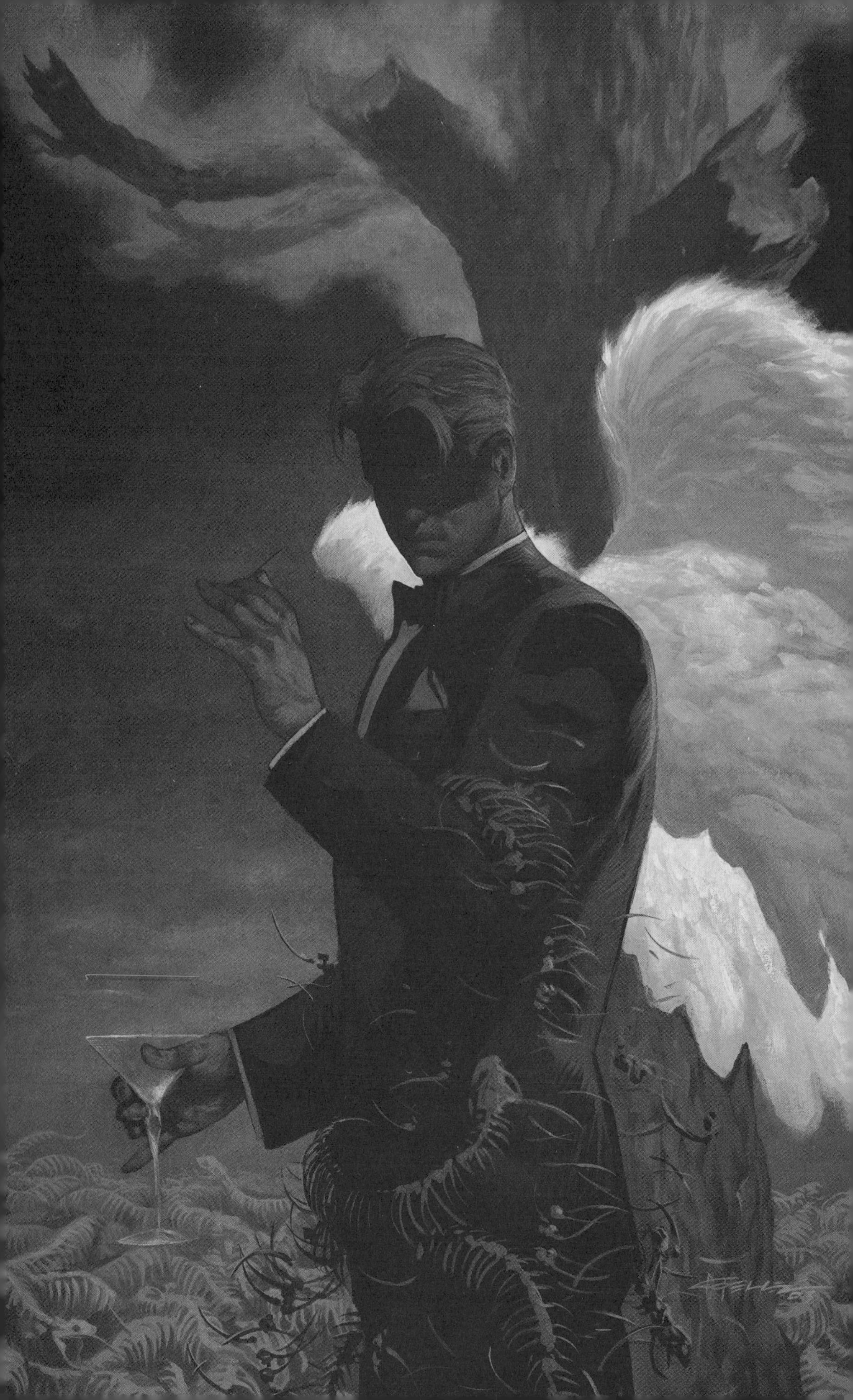

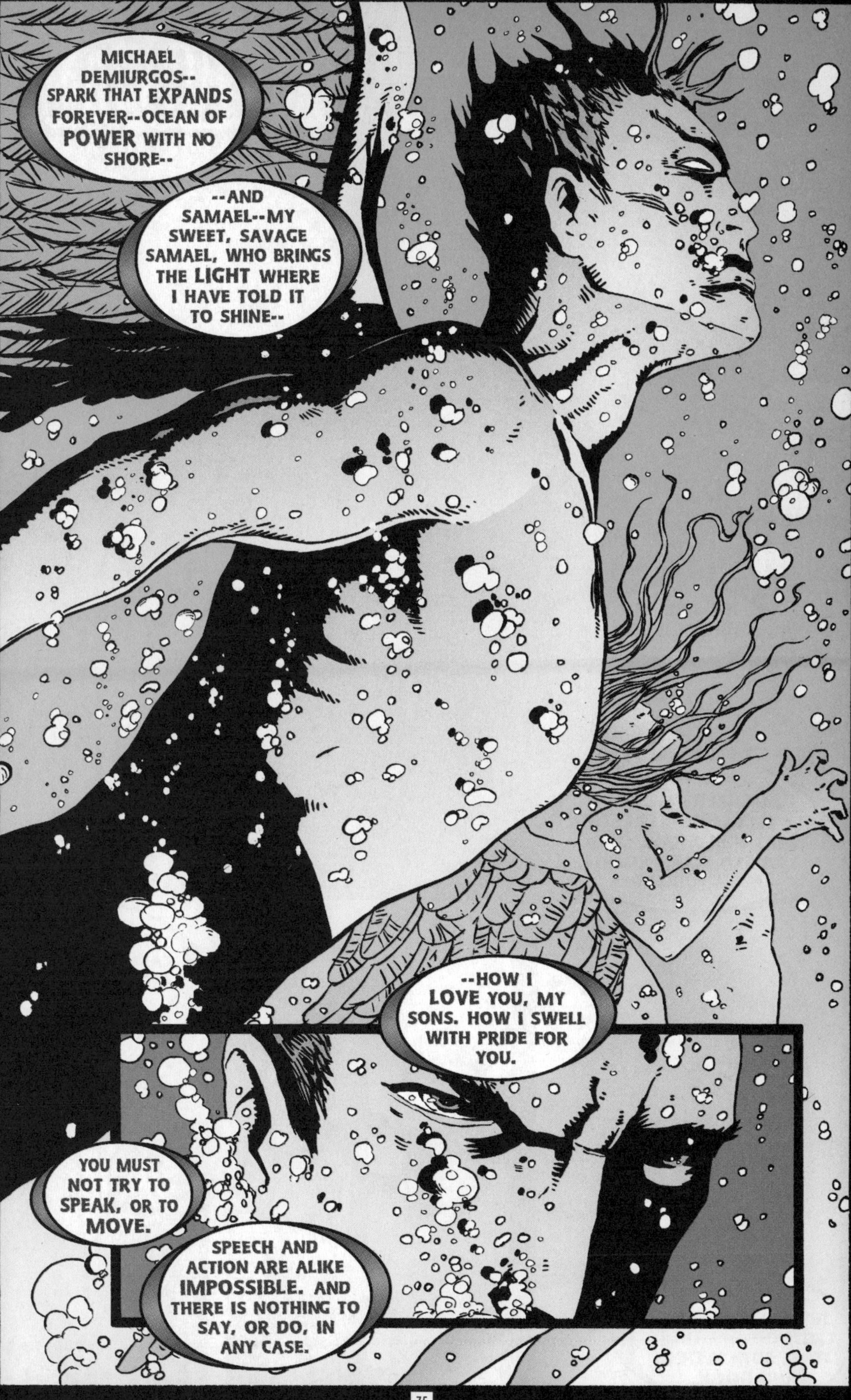
MICHAEL DEMIURGOS--SPARK THAT EXPANDS FOREVER--OCEAN OF POWER WITH NO SHORE--
--AND SAMAEL--MY SWEET, SAVAGE SAMAEL, WHO BRINGS THE LIGHT WHERE I HAVE TOLD IT TO SHINE--
--HOW I LOVE YOU, MY SONS. HOW I SWELL WITH PRIDE FOR YOU.
YOU MUST NOT TRY TO SPEAK, OR TO MOVE.
SPEECH AND ACTION ARE ALIKE IMPOSSIBLE. AND THERE IS NOTHING TO SAY, OR DO, IN ANY CASE.

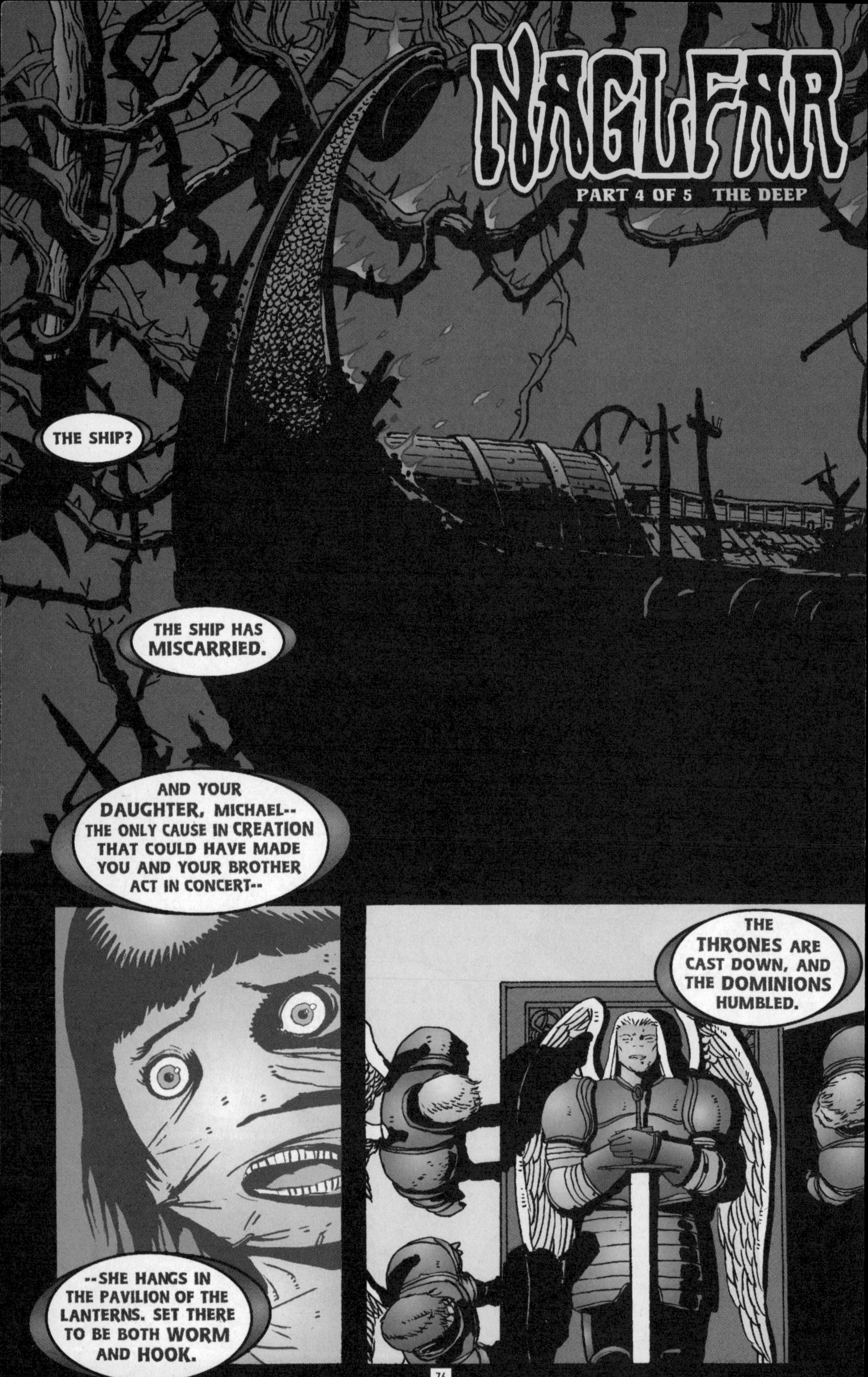
NAGLFAR
PART 4 OF 5 THE DEEP
THE SHIP?
THE SHIP HAS MISCARRIED.
AND YOUR DAUGHTER, MICHAEL-- THE ONLY CAUSE IN CREATION THAT COULD HAVE MADE YOU AND YOUR BROTHER ACT IN CONCERT--
--SHE HANGS IN THE PAVILION OF THE LANTERNS. SET THERE TO BE BOTH WORM AND HOOK.
THE THRONES ARE CAST DOWN, AND THE DOMINIONS HUMBLED.

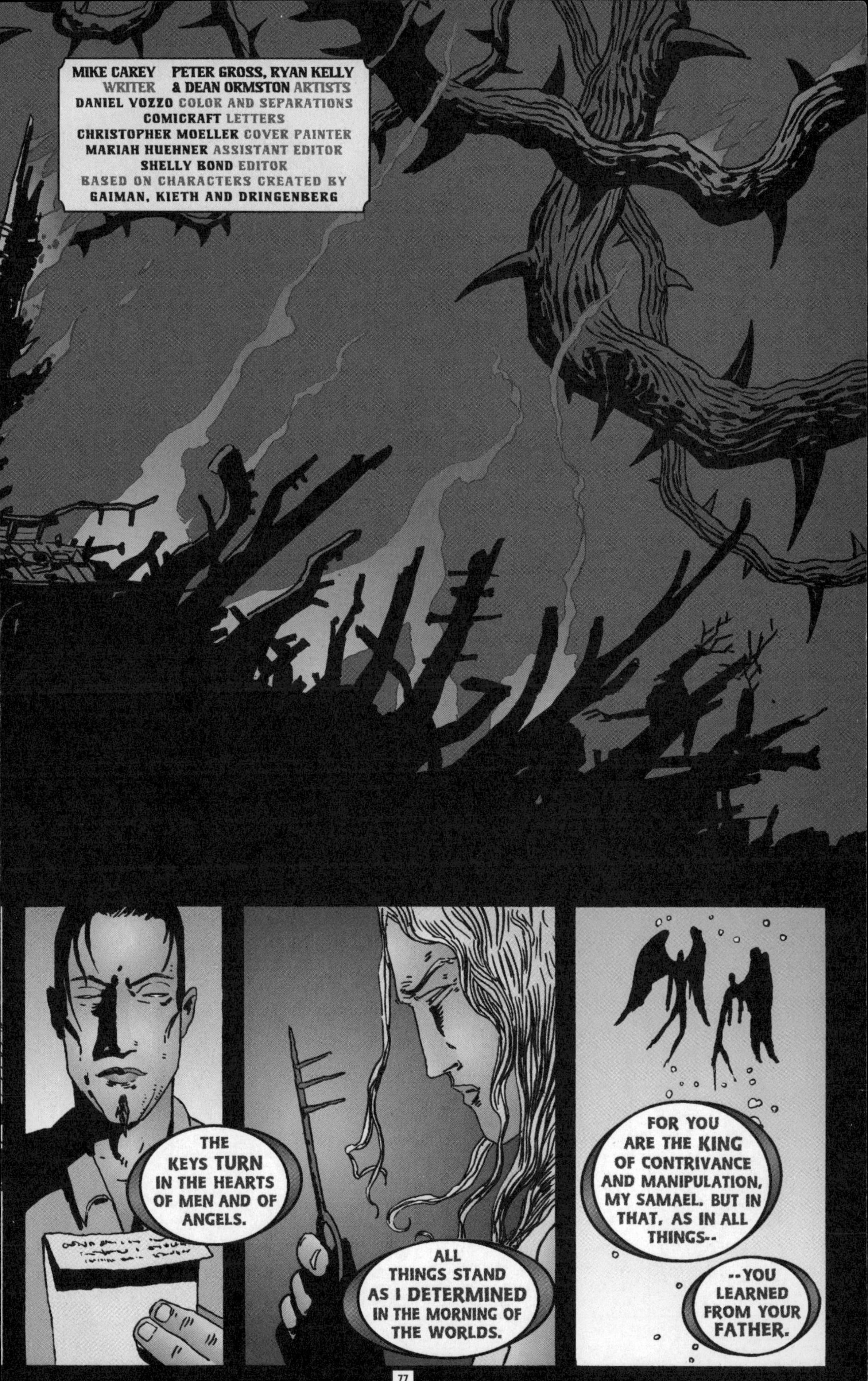
MIKE CAREY WRITER
PETER GROSS, RYAN KELLY & DEAN ORMSTON ARTISTS
DANIEL VOZZO COLOR AND SEPARATIONS
COMICRAFT LETTERS
CHRISTOPHER MOELLER COVER PAINTER
MARIAH HUEHNER ASSISTANT EDITOR
SHELLY BOND EDITOR
BASED ON CHARACTERS CREATED BY GAIMAN, KIETH AND DRINGENBERG
THE KEYS TURN IN THE HEARTS OF MEN AND OF ANGELS.
ALL THINGS STAND AS I DETERMINED IN THE MORNING OF THE WORLDS.
FOR YOU ARE THE KING OF CONTRIVANCE AND MANIPULATION, MY SAMAEL. BUT IN THAT, AS IN ALL THINGS--
--YOU LEARNED FROM YOUR FATHER.

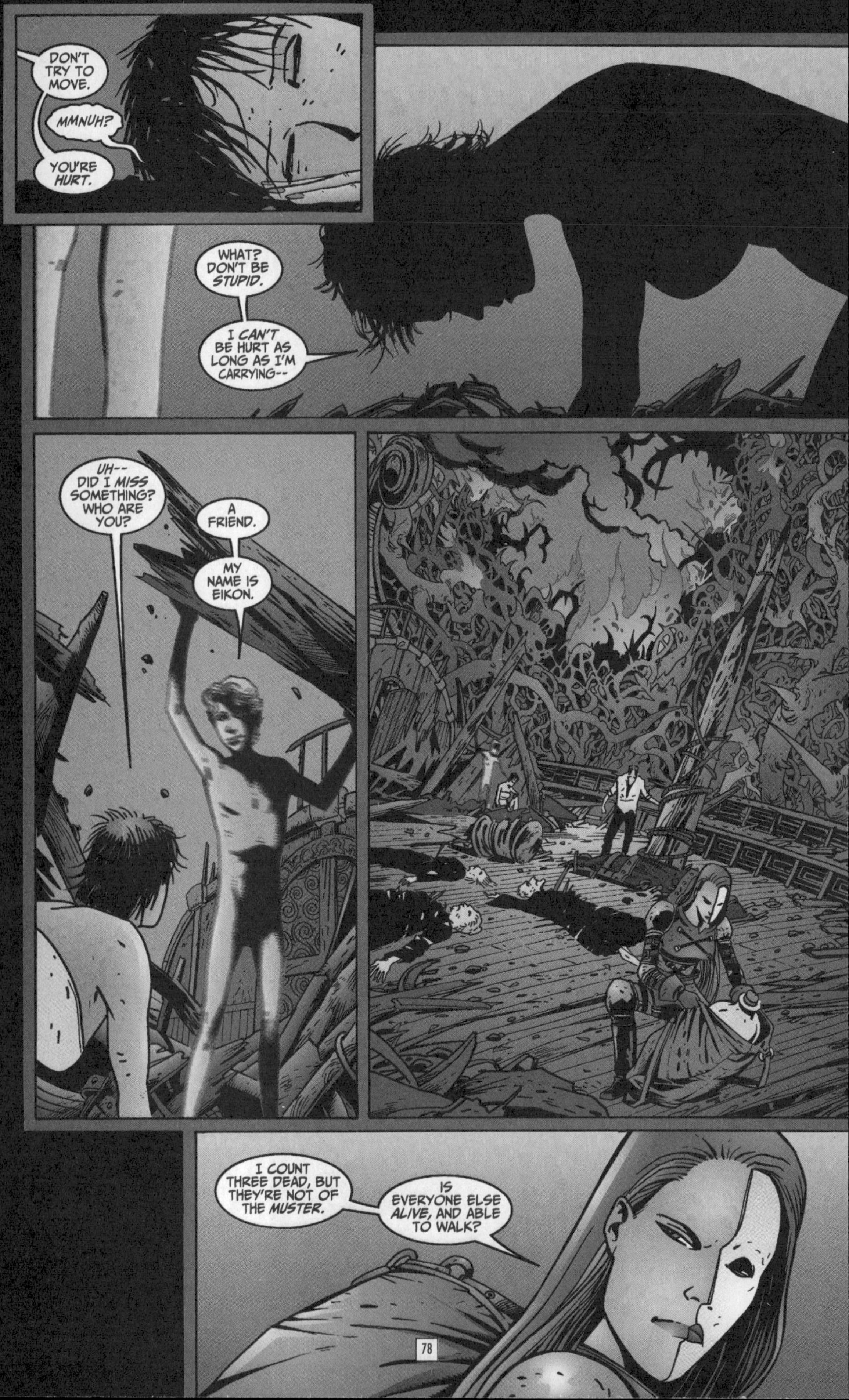
DON'T TRY TO MOVE.
MMNUH?
YOU'RE HURT.
WHAT? DON'T BE STUPID.
I CAN'T BE HURT AS LONG AS I'M CARRYING--
UH-- DID I MISS SOMETHING? WHO ARE YOU?
A FRIEND.
MY NAME IS EIKON.
I COUNT THREE DEAD, BUT THEY'RE NOT OF THE MUSTER.
IS EVERYONE ELSE ALIVE, AND ABLE TO WALK?

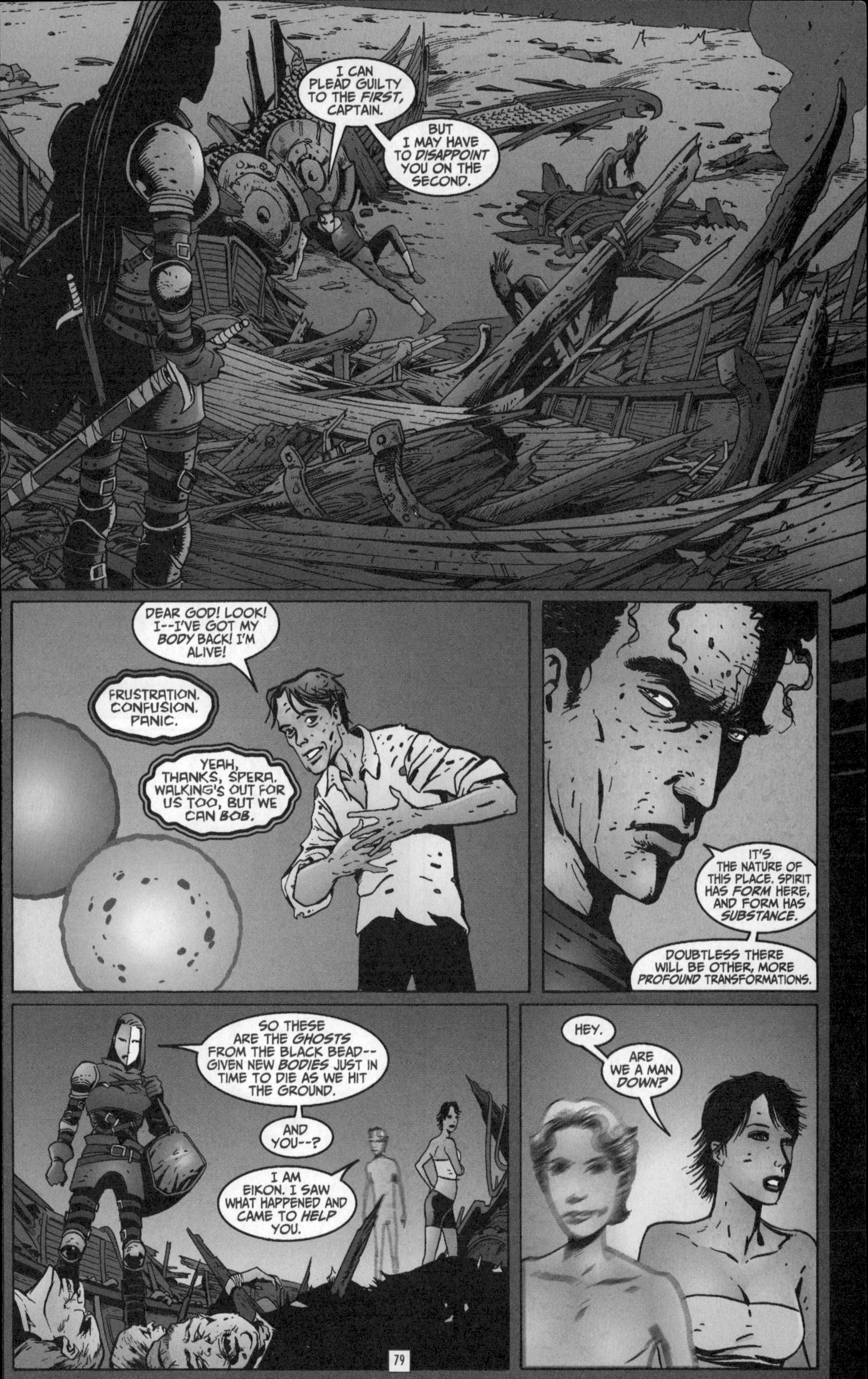

I CAN PLEAD GUILTY TO THE *FIRST*, CAPTAIN.
BUT I MAY HAVE TO *DISAPPOINT* YOU ON THE SECOND.
DEAR GOD! LOOK! I--I'VE GOT MY *BODY* BACK! I'M ALIVE!
FRUSTRATION. CONFUSION. PANIC.
YEAH, THANKS, SPERA. WALKING'S OUT FOR US TOO, BUT WE CAN *BOB*.
IT'S THE NATURE OF THIS PLACE. SPIRIT HAS *FORM* HERE, AND FORM HAS *SUBSTANCE*.
DOUBTLESS THERE WILL BE OTHER, MORE *PROFOUND* TRANSFORMATIONS.
SO THESE ARE THE *GHOSTS* FROM THE BLACK BEAD-- GIVEN NEW *BODIES* JUST IN TIME TO DIE AS WE HIT THE GROUND.
AND YOU--?
I AM EIKON. I SAW WHAT HAPPENED AND CAME TO *HELP* YOU.
HEY.
ARE WE A MAN *DOWN*?

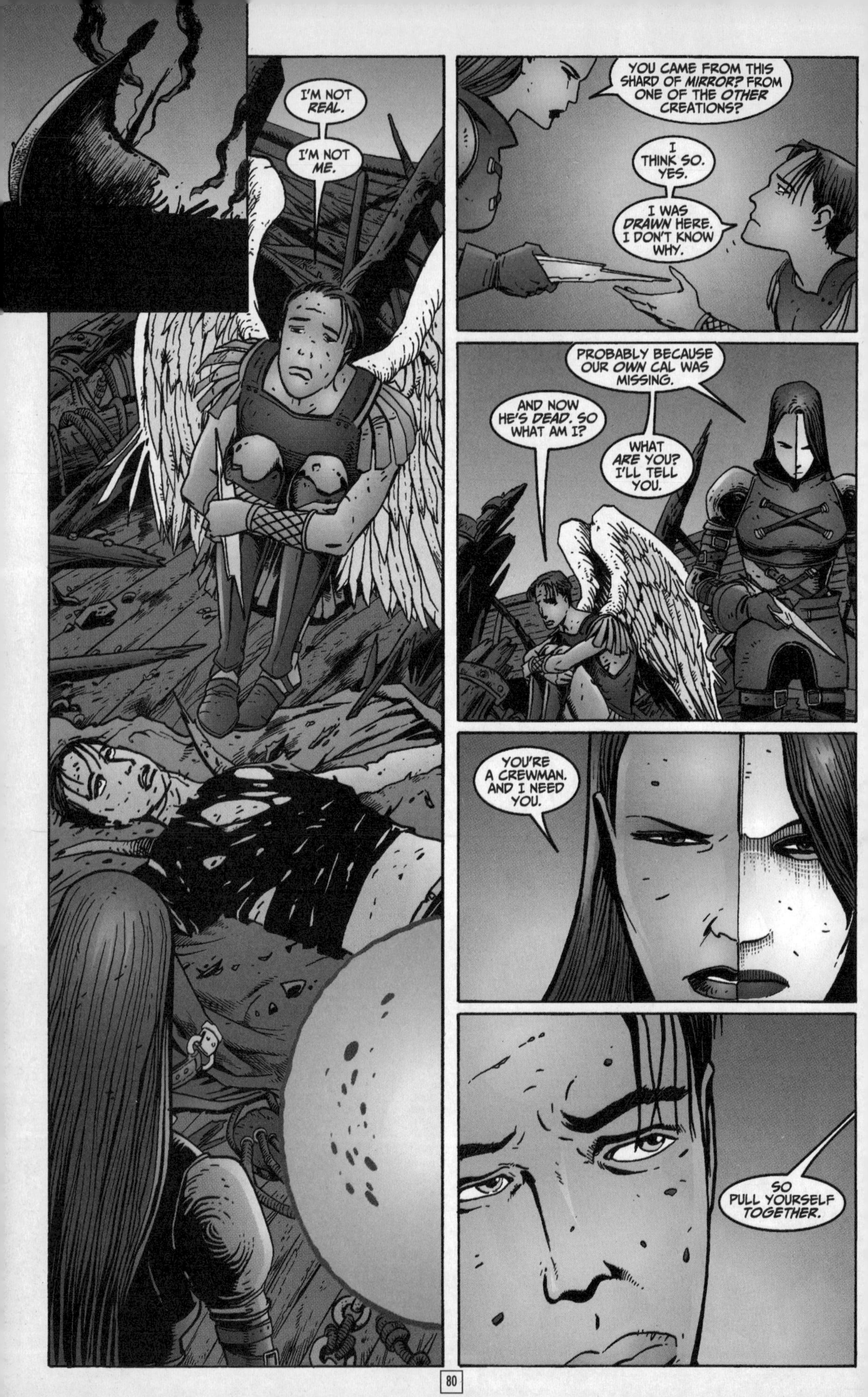
I'M NOT REAL.
I'M NOT ME.
YOU CAME FROM THIS SHARD OF MIRROR? FROM ONE OF THE OTHER CREATIONS?
I THINK SO. YES.
I WAS DRAWN HERE. I DON'T KNOW WHY.
PROBABLY BECAUSE OUR OWN CAL WAS MISSING.
AND NOW HE'S DEAD. SO WHAT AM I?
WHAT ARE YOU? I'LL TELL YOU.
YOU'RE A CREWMAN. AND I NEED YOU.
SO PULL YOURSELF TOGETHER.

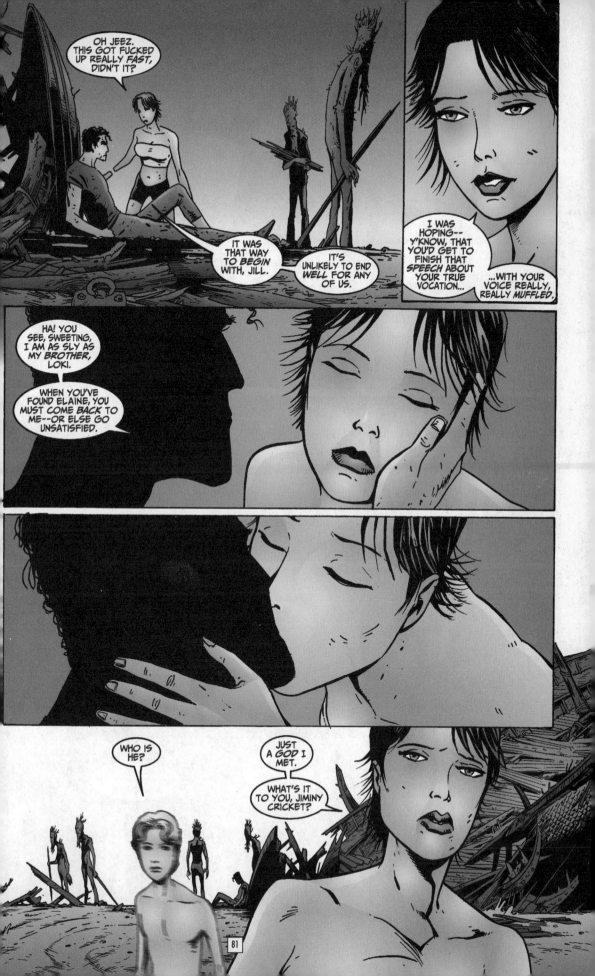

OH JEEZ. THIS GOT FUCKED UP REALLY FAST, DIDN'T IT?

IT WAS THAT WAY TO BEGIN WITH, JILL.

IT'S UNLIKELY TO END WELL FOR ANY OF US.

I WAS HOPING-- Y'KNOW, THAT YOU'D GET TO FINISH THAT SPEECH ABOUT YOUR TRUE VOCATION...

...WITH YOUR VOICE REALLY, REALLY MUFFLED.

HA! YOU SEE, SWEETING, I AM AS SLY AS MY BROTHER, LOKI.

WHEN YOU'VE FOUND ELAINE, YOU MUST COME BACK TO ME--OR ELSE GO UNSATISFIED.

WHO IS HE?

JUST A GOD I MET.

WHAT'S IT TO YOU, JIMINY CRICKET?

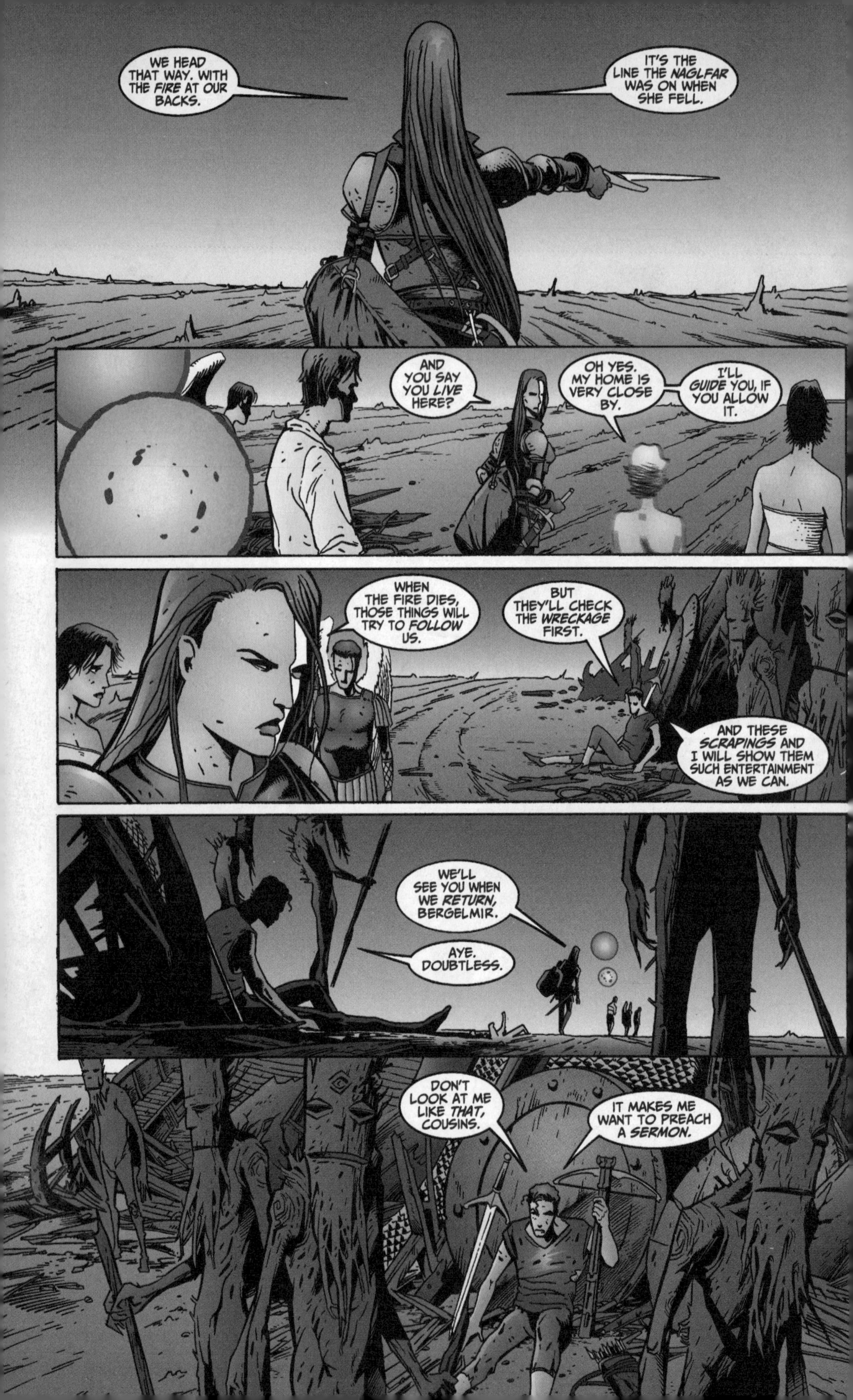
WE HEAD THAT WAY. WITH THE *FIRE* AT OUR BACKS.
IT'S THE LINE THE *NAGLFAR* WAS ON WHEN SHE FELL.
AND YOU SAY YOU *LIVE* HERE?
OH YES. MY HOME IS VERY CLOSE BY.
I'LL *GUIDE* YOU, IF YOU ALLOW IT.
WHEN THE FIRE DIES, THOSE THINGS WILL TRY TO *FOLLOW* US.
BUT THEY'LL CHECK THE *WRECKAGE* FIRST.
AND THESE *SCRAPINGS* AND I WILL SHOW THEM SUCH ENTERTAINMENT AS WE CAN.
WE'LL SEE YOU WHEN WE *RETURN*, BERGELMIR.
AYE. DOUBTLESS.
DON'T LOOK AT ME LIKE *THAT*, COUSINS.
IT MAKES ME WANT TO PREACH A *SERMON*.

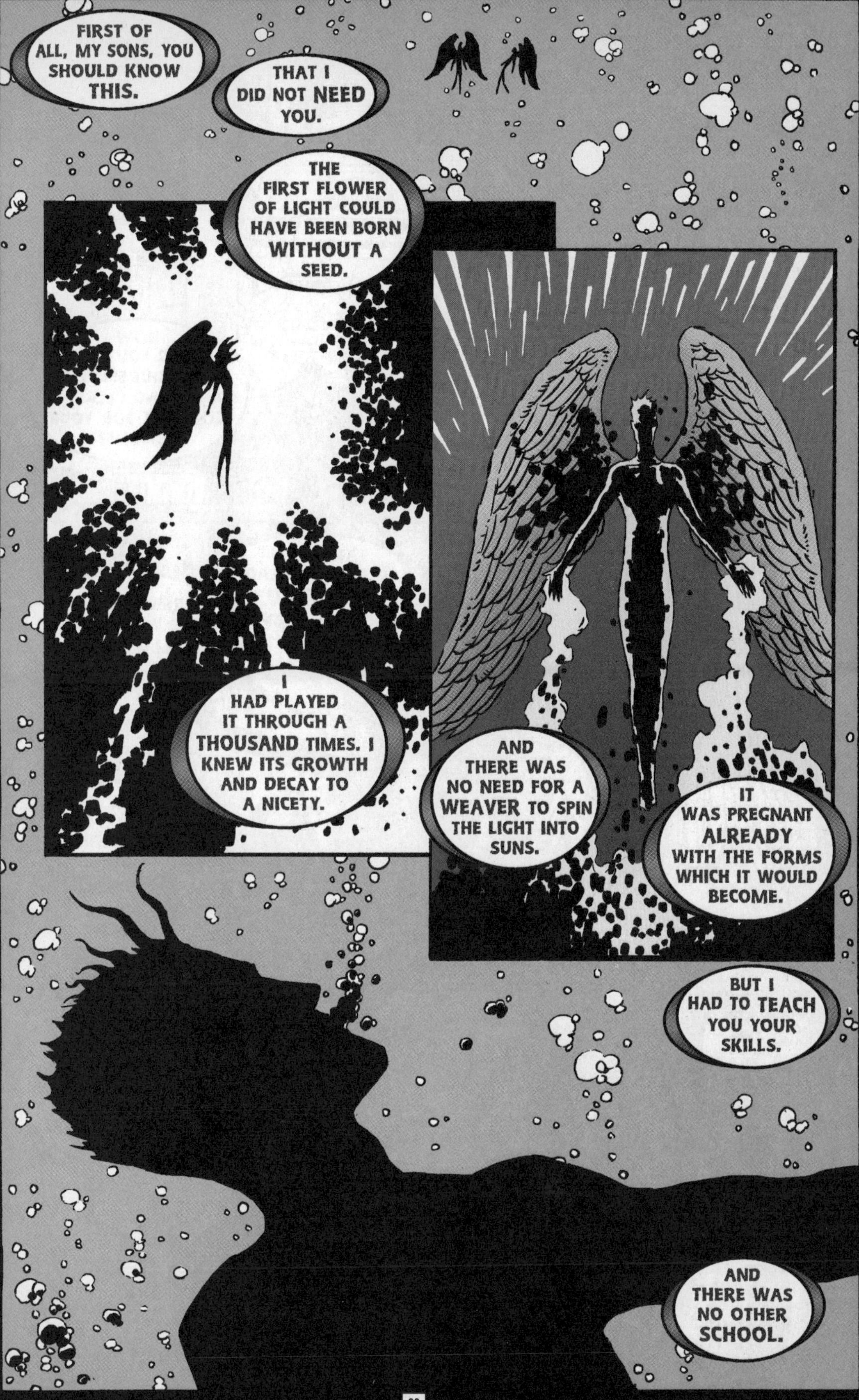
FIRST OF ALL, MY SONS, YOU SHOULD KNOW THIS.
THAT I DID NOT NEED YOU.
THE FIRST FLOWER OF LIGHT COULD HAVE BEEN BORN WITHOUT A SEED.
I HAD PLAYED IT THROUGH A THOUSAND TIMES. I KNEW ITS GROWTH AND DECAY TO A NICETY.
AND THERE WAS NO NEED FOR A WEAVER TO SPIN THE LIGHT INTO SUNS.
IT WAS PREGNANT ALREADY WITH THE FORMS WHICH IT WOULD BECOME.
BUT I HAD TO TEACH YOU YOUR SKILLS.
AND THERE WAS NO OTHER SCHOOL.

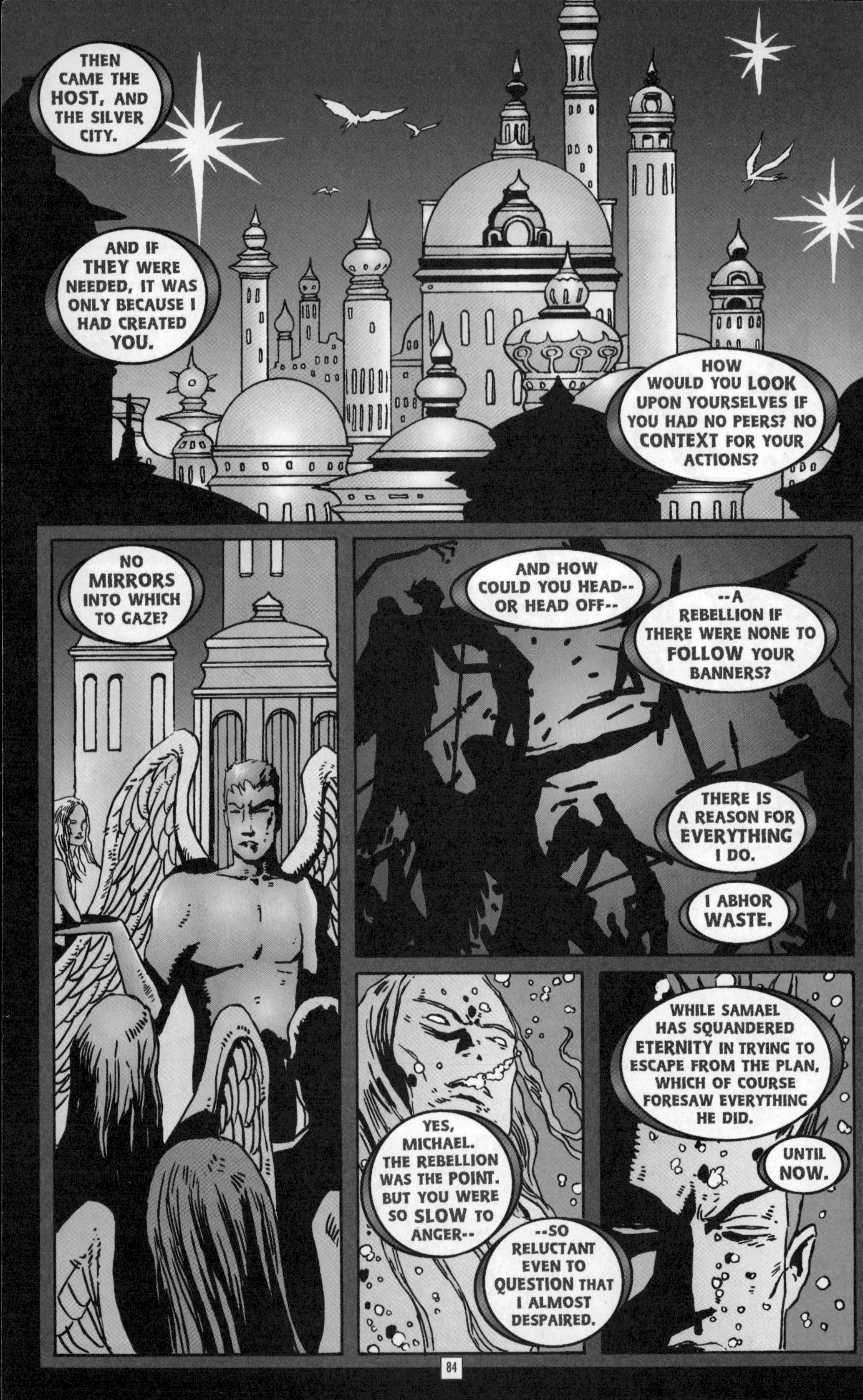
THEN CAME THE HOST, AND THE SILVER CITY.
AND IF THEY WERE NEEDED, IT WAS ONLY BECAUSE I HAD CREATED YOU.
HOW WOULD YOU LOOK UPON YOURSELVES IF YOU HAD NO PEERS? NO CONTEXT FOR YOUR ACTIONS?
NO MIRRORS INTO WHICH TO GAZE?
AND HOW COULD YOU HEAD-- OR HEAD OFF--
--A REBELLION IF THERE WERE NONE TO FOLLOW YOUR BANNERS?
THERE IS A REASON FOR EVERYTHING I DO.
I ABHOR WASTE.
YES, MICHAEL. THE REBELLION WAS THE POINT. BUT YOU WERE SO SLOW TO ANGER--
--SO RELUCTANT EVEN TO QUESTION THAT I ALMOST DESPAIRED.
WHILE SAMAEL HAS SQUANDERED ETERNITY IN TRYING TO ESCAPE FROM THE PLAN, WHICH OF COURSE FORESAW EVERYTHING HE DID.
UNTIL NOW.

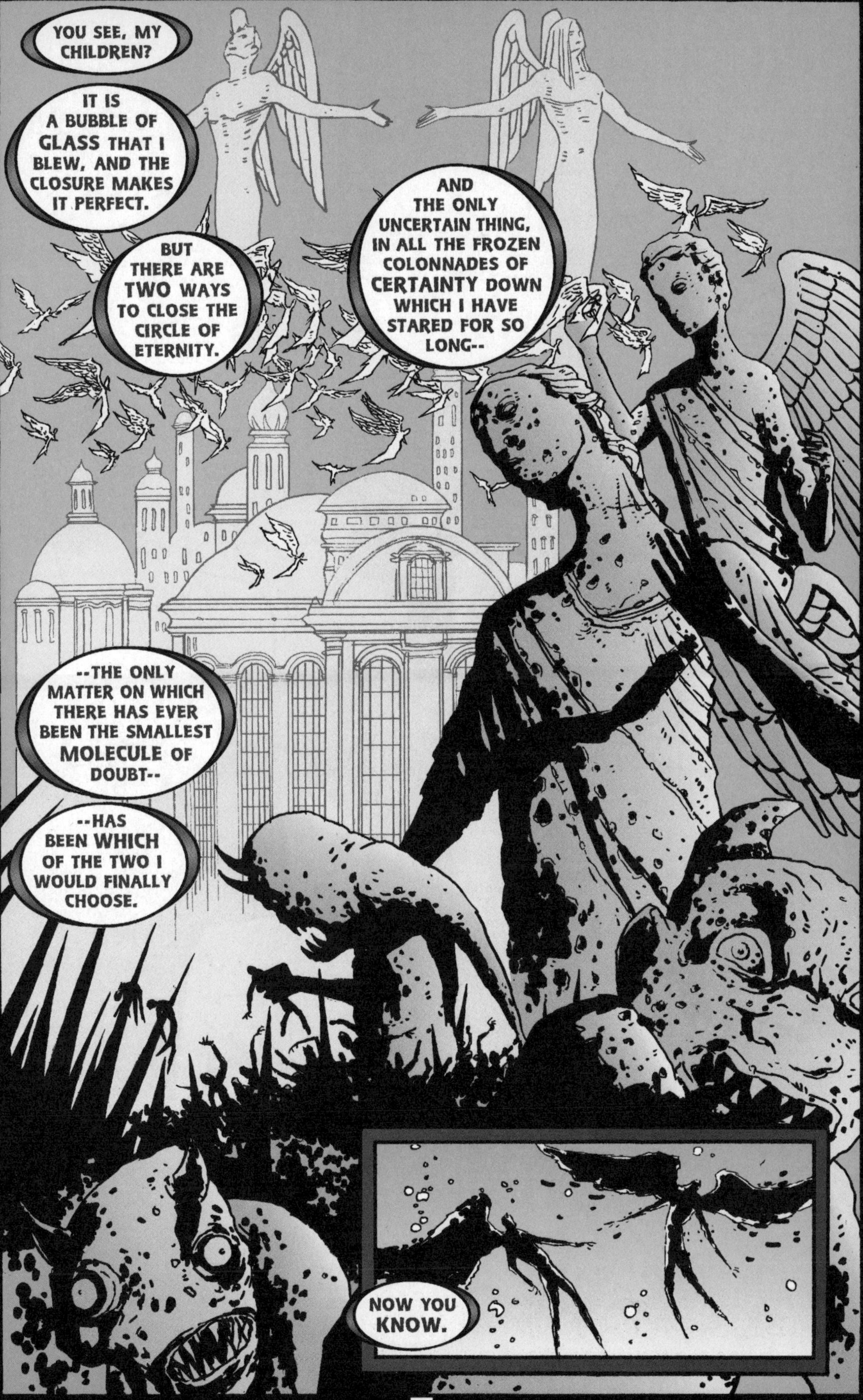
YOU SEE, MY CHILDREN?
IT IS A BUBBLE OF GLASS THAT I BLEW, AND THE CLOSURE MAKES IT PERFECT.
BUT THERE ARE TWO WAYS TO CLOSE THE CIRCLE OF ETERNITY.
AND THE ONLY UNCERTAIN THING, IN ALL THE FROZEN COLONNADES OF CERTAINTY DOWN WHICH I HAVE STARED FOR SO LONG--
--THE ONLY MATTER ON WHICH THERE HAS EVER BEEN THE SMALLEST MOLECULE OF DOUBT--
--HAS BEEN WHICH OF THE TWO I WOULD FINALLY CHOOSE.
NOW YOU KNOW.

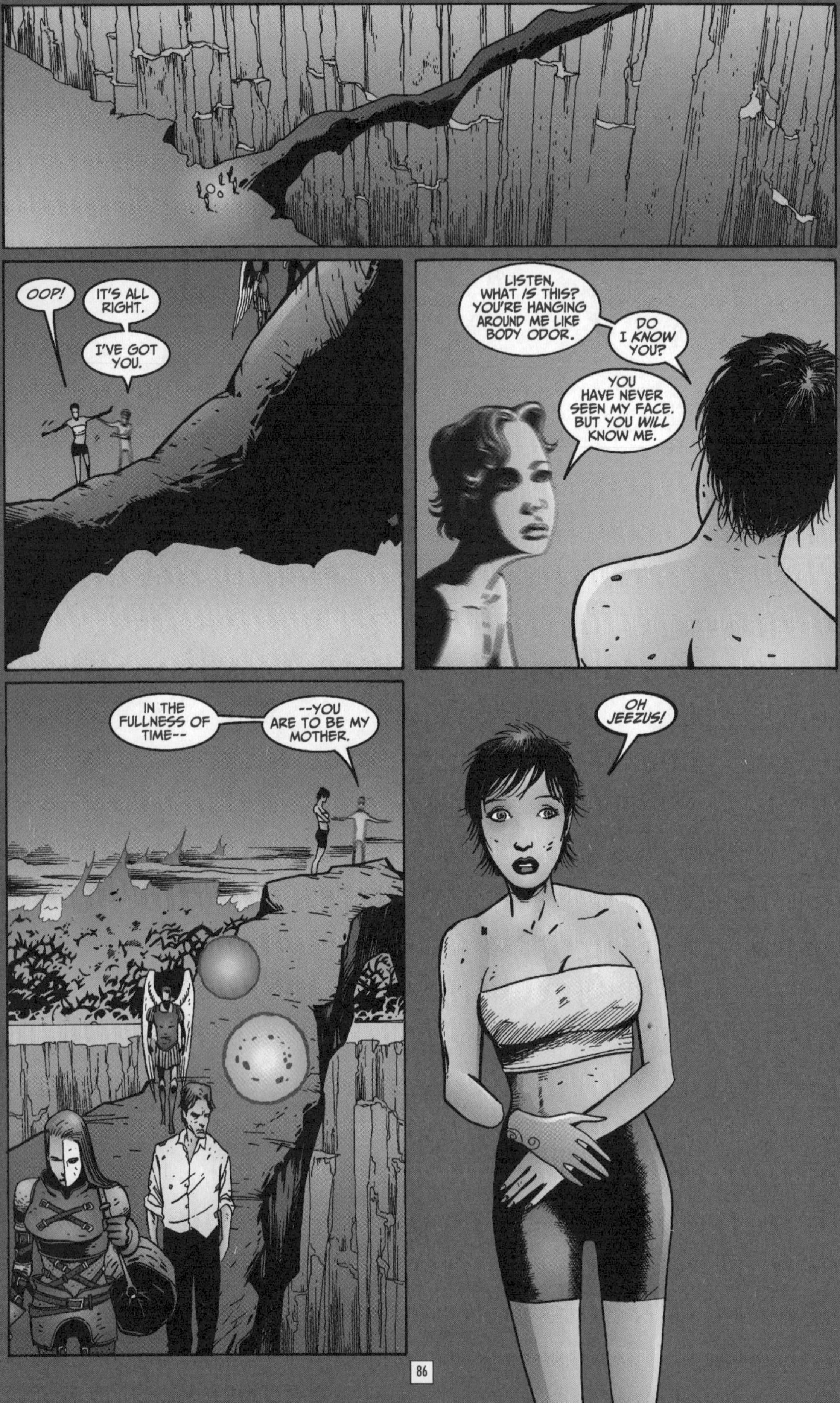
OOP!
IT'S ALL RIGHT.
I'VE GOT YOU.
LISTEN, WHAT *IS* THIS? YOU'RE HANGING AROUND ME LIKE BODY ODOR.
DO I *KNOW* YOU?
YOU HAVE NEVER SEEN MY FACE. BUT YOU *WILL* KNOW ME.
IN THE FULLNESS OF TIME--
--YOU ARE TO BE MY MOTHER.
OH JEEZUS!

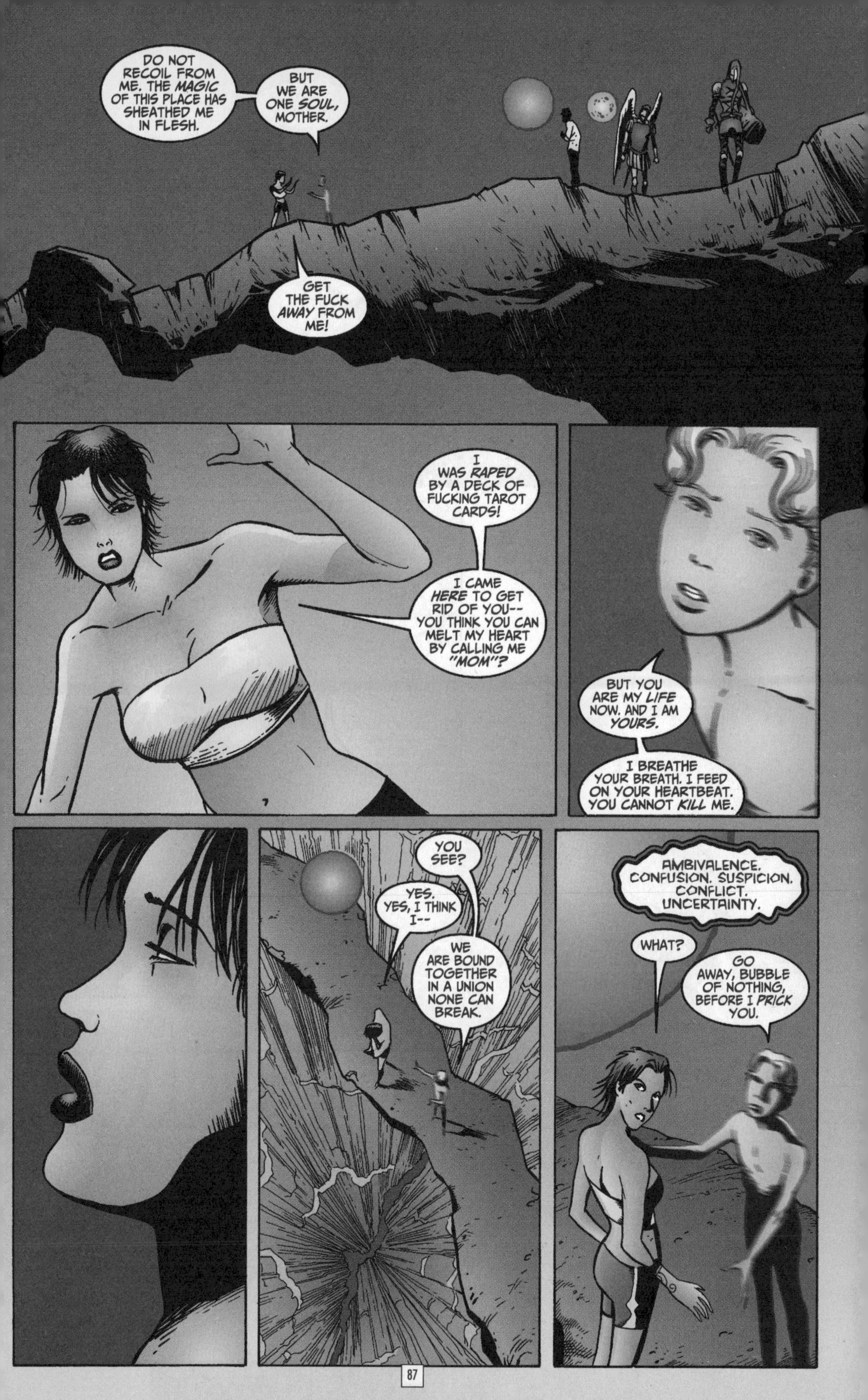
DO NOT RECOIL FROM ME. THE MAGIC OF THIS PLACE HAS SHEATHED ME IN FLESH.
BUT WE ARE ONE SOUL, MOTHER.
GET THE FUCK AWAY FROM ME!
I WAS RAPED BY A DECK OF FUCKING TAROT CARDS!
I CAME HERE TO GET RID OF YOU-- YOU THINK YOU CAN MELT MY HEART BY CALLING ME "MOM"?
BUT YOU ARE MY LIFE NOW. AND I AM YOURS.
I BREATHE YOUR BREATH. I FEED ON YOUR HEARTBEAT. YOU CANNOT KILL ME.
YOU SEE?
YES. YES, I THINK I--
WE ARE BOUND TOGETHER IN A UNION NONE CAN BREAK.
AMBIVALENCE. CONFUSION. SUSPICION. CONFLICT. UNCERTAINTY.
WHAT?
GO AWAY, BUBBLE OF NOTHING, BEFORE I PRICK YOU.

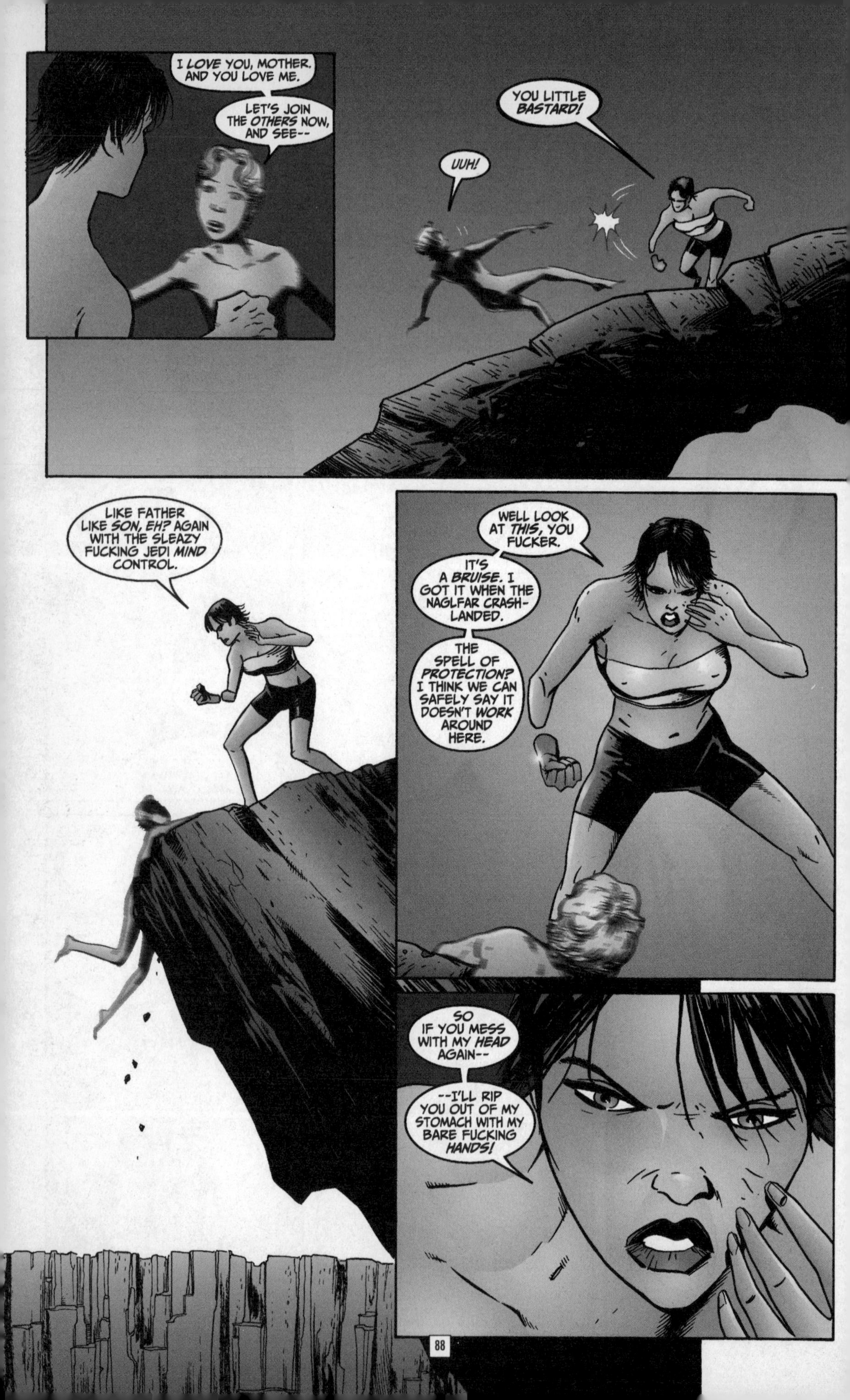

I LOVE YOU, MOTHER. AND YOU LOVE ME.
LET'S JOIN THE OTHERS NOW, AND SEE--
YOU LITTLE BASTARD!
UUH!
LIKE FATHER LIKE SON, EH? AGAIN WITH THE SLEAZY FUCKING JEDI MIND CONTROL.
WELL LOOK AT THIS, YOU FUCKER.
IT'S A BRUISE. I GOT IT WHEN THE NAGLFAR CRASH-LANDED.
THE SPELL OF PROTECTION? I THINK WE CAN SAFELY SAY IT DOESN'T WORK AROUND HERE.
SO IF YOU MESS WITH MY HEAD AGAIN--
--I'LL RIP YOU OUT OF MY STOMACH WITH MY BARE FUCKING HANDS!

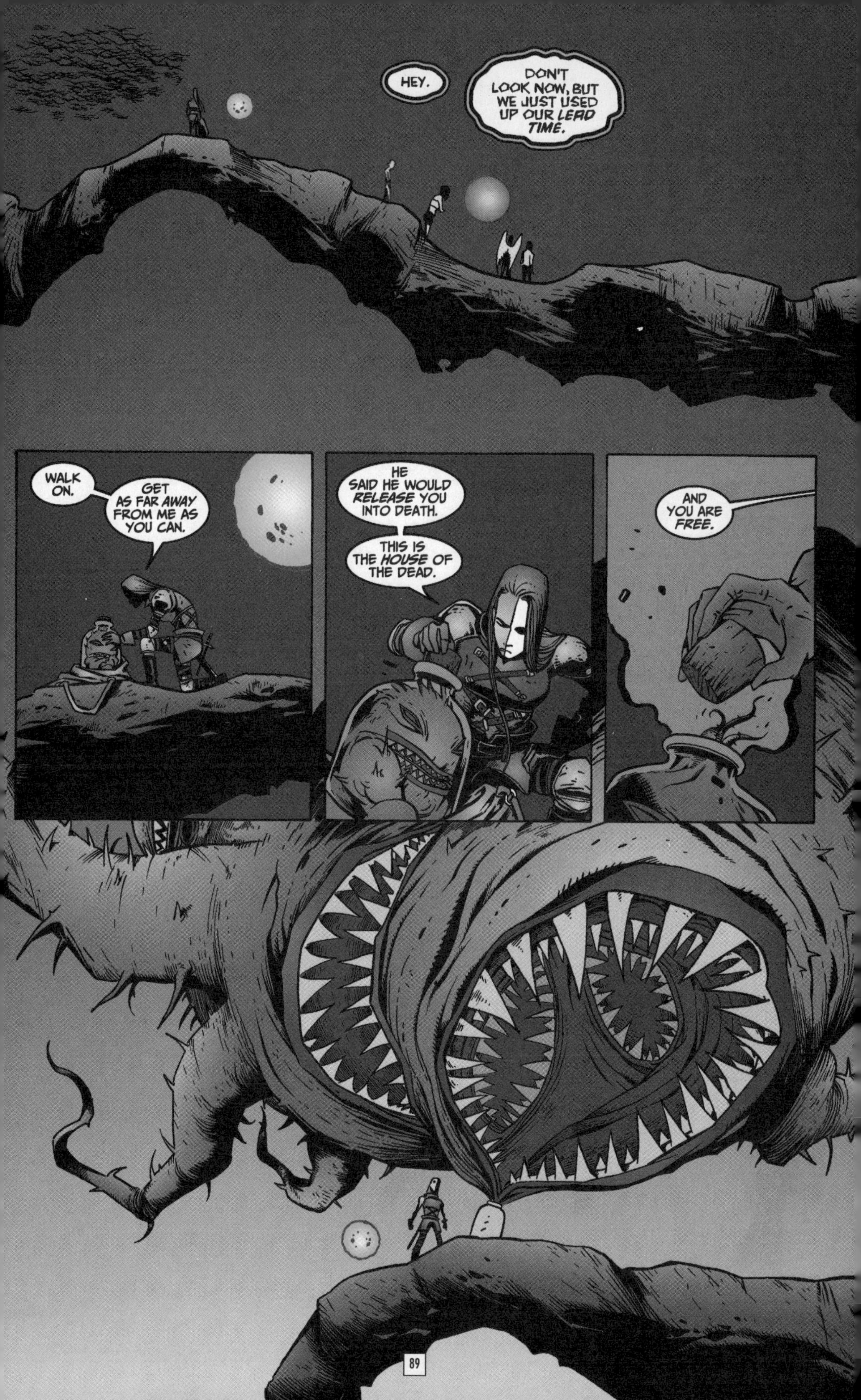
HEY.
DON'T LOOK NOW, BUT WE JUST USED UP OUR LEAD TIME.
WALK ON.
GET AS FAR AWAY FROM ME AS YOU CAN.
HE SAID HE WOULD RELEASE YOU INTO DEATH.
THIS IS THE HOUSE OF THE DEAD.
AND YOU ARE FREE.

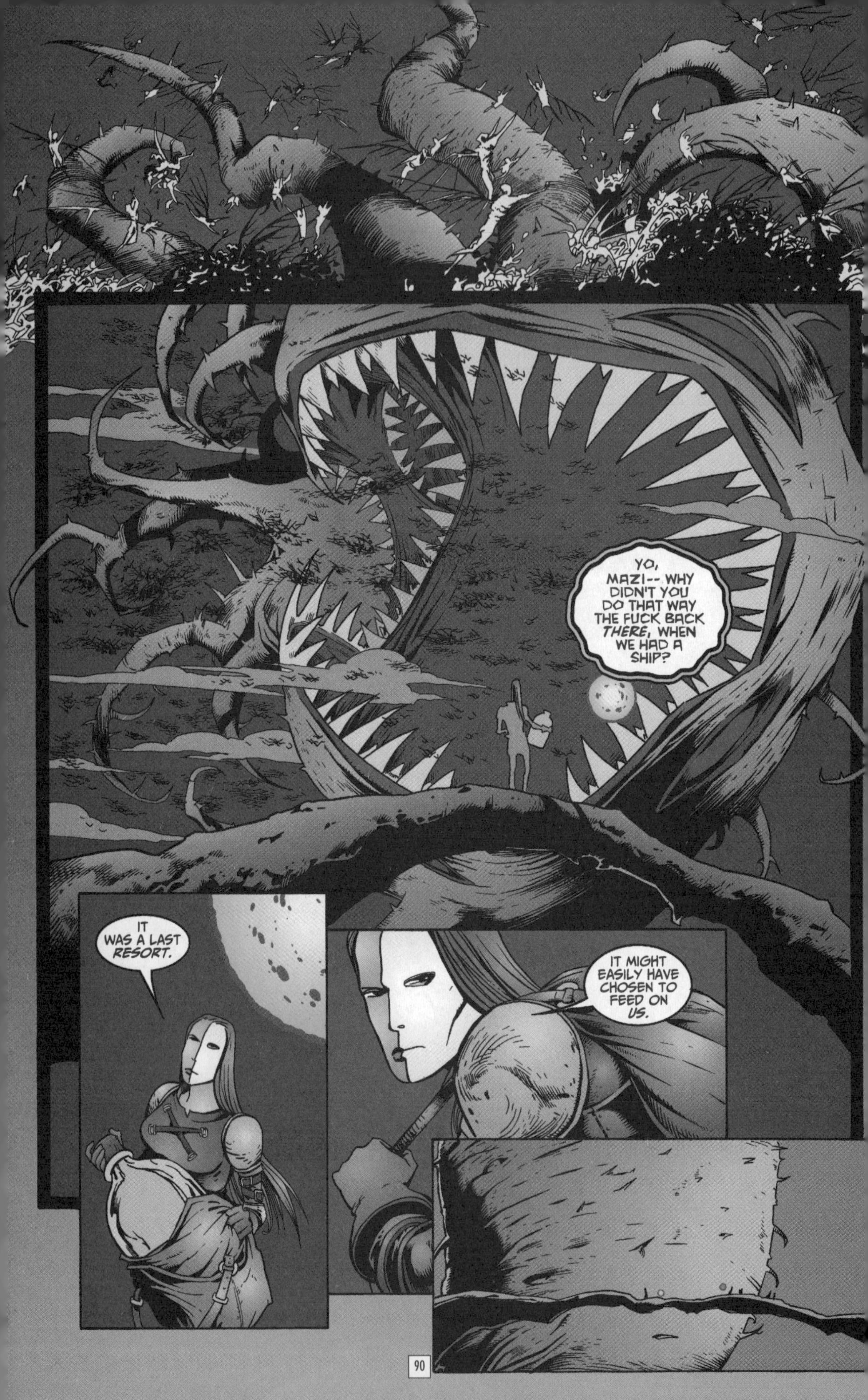

YO, MAZI-- WHY DIDN'T YOU DO THAT WAY THE FUCK BACK *THERE*, WHEN WE HAD A SHIP?
IT WAS A LAST *RESORT.*
IT MIGHT EASILY HAVE CHOSEN TO FEED ON *US.*

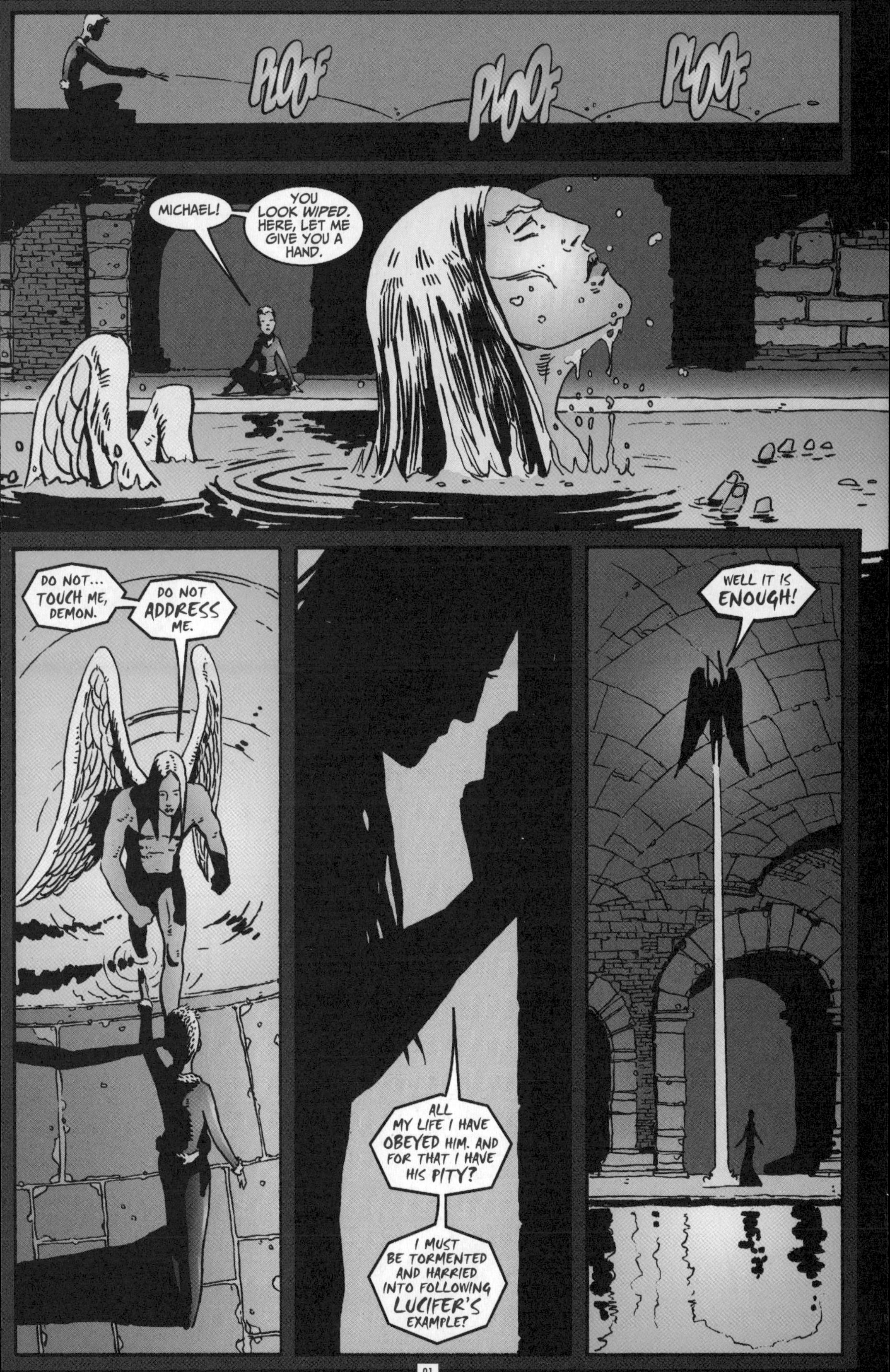
PLOOF
PLOOF
PLOOF
MICHAEL!
YOU LOOK WIPED. HERE, LET ME GIVE YOU A HAND.
DO NOT... TOUCH ME, DEMON.
DO NOT ADDRESS ME.
ALL MY LIFE I HAVE OBEYED HIM. AND FOR THAT I HAVE HIS PITY?
I MUST BE TORMENTED AND HARRIED INTO FOLLOWING LUCIFER'S EXAMPLE?
WELL IT IS ENOUGH!

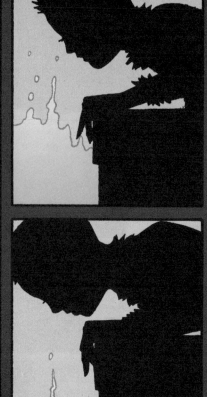

THERE.

I WANTED TO BE SURE I HADN'T *MISSED* ANYTHING.

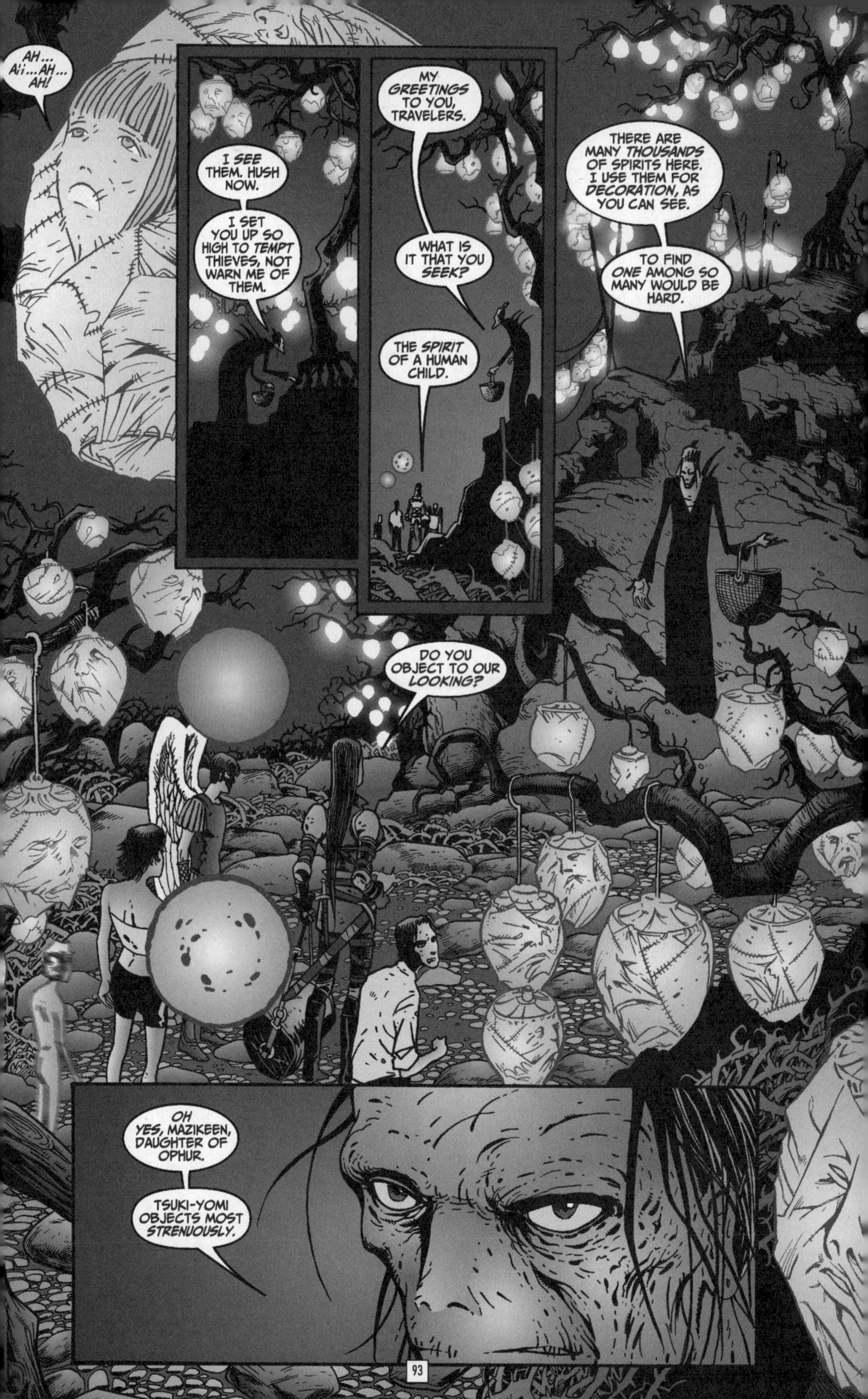
AH... AI...AH... AH!
I SEE THEM. HUSH NOW.
I SET YOU UP SO HIGH TO TEMPT THIEVES, NOT WARN ME OF THEM.
MY GREETINGS TO YOU, TRAVELERS.
WHAT IS IT THAT YOU SEEK?
THE SPIRIT OF A HUMAN CHILD.
THERE ARE MANY THOUSANDS OF SPIRITS HERE. I USE THEM FOR DECORATION, AS YOU CAN SEE.
TO FIND ONE AMONG SO MANY WOULD BE HARD.
DO YOU OBJECT TO OUR LOOKING?
OH YES, MAZIKEEN, DAUGHTER OF OPHUR.
TSUKI-YOMI OBJECTS MOST STRENUOUSLY.

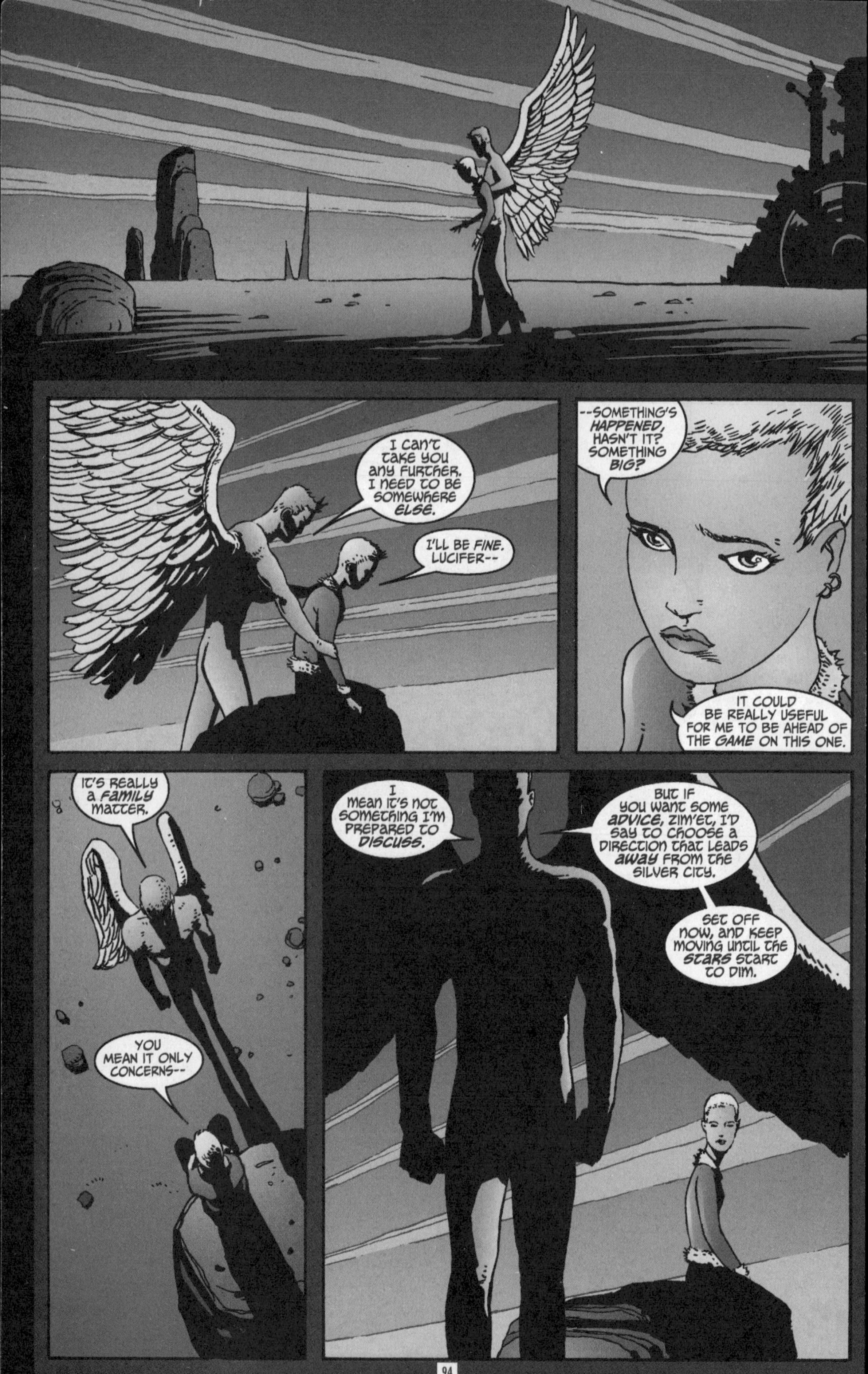
I CAN'T TAKE YOU ANY FURTHER. I NEED TO BE SOMEWHERE ELSE.
I'LL BE FINE. LUCIFER--
--SOMETHING'S HAPPENED, HASN'T IT? SOMETHING BIG?
IT COULD BE REALLY USEFUL FOR ME TO BE AHEAD OF THE GAME ON THIS ONE.
IT'S REALLY A FAMILY MATTER.
YOU MEAN IT ONLY CONCERNS--
I MEAN IT'S NOT SOMETHING I'M PREPARED TO DISCUSS.
BUT IF YOU WANT SOME ADVICE, ZIM'ET, I'D SAY TO CHOOSE A DIRECTION THAT LEADS AWAY FROM THE SILVER CITY.
SET OFF NOW, AND KEEP MOVING UNTIL THE STARS START TO DIM.

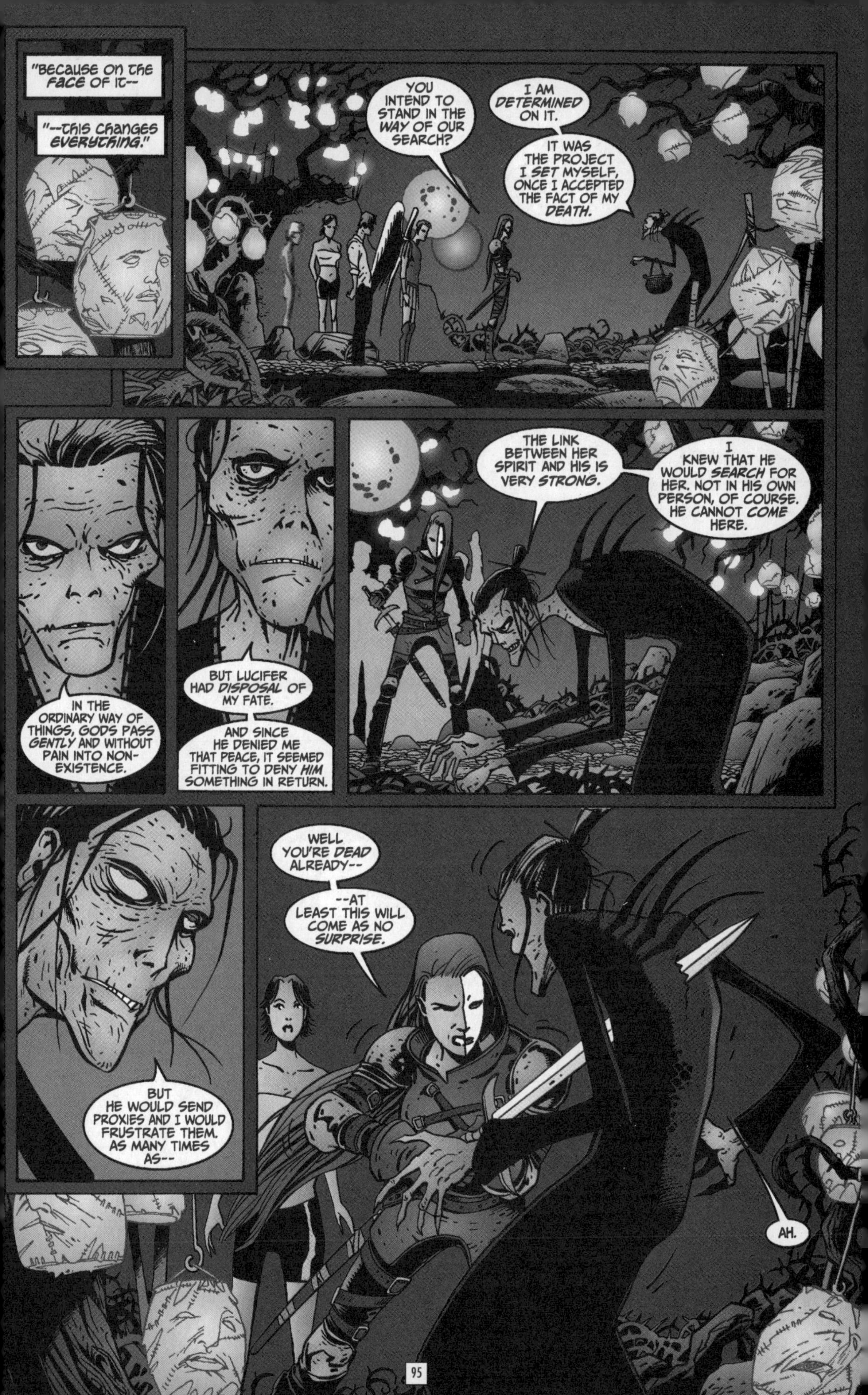

"Because on the face of it--
"--this changes everything."
YOU INTEND TO STAND IN THE WAY OF OUR SEARCH?
I AM DETERMINED ON IT.
IT WAS THE PROJECT I SET MYSELF, ONCE I ACCEPTED THE FACT OF MY DEATH.
IN THE ORDINARY WAY OF THINGS, GODS PASS GENTLY AND WITHOUT PAIN INTO NON-EXISTENCE.
BUT LUCIFER HAD DISPOSAL OF MY FATE.
AND SINCE HE DENIED ME THAT PEACE, IT SEEMED FITTING TO DENY HIM SOMETHING IN RETURN.
THE LINK BETWEEN HER SPIRIT AND HIS IS VERY STRONG.
I KNEW THAT HE WOULD SEARCH FOR HER. NOT IN HIS OWN PERSON, OF COURSE. HE CANNOT COME HERE.
BUT HE WOULD SEND PROXIES AND I WOULD FRUSTRATE THEM. AS MANY TIMES AS--
WELL YOU'RE DEAD ALREADY--
--AT LEAST THIS WILL COME AS NO SURPRISE.
AH.

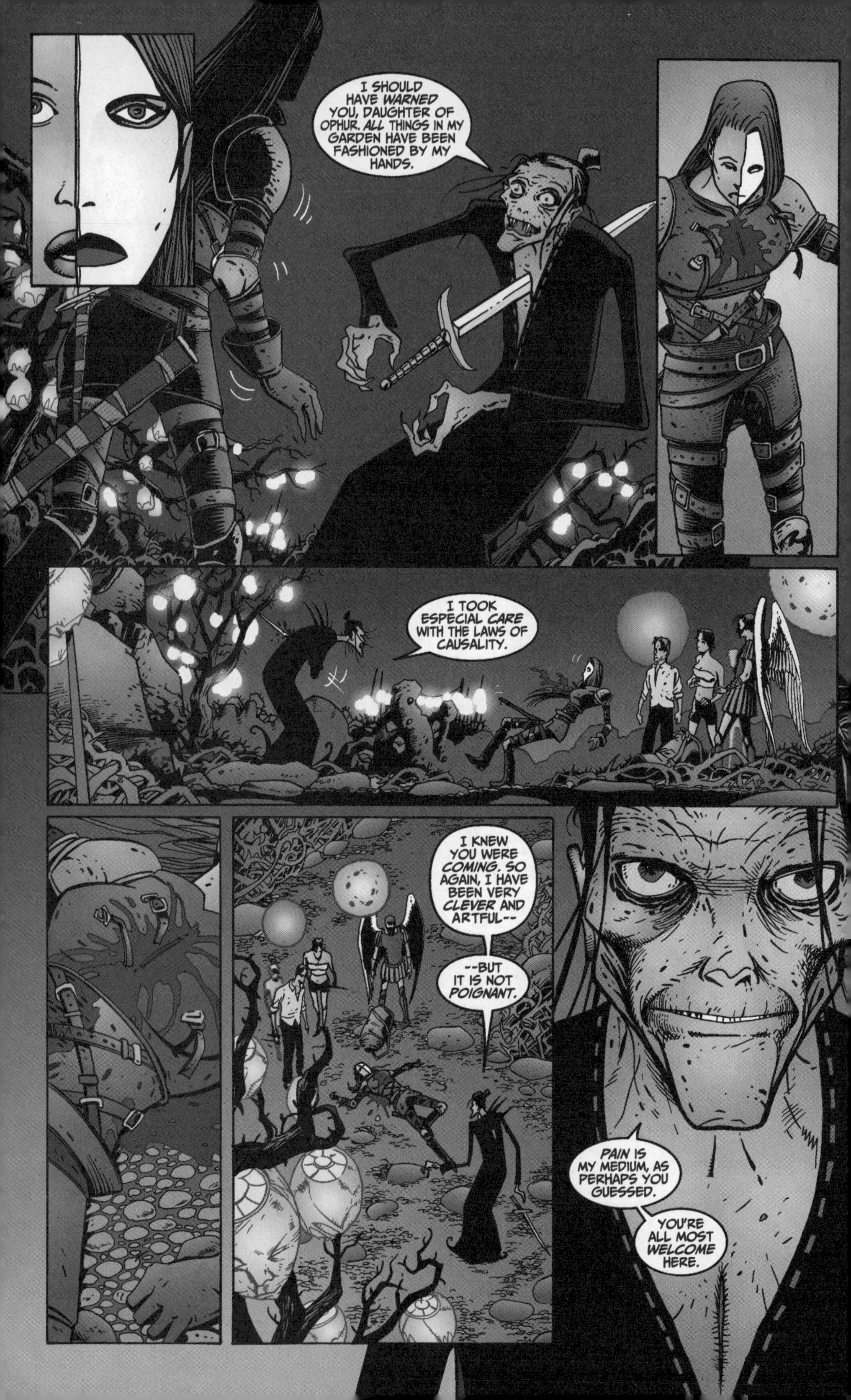
I SHOULD HAVE WARNED YOU, DAUGHTER OF OPHUR. ALL THINGS IN MY GARDEN HAVE BEEN FASHIONED BY MY HANDS.
I TOOK ESPECIAL CARE WITH THE LAWS OF CAUSALITY.
I KNEW YOU WERE COMING. SO AGAIN, I HAVE BEEN VERY CLEVER AND ARTFUL--
--BUT IT IS NOT POIGNANT.
PAIN IS MY MEDIUM, AS PERHAPS YOU GUESSED.
YOU'RE ALL MOST WELCOME HERE.

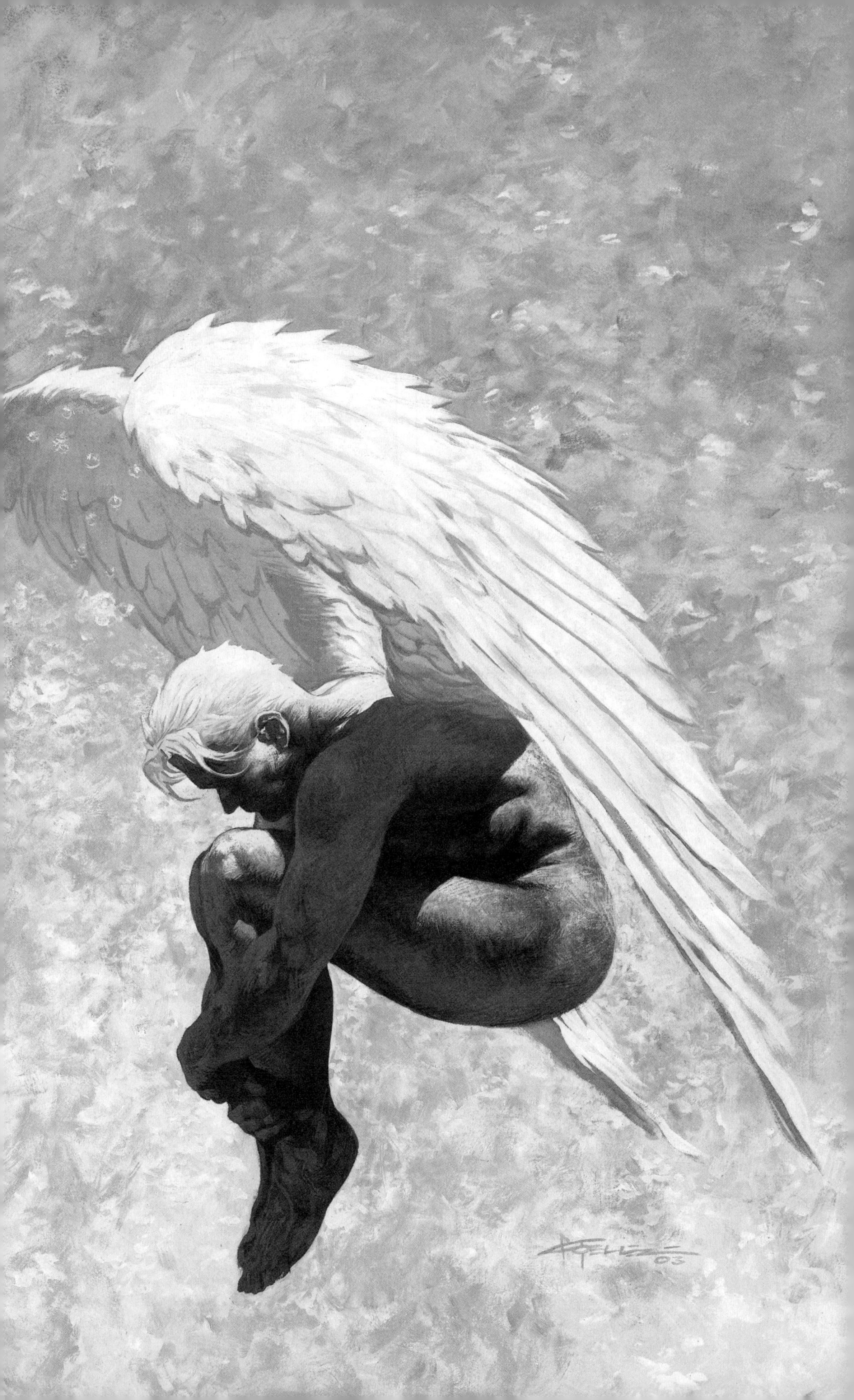

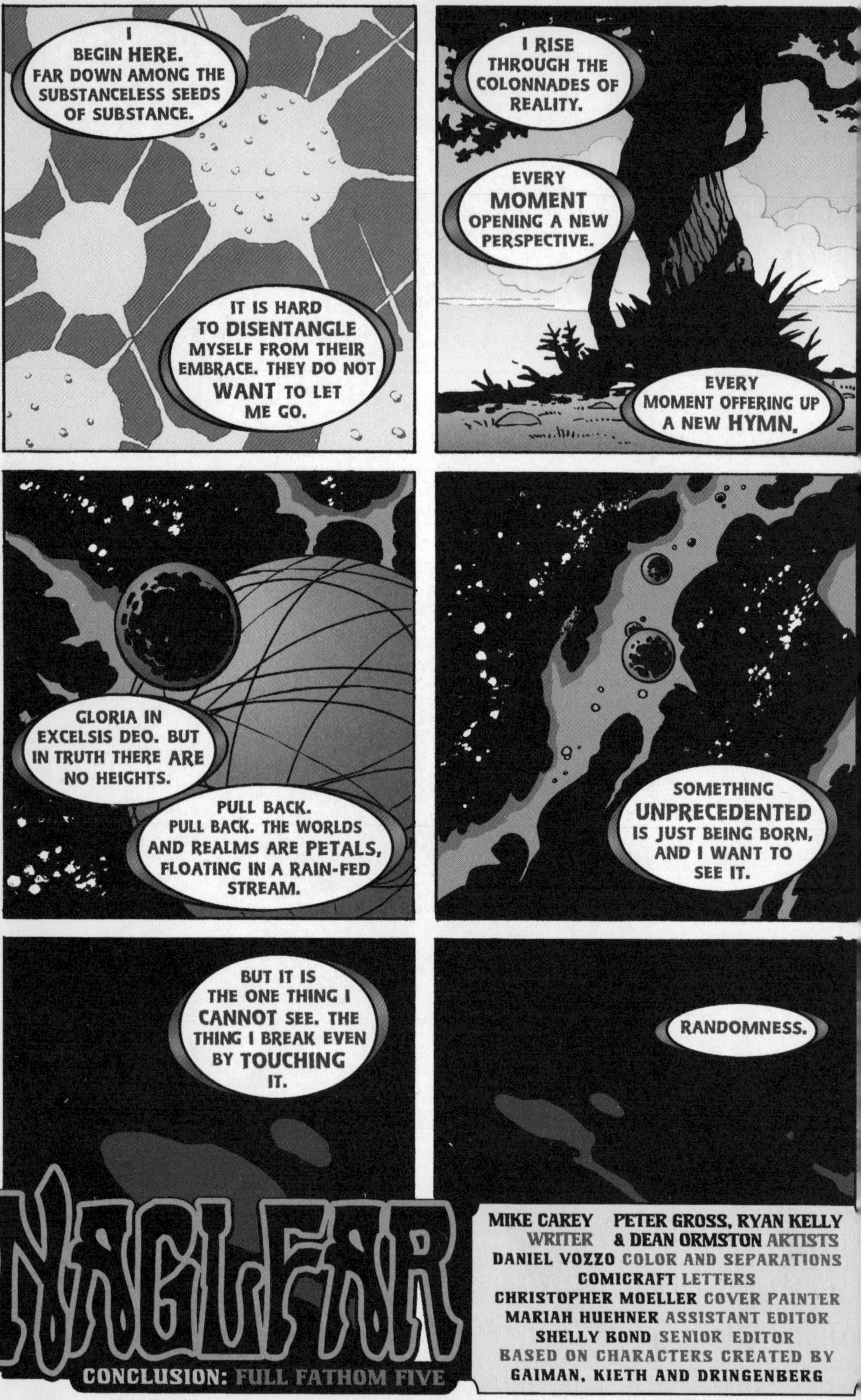
I BEGIN HERE. FAR DOWN AMONG THE SUBSTANCELESS SEEDS OF SUBSTANCE.
IT IS HARD TO DISENTANGLE MYSELF FROM THEIR EMBRACE. THEY DO NOT WANT TO LET ME GO.
I RISE THROUGH THE COLONNADES OF REALITY.
EVERY MOMENT OPENING A NEW PERSPECTIVE.
EVERY MOMENT OFFERING UP A NEW HYMN.
GLORIA IN EXCELSIS DEO. BUT IN TRUTH THERE ARE NO HEIGHTS.
PULL BACK. PULL BACK. THE WORLDS AND REALMS ARE PETALS, FLOATING IN A RAIN-FED STREAM.
SOMETHING UNPRECEDENTED IS JUST BEING BORN, AND I WANT TO SEE IT.
BUT IT IS THE ONE THING I CANNOT SEE. THE THING I BREAK EVEN BY TOUCHING IT.
RANDOMNESS.

# NAGLFAR

## CONCLUSION: FULL FATHOM FIVE

MIKE CAREY WRITER
PETER GROSS, RYAN KELLY & DEAN ORMSTON ARTISTS
DANIEL VOZZO COLOR AND SEPARATIONS
COMICRAFT LETTERS
CHRISTOPHER MOELLER COVER PAINTER
MARIAH HUEHNER ASSISTANT EDITOR
SHELLY BOND SENIOR EDITOR
BASED ON CHARACTERS CREATED BY GAIMAN, KIETH AND DRINGENBERG

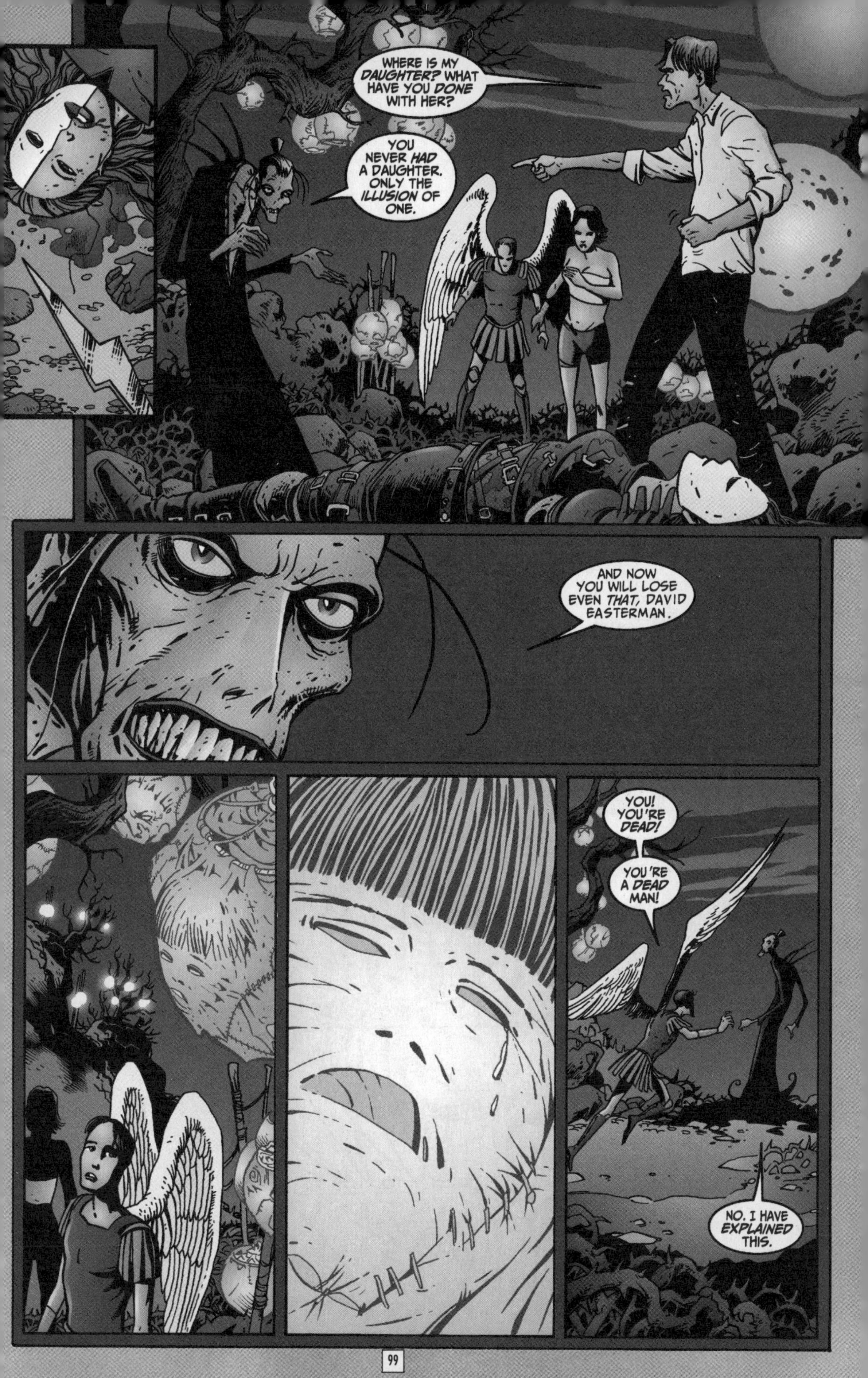
WHERE IS MY *DAUGHTER?* WHAT HAVE YOU *DONE* WITH HER?
YOU NEVER *HAD* A DAUGHTER. ONLY THE *ILLUSION* OF ONE.
AND NOW YOU WILL LOSE EVEN *THAT,* DAVID EASTERMAN.
YOU! YOU'RE *DEAD!*
YOU'RE A *DEAD* MAN!
NO. I HAVE *EXPLAINED* THIS.

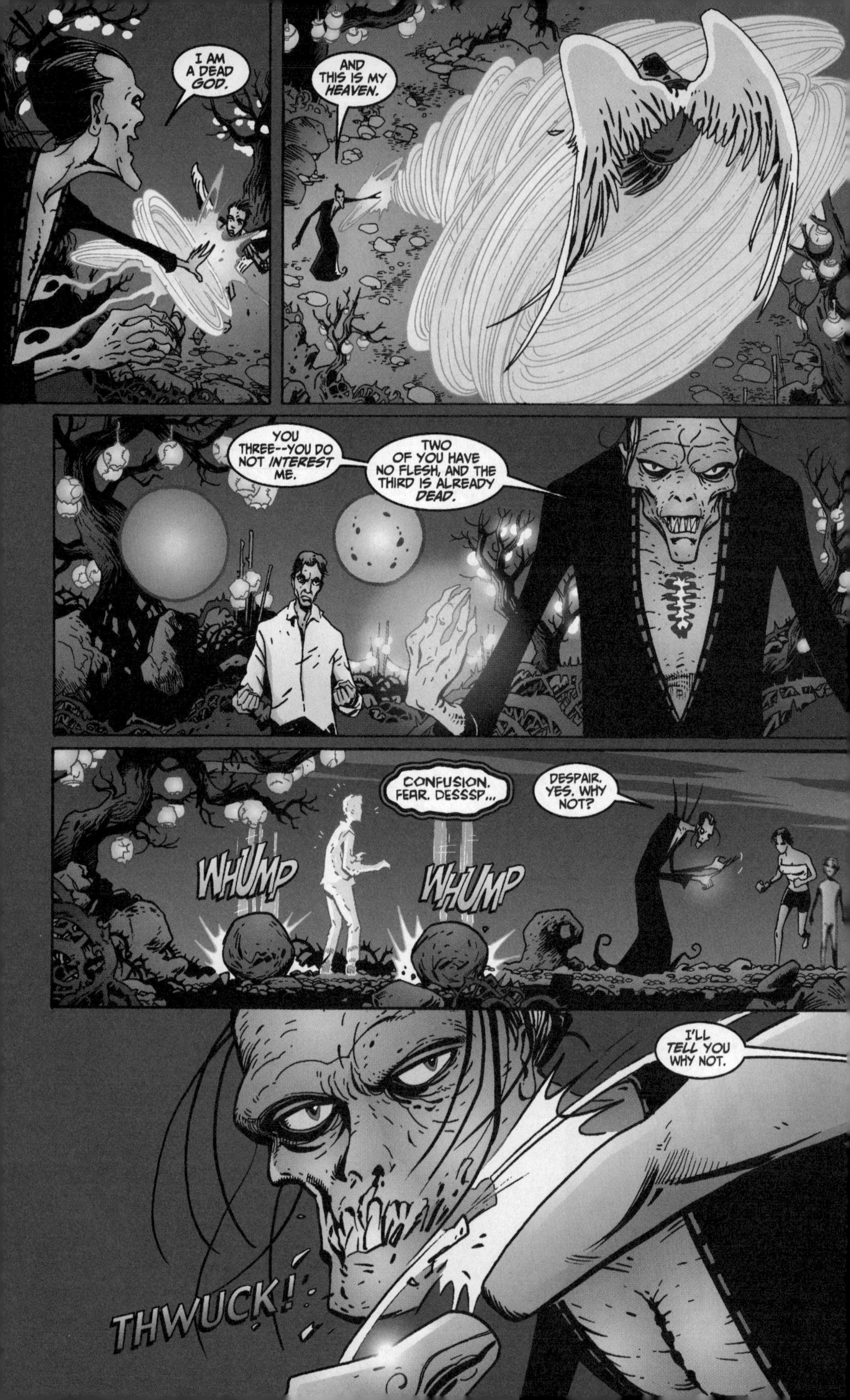
I AM A DEAD GOD.
AND THIS IS MY HEAVEN.
YOU THREE--YOU DO NOT INTEREST ME.
TWO OF YOU HAVE NO FLESH, AND THE THIRD IS ALREADY DEAD.
CONFUSION. FEAR. DESSSP...
DESPAIR. YES. WHY NOT?
WHUMP
WHUMP
I'LL TELL YOU WHY NOT.
THWUCK!

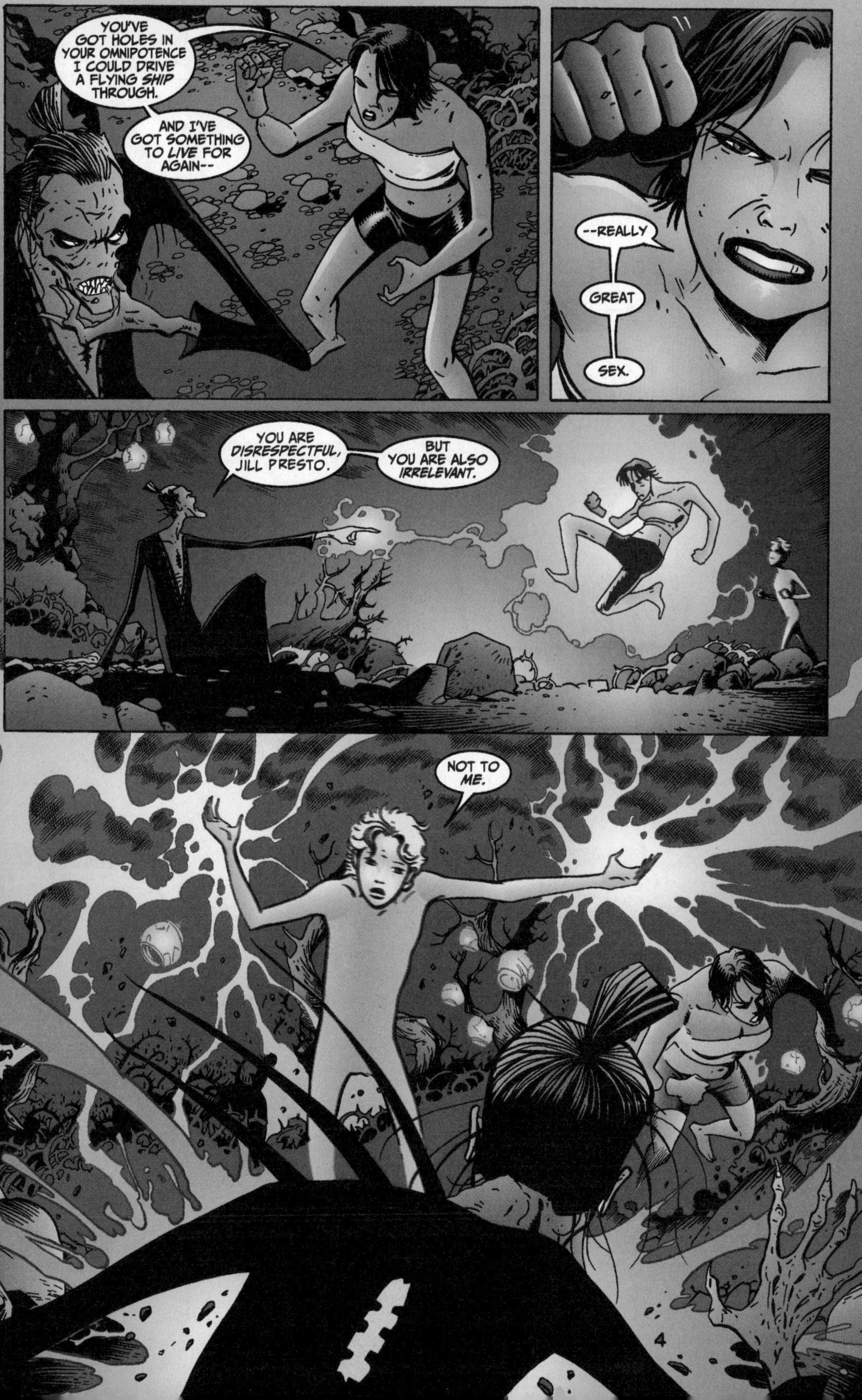

YOU'VE GOT HOLES IN YOUR OMNIPOTENCE I COULD DRIVE A FLYING SHIP THROUGH.
AND I'VE GOT SOMETHING TO LIVE FOR AGAIN--
--REALLY
GREAT
SEX.
YOU ARE DISRESPECTFUL, JILL PRESTO.
BUT YOU ARE ALSO IRRELEVANT.
NOT TO ME.

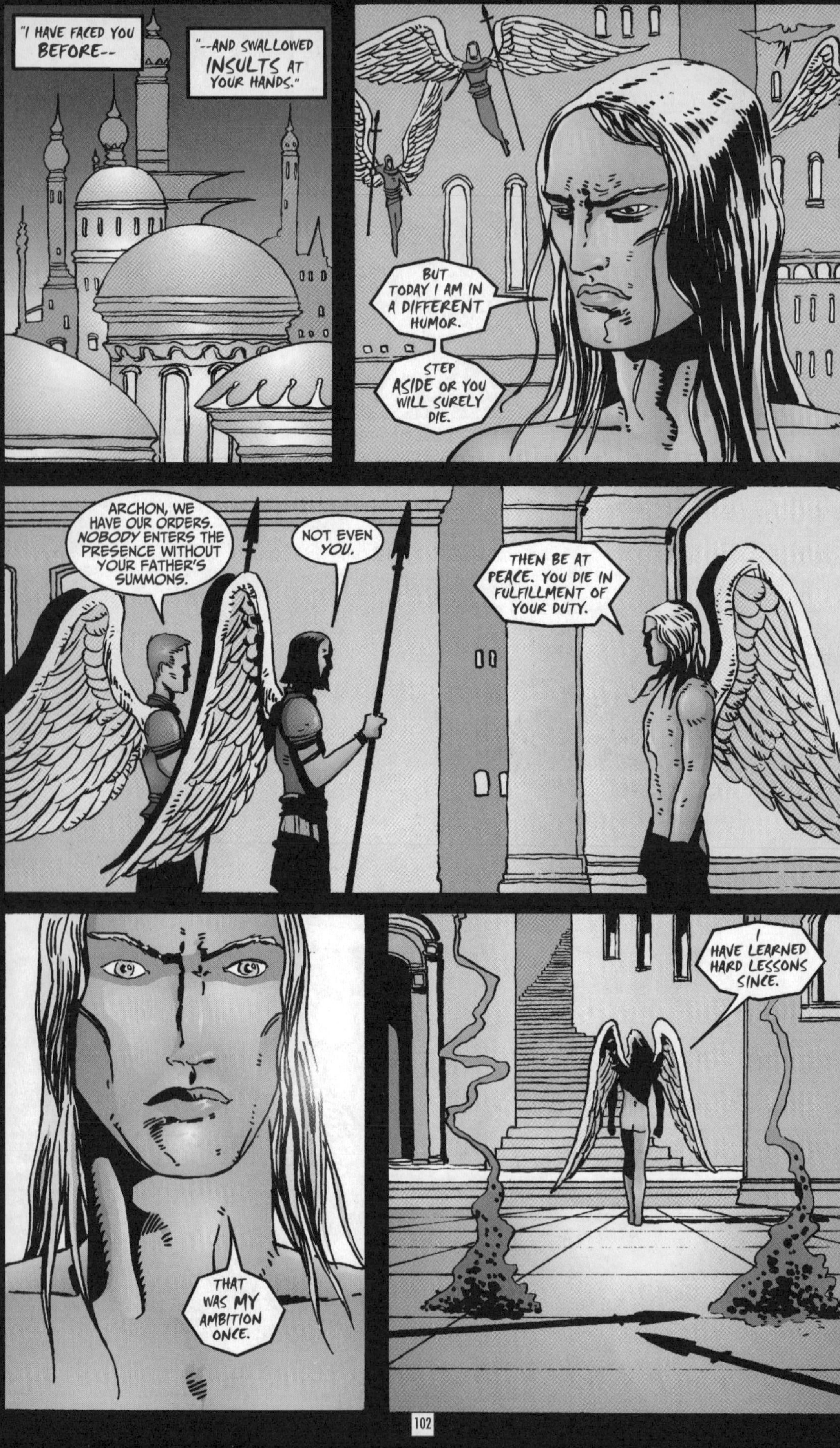
"I HAVE FACED YOU BEFORE--
"--AND SWALLOWED INSULTS AT YOUR HANDS."
BUT TODAY I AM IN A DIFFERENT HUMOR.
STEP ASIDE OR YOU WILL SURELY DIE.
ARCHON, WE HAVE OUR ORDERS. NOBODY ENTERS THE PRESENCE WITHOUT YOUR FATHER'S SUMMONS.
NOT EVEN YOU.
THEN BE AT PEACE. YOU DIE IN FULFILLMENT OF YOUR DUTY.
THAT WAS MY AMBITION ONCE.
I HAVE LEARNED HARD LESSONS SINCE.

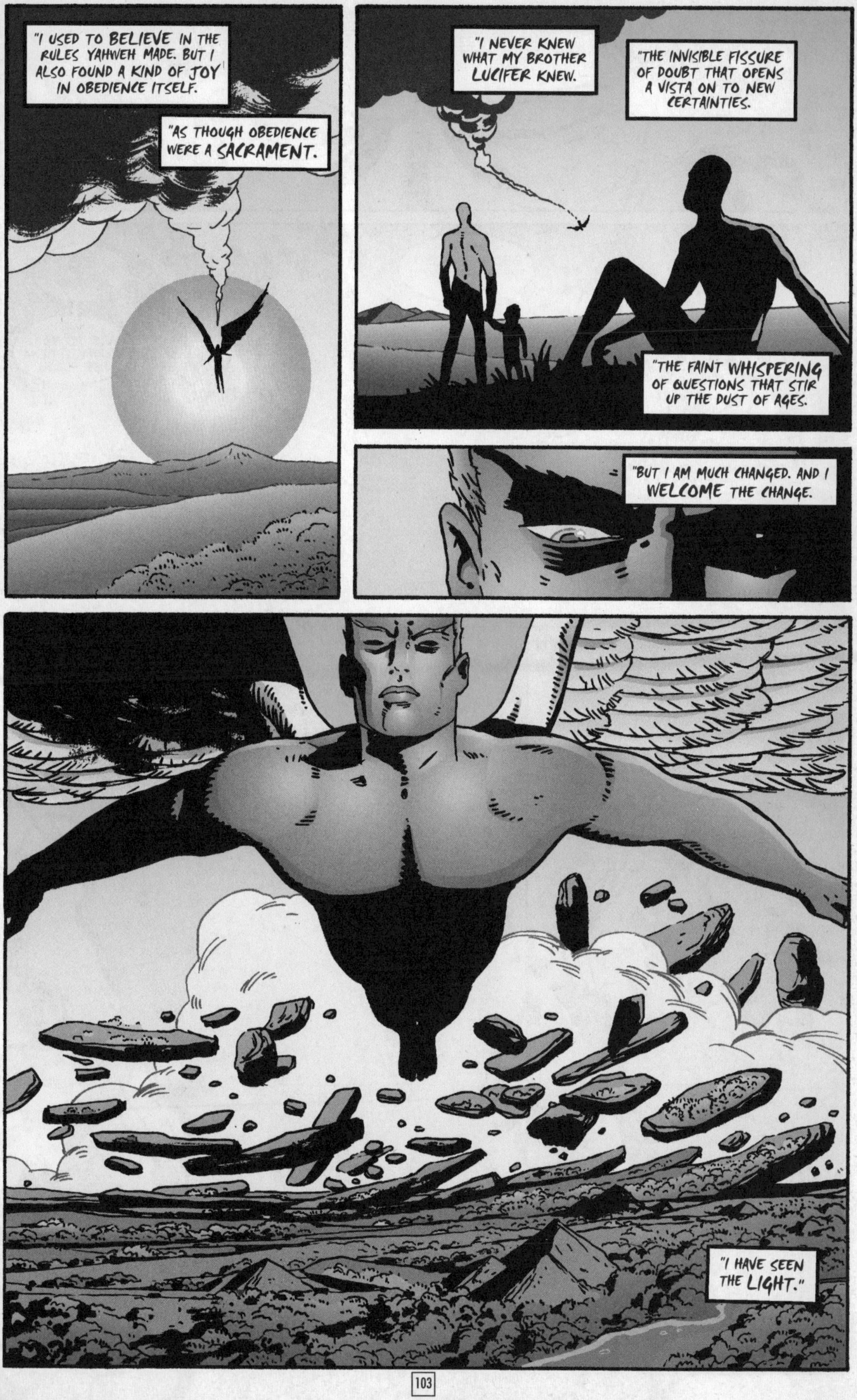
"I USED TO BELIEVE IN THE RULES YAHWEH MADE. BUT I ALSO FOUND A KIND OF JOY IN OBEDIENCE ITSELF.
"AS THOUGH OBEDIENCE WERE A SACRAMENT.
"I NEVER KNEW WHAT MY BROTHER LUCIFER KNEW.
"THE INVISIBLE FISSURE OF DOUBT THAT OPENS A VISTA ON TO NEW CERTAINTIES.
"THE FAINT WHISPERING OF QUESTIONS THAT STIR UP THE DUST OF AGES.
"BUT I AM MUCH CHANGED. AND I WELCOME THE CHANGE.
"I HAVE SEEN THE LIGHT."

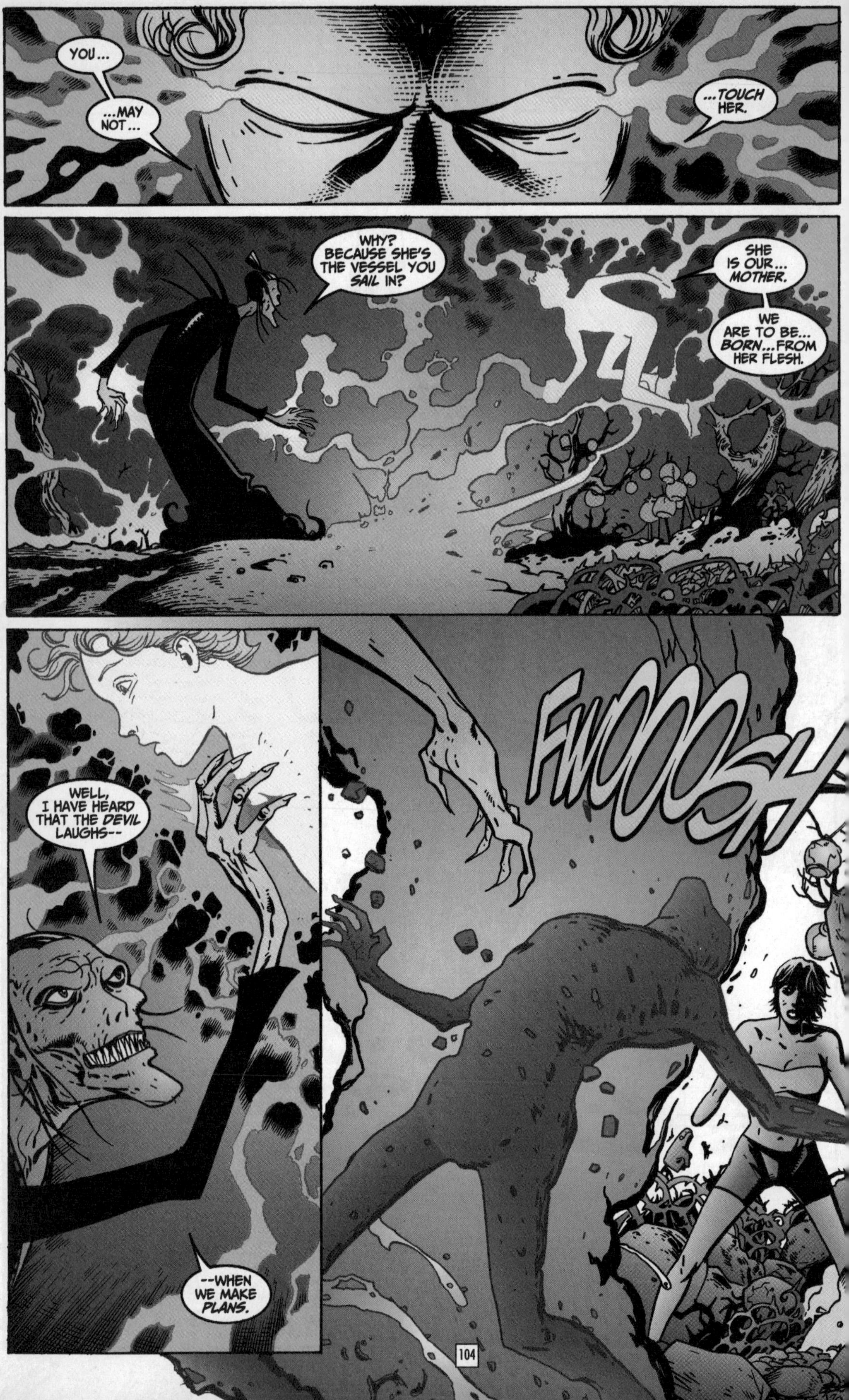
YOU...
...MAY NOT...
...TOUCH HER.
WHY? BECAUSE SHE'S THE VESSEL YOU *SAIL* IN?
SHE IS OUR... *MOTHER*.
WE ARE TO BE... *BORN*...FROM HER FLESH.
WELL, I HAVE HEARD THAT THE *DEVIL* LAUGHS--
FWOOOSH
--WHEN WE MAKE *PLANS*.

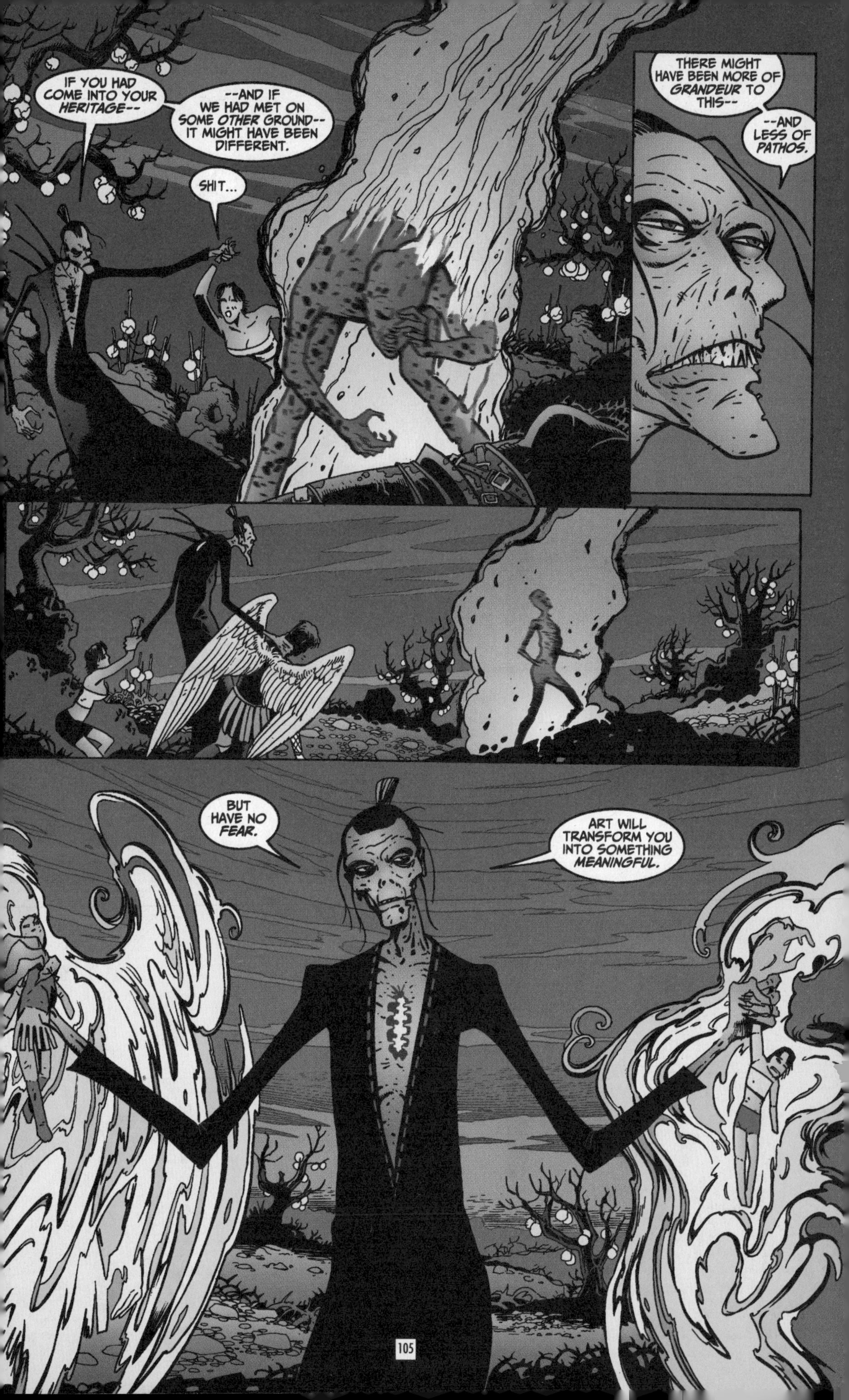
IF YOU HAD COME INTO YOUR HERITAGE--
--AND IF WE HAD MET ON SOME OTHER GROUND-- IT MIGHT HAVE BEEN DIFFERENT.
SHIT...
THERE MIGHT HAVE BEEN MORE OF GRANDEUR TO THIS--
--AND LESS OF PATHOS.
BUT HAVE NO FEAR.
ART WILL TRANSFORM YOU INTO SOMETHING MEANINGFUL.

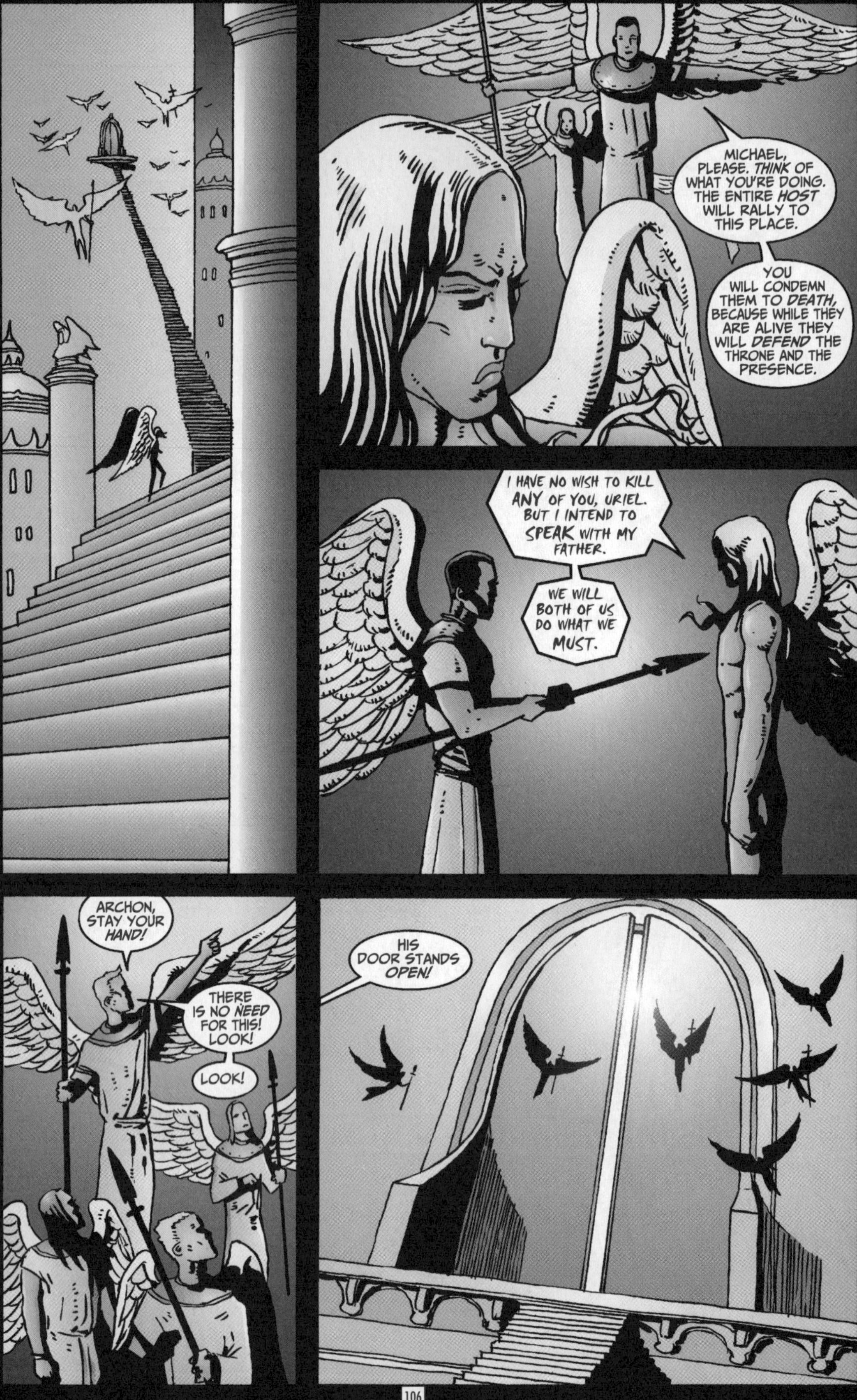
MICHAEL, PLEASE. THINK OF WHAT YOU'RE DOING. THE ENTIRE HOST WILL RALLY TO THIS PLACE.
YOU WILL CONDEMN THEM TO DEATH, BECAUSE WHILE THEY ARE ALIVE THEY WILL DEFEND THE THRONE AND THE PRESENCE.
I HAVE NO WISH TO KILL ANY OF YOU, URIEL. BUT I INTEND TO SPEAK WITH MY FATHER.
WE WILL BOTH OF US DO WHAT WE MUST.
ARCHON, STAY YOUR HAND!
THERE IS NO NEED FOR THIS! LOOK!
LOOK!
HIS DOOR STANDS OPEN!

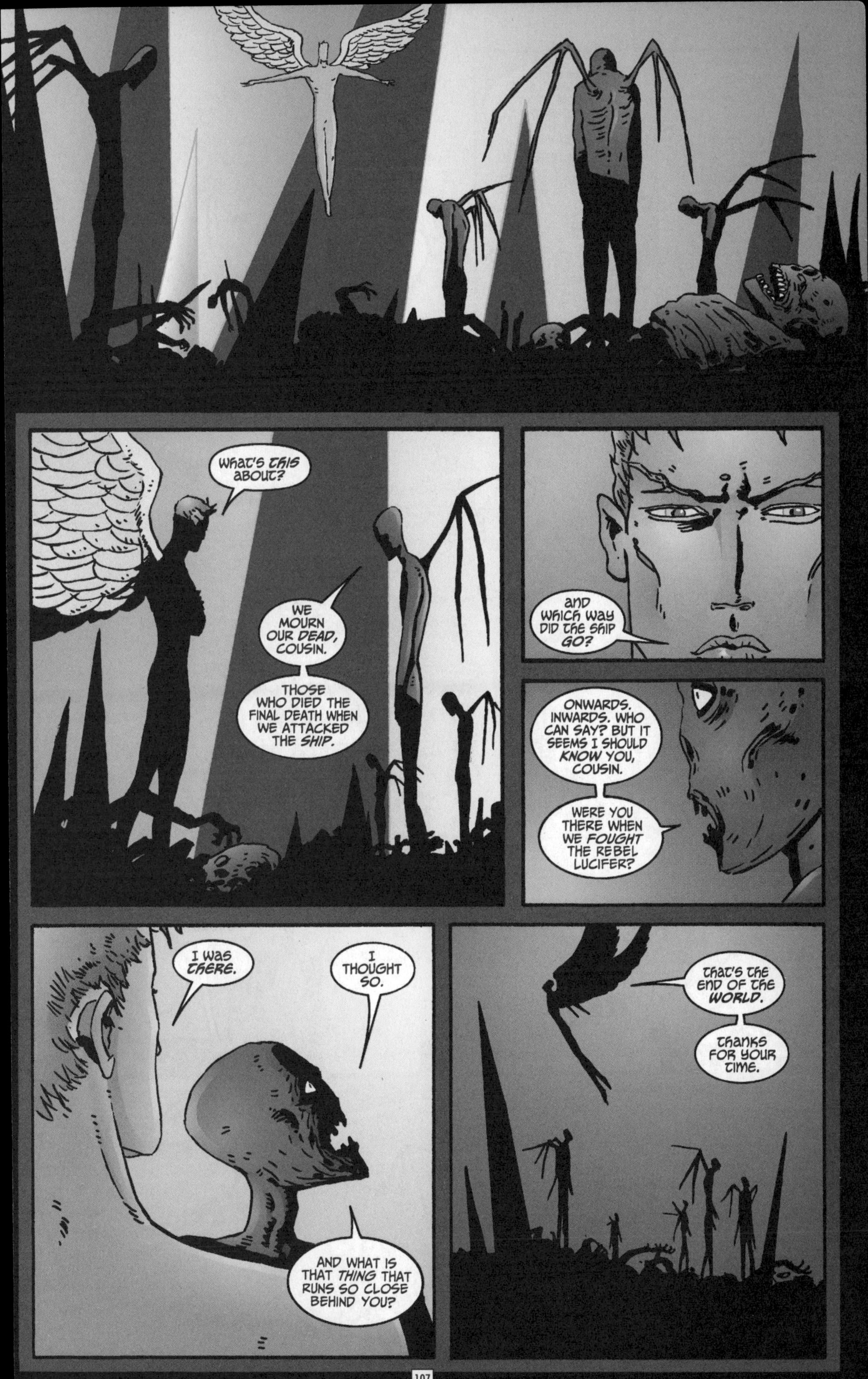
What's THIS about?
WE MOURN OUR DEAD, COUSIN.
THOSE WHO DIED THE FINAL DEATH WHEN WE ATTACKED THE SHIP.
and WHICH WAY DID THE SHIP GO?
ONWARDS. INWARDS. WHO CAN SAY? BUT IT SEEMS I SHOULD KNOW YOU, COUSIN.
WERE YOU THERE WHEN WE FOUGHT THE REBEL LUCIFER?
I WAS THERE.
I THOUGHT SO.
AND WHAT IS THAT THING THAT RUNS SO CLOSE BEHIND YOU?
THAT'S THE END OF THE WORLD.
THANKS FOR YOUR TIME.

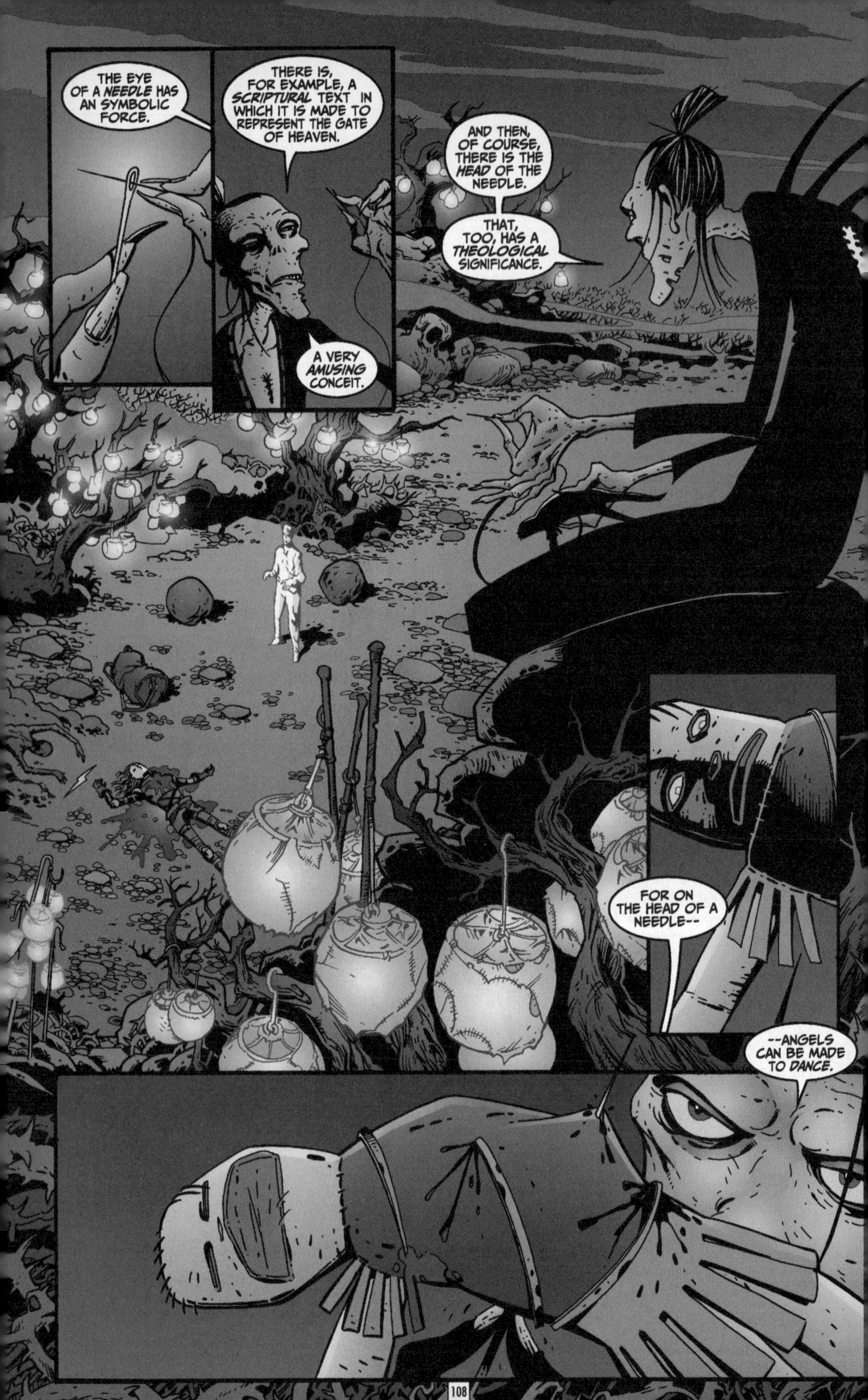
THE EYE OF A NEEDLE HAS AN SYMBOLIC FORCE.
THERE IS, FOR EXAMPLE, A SCRIPTURAL TEXT IN WHICH IT IS MADE TO REPRESENT THE GATE OF HEAVEN.
A VERY AMUSING CONCEIT.
AND THEN, OF COURSE, THERE IS THE HEAD OF THE NEEDLE.
THAT, TOO, HAS A THEOLOGICAL SIGNIFICANCE.
FOR ON THE HEAD OF A NEEDLE--
--ANGELS CAN BE MADE TO DANCE.

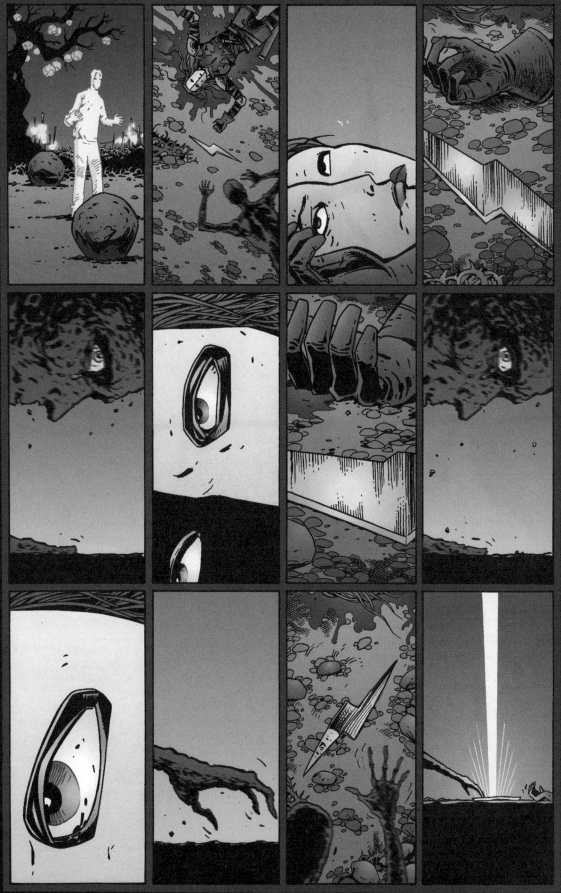

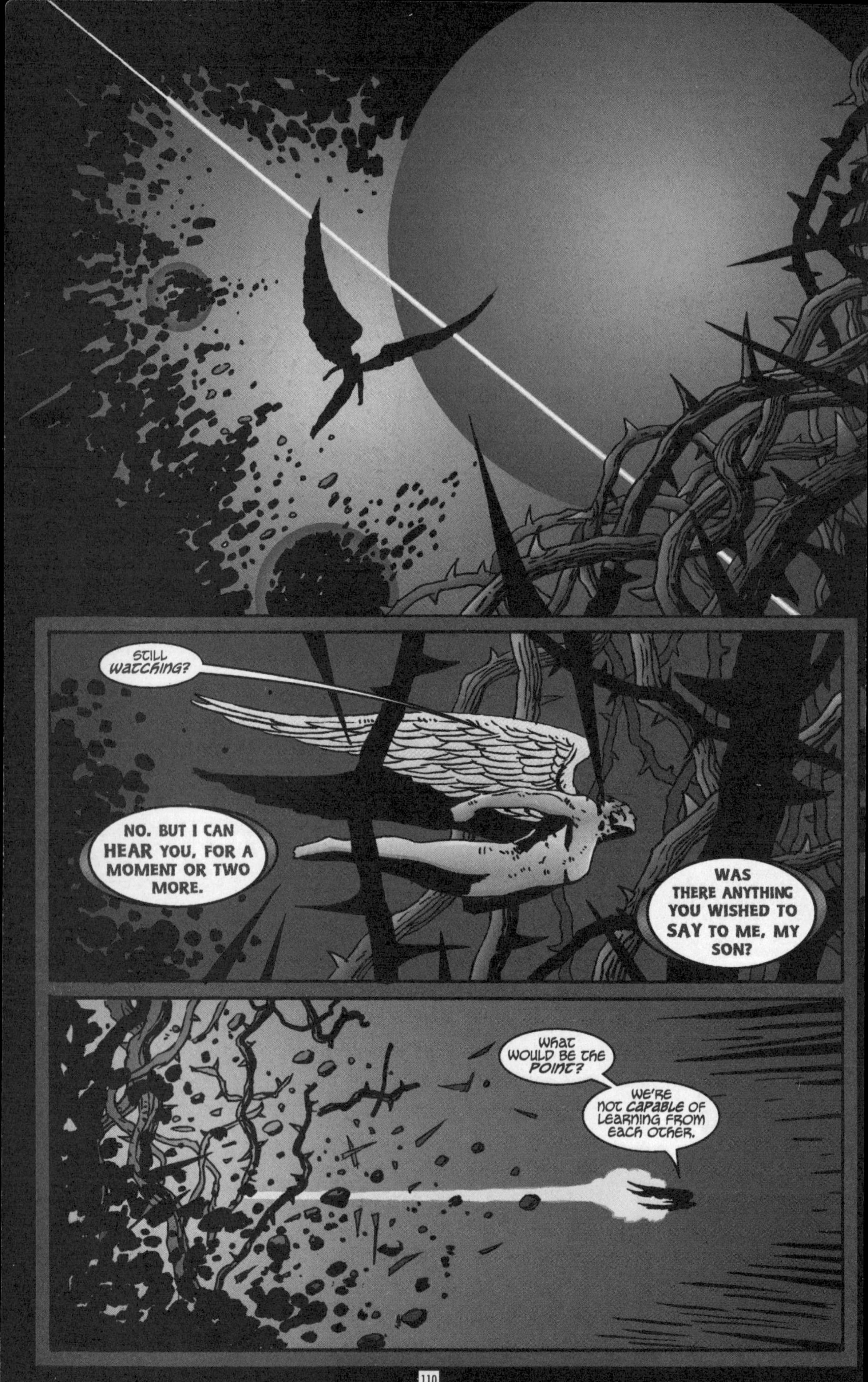
STILL WATCHING?
NO. BUT I CAN HEAR YOU, FOR A MOMENT OR TWO MORE.
WAS THERE ANYTHING YOU WISHED TO SAY TO ME, MY SON?
WHAT WOULD BE THE POINT?
WE'RE NOT CAPABLE OF LEARNING FROM EACH OTHER.

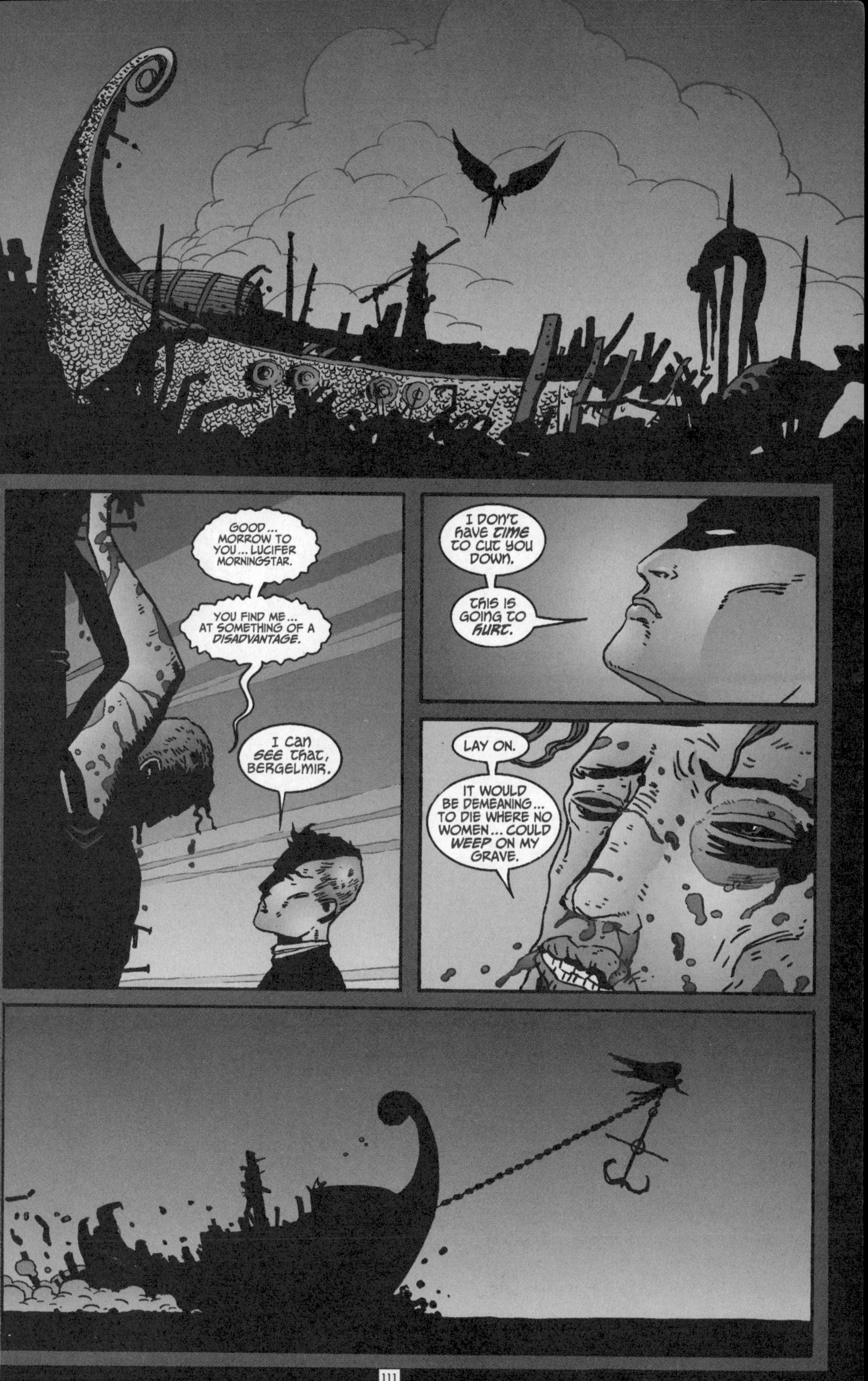
GOOD... MORROW TO YOU... LUCIFER MORNINGSTAR.
YOU FIND ME... AT SOMETHING OF A DISADVANTAGE.
I CAN SEE THAT, BERGELMIR.
I DON'T HAVE TIME TO CUT YOU DOWN.
THIS IS GOING TO HURT.
LAY ON.
IT WOULD BE DEMEANING... TO DIE WHERE NO WOMEN... COULD WEEP ON MY GRAVE.

WHAT IS THIS?

A PIECE OF SOMEWHERE ELSE, SHINING IN MY GARDEN?

IS THERE A MEANING TO THIS, SPAWN OF THE BASANOS?

SPEAK.

GUUUUH!

A... B... BEAC... BEACON...

BUT THERE IS NOBODY TO--

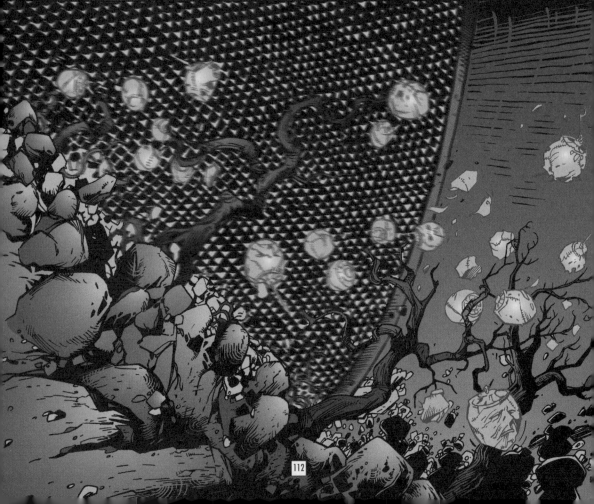

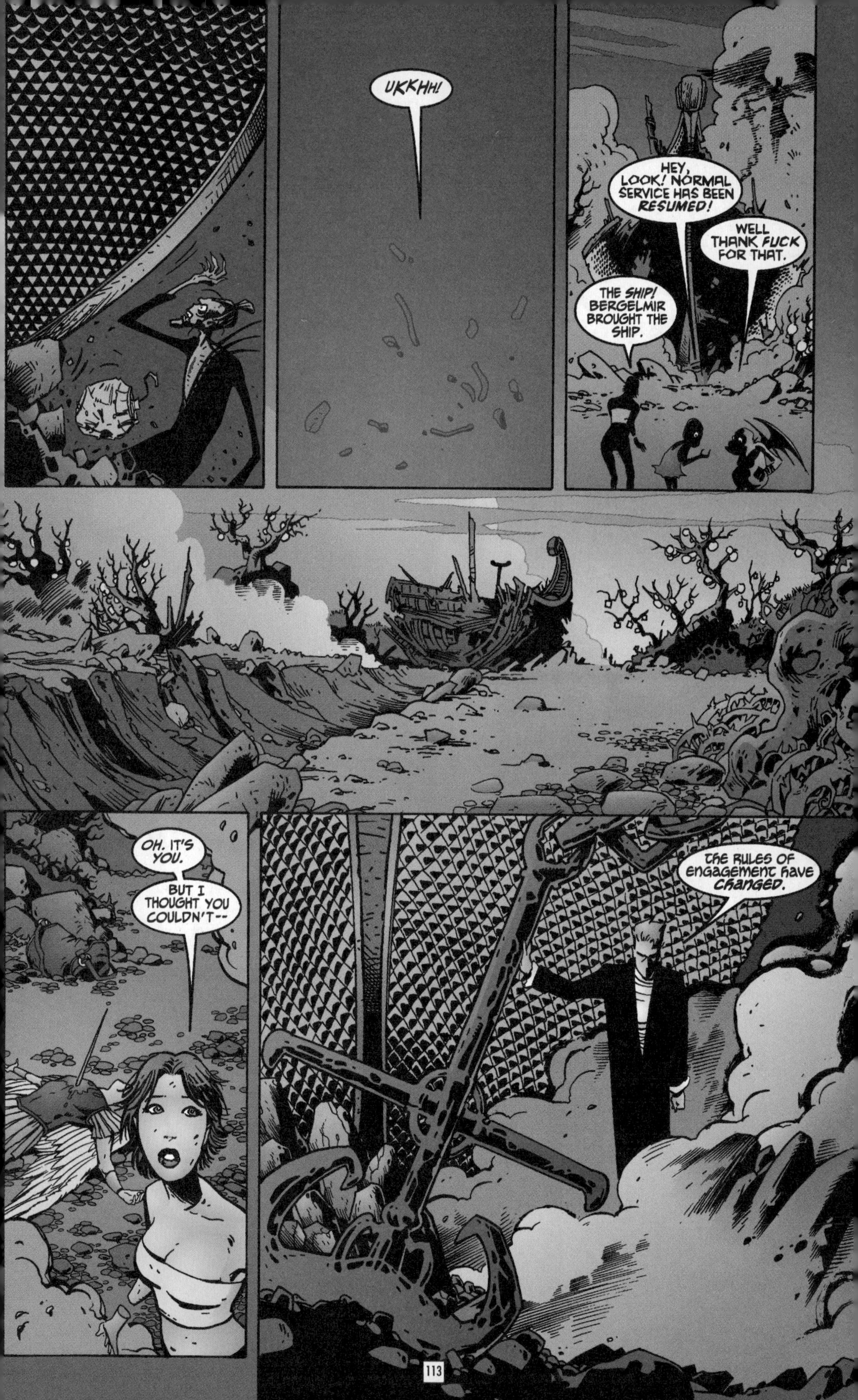
UKKHH!
HEY, LOOK! NORMAL SERVICE HAS BEEN RESUMED!
WELL THANK FUCK FOR THAT.
THE SHIP! BERGELMIR BROUGHT THE SHIP.
OH. IT'S YOU.
BUT I THOUGHT YOU COULDN'T--
THE RULES OF ENGAGEMENT HAVE CHANGED.

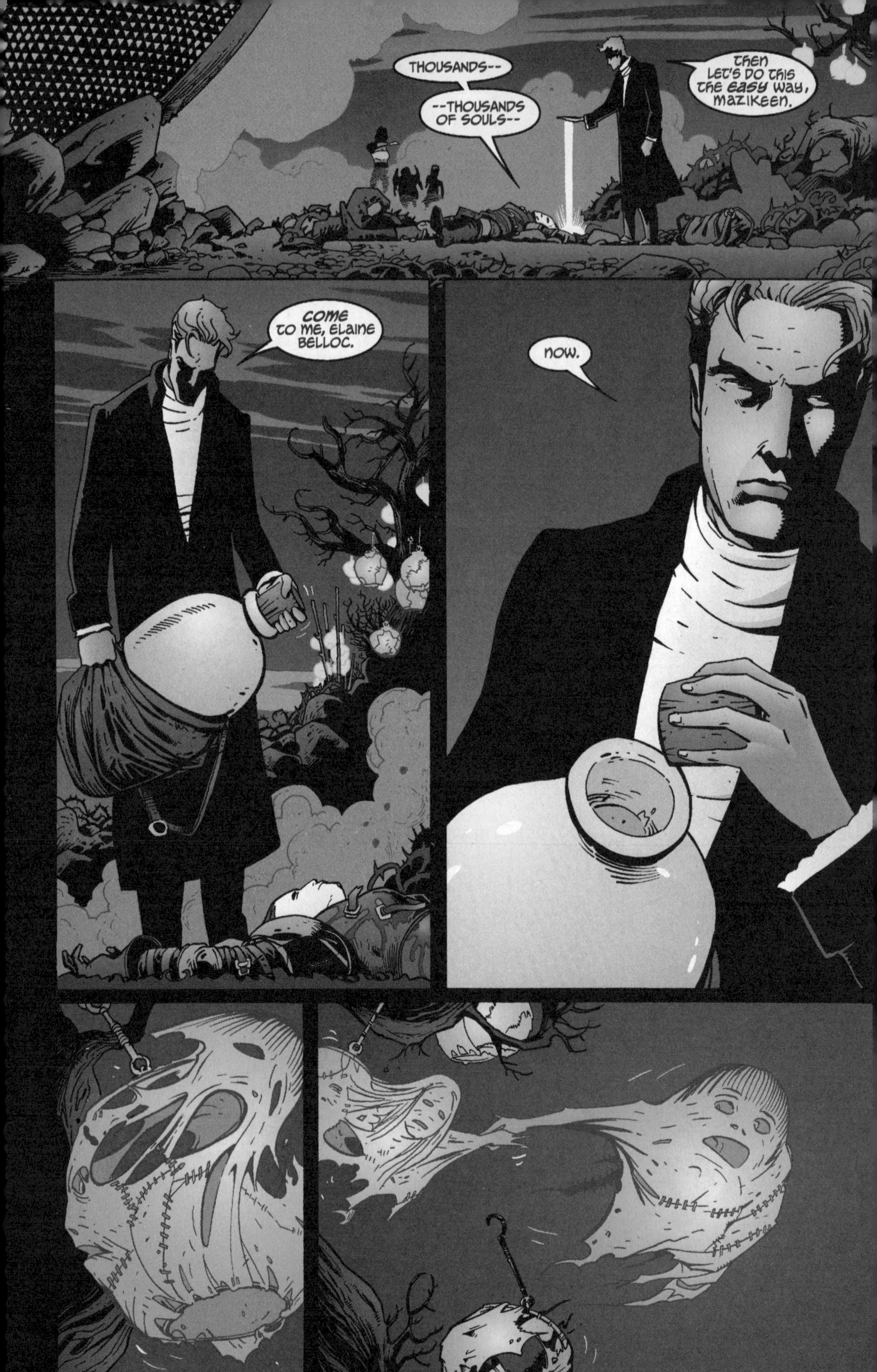
THOUSANDS--
--THOUSANDS OF SOULS--
THEN LET'S DO THIS THE EASY WAY, MAZIKEEN.
COME TO ME, ELAINE BELLOC.
NOW.

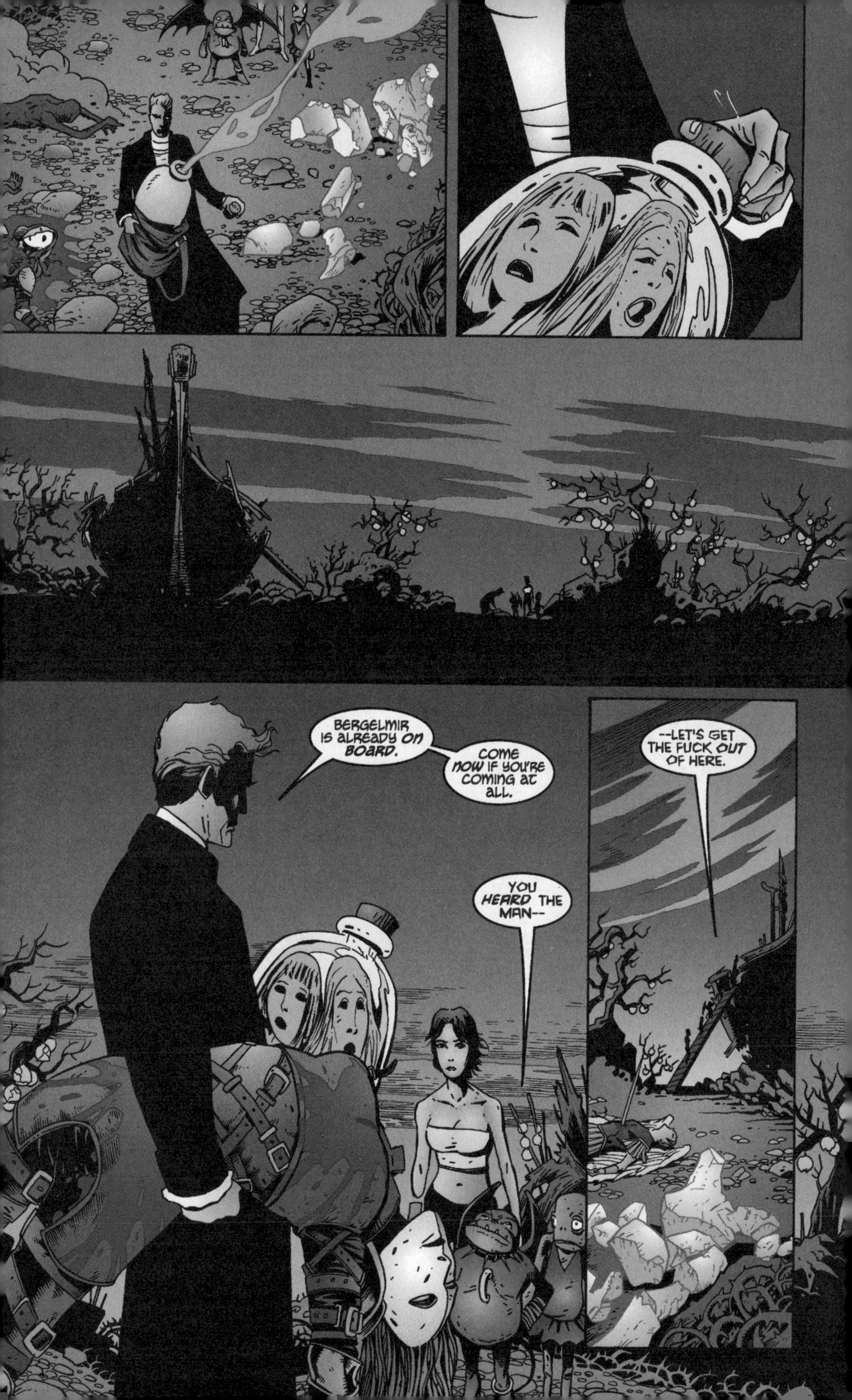
BERGELMIR IS ALREADY ON BOARD.
COME NOW IF YOU'RE COMING AT ALL.
YOU HEARD THE MAN--
--LET'S GET THE FUCK OUT OF HERE.

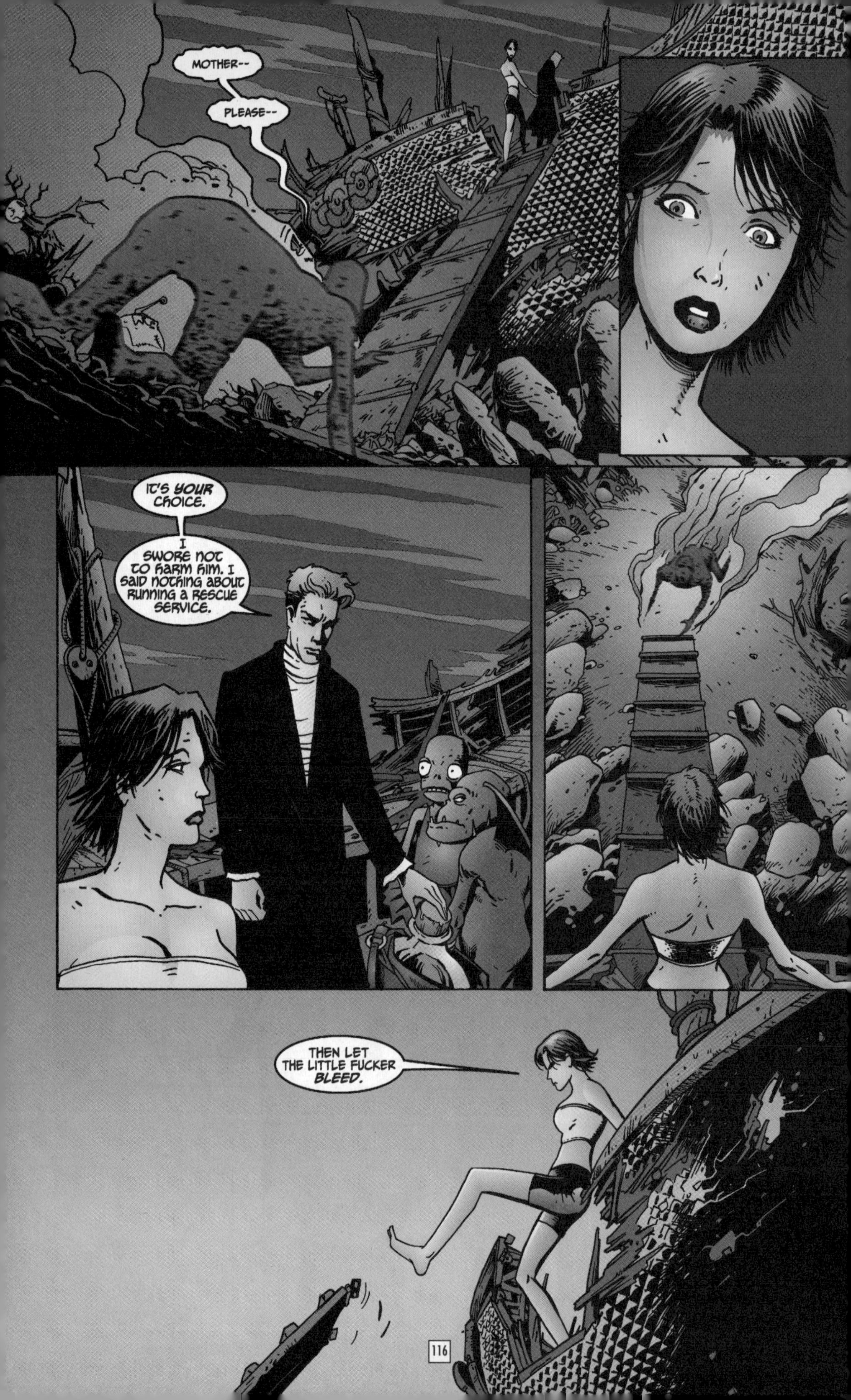
MOTHER--
PLEASE--
IT'S YOUR CHOICE.
I SWORE NOT TO HARM HIM. I SAID NOTHING ABOUT RUNNING A RESCUE SERVICE.
THEN LET THE LITTLE FUCKER BLEED.

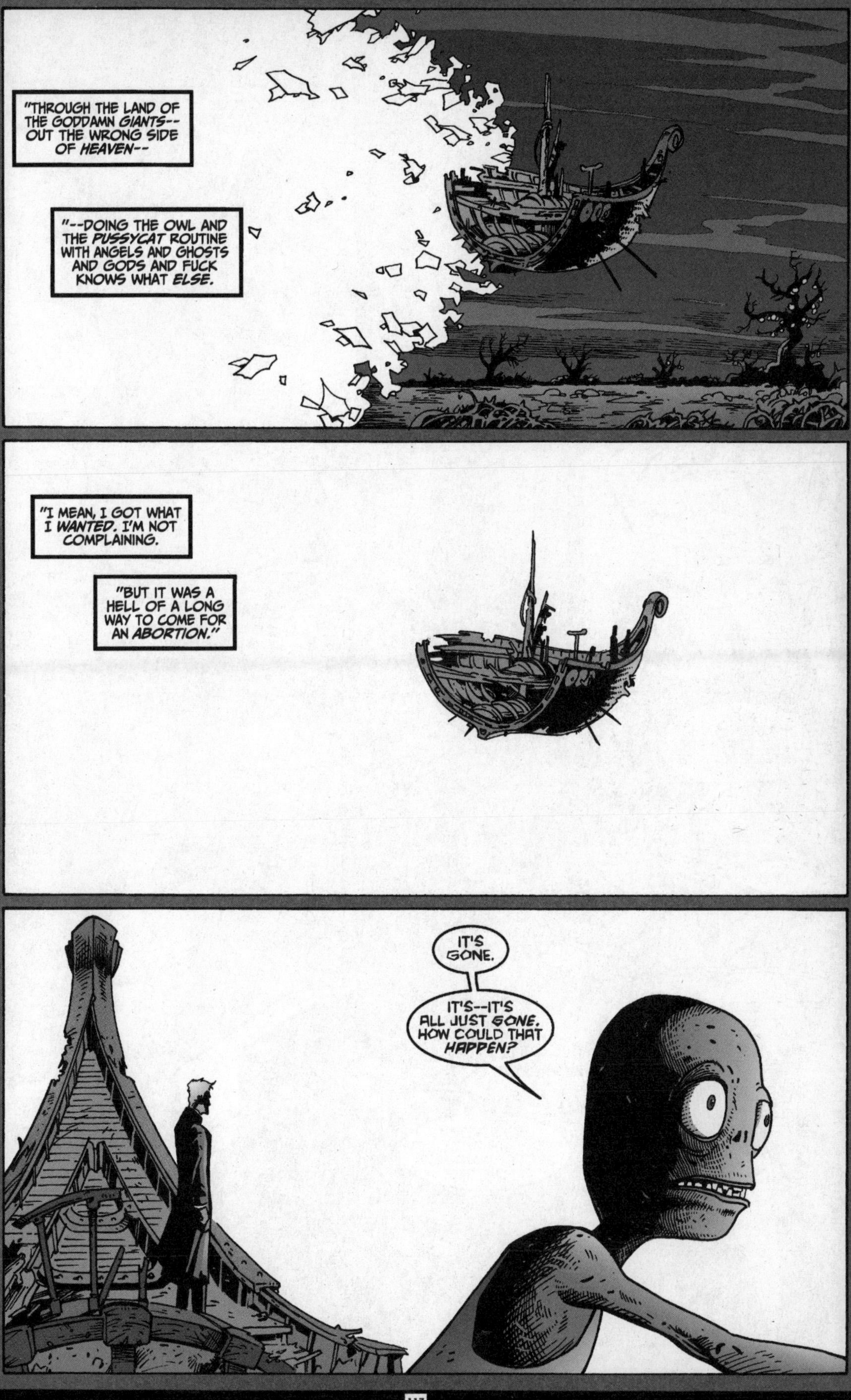
"THROUGH THE LAND OF THE GODDAMN GIANTS-- OUT THE WRONG SIDE OF HEAVEN--
"--DOING THE OWL AND THE PUSSYCAT ROUTINE WITH ANGELS AND GHOSTS AND GODS AND FUCK KNOWS WHAT ELSE.
"I MEAN, I GOT WHAT I WANTED. I'M NOT COMPLAINING.
"BUT IT WAS A HELL OF A LONG WAY TO COME FOR AN ABORTION."
IT'S GONE.
IT'S--IT'S ALL JUST GONE. HOW COULD THAT HAPPEN?

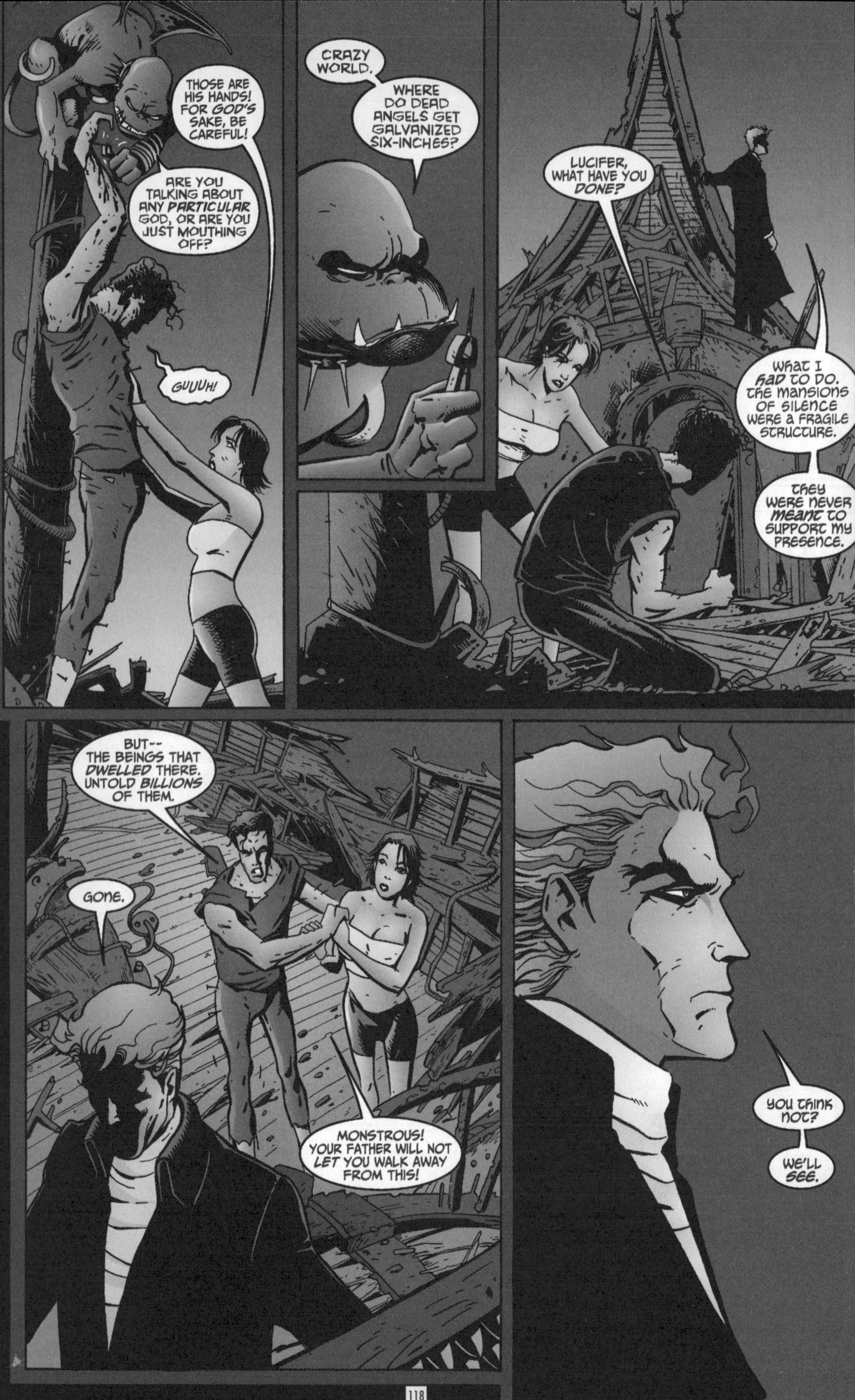
THOSE ARE HIS HANDS! FOR GOD'S SAKE, BE CAREFUL!
ARE YOU TALKING ABOUT ANY PARTICULAR GOD, OR ARE YOU JUST MOUTHING OFF?
GUUUH!
CRAZY WORLD.
WHERE DO DEAD ANGELS GET GALVANIZED SIX-INCHES?
LUCIFER, WHAT HAVE YOU DONE?
WHAT I HAD TO DO. THE MANSIONS OF SILENCE WERE A FRAGILE STRUCTURE.
THEY WERE NEVER MEANT TO SUPPORT MY PRESENCE.
BUT-- THE BEINGS THAT DWELLED THERE. UNTOLD BILLIONS OF THEM.
GONE.
MONSTROUS! YOUR FATHER WILL NOT LET YOU WALK AWAY FROM THIS!
YOU THINK NOT?
WE'LL SEE.

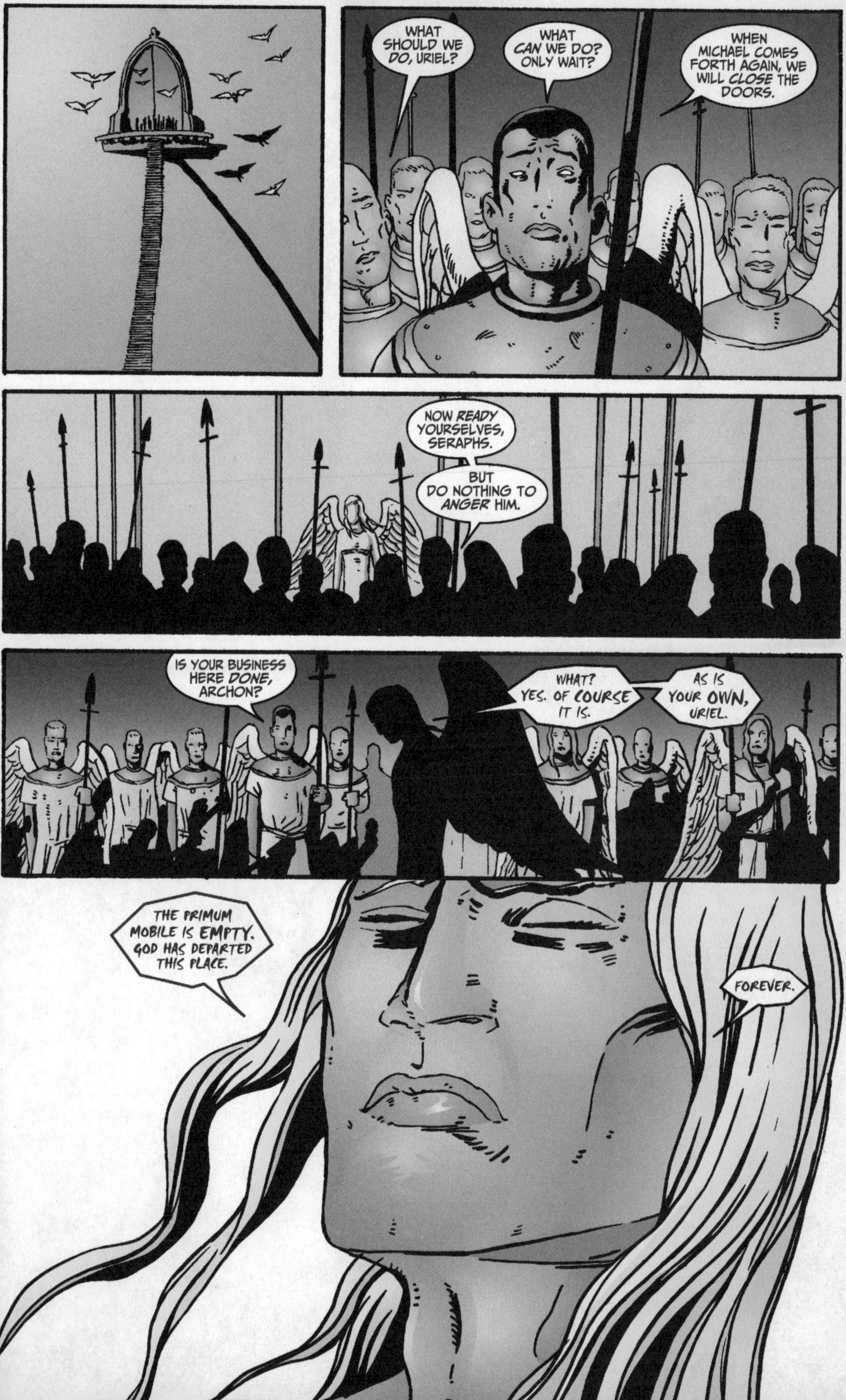

WHAT SHOULD WE DO, URIEL?
WHAT CAN WE DO? ONLY WAIT?
WHEN MICHAEL COMES FORTH AGAIN, WE WILL CLOSE THE DOORS.
NOW READY YOURSELVES, SERAPHS.
BUT DO NOTHING TO ANGER HIM.
IS YOUR BUSINESS HERE DONE, ARCHON?
WHAT? YES. OF COURSE IT IS.
AS IS YOUR OWN, URIEL.
THE PRIMUM MOBILE IS EMPTY. GOD HAS DEPARTED THIS PLACE.
FOREVER.

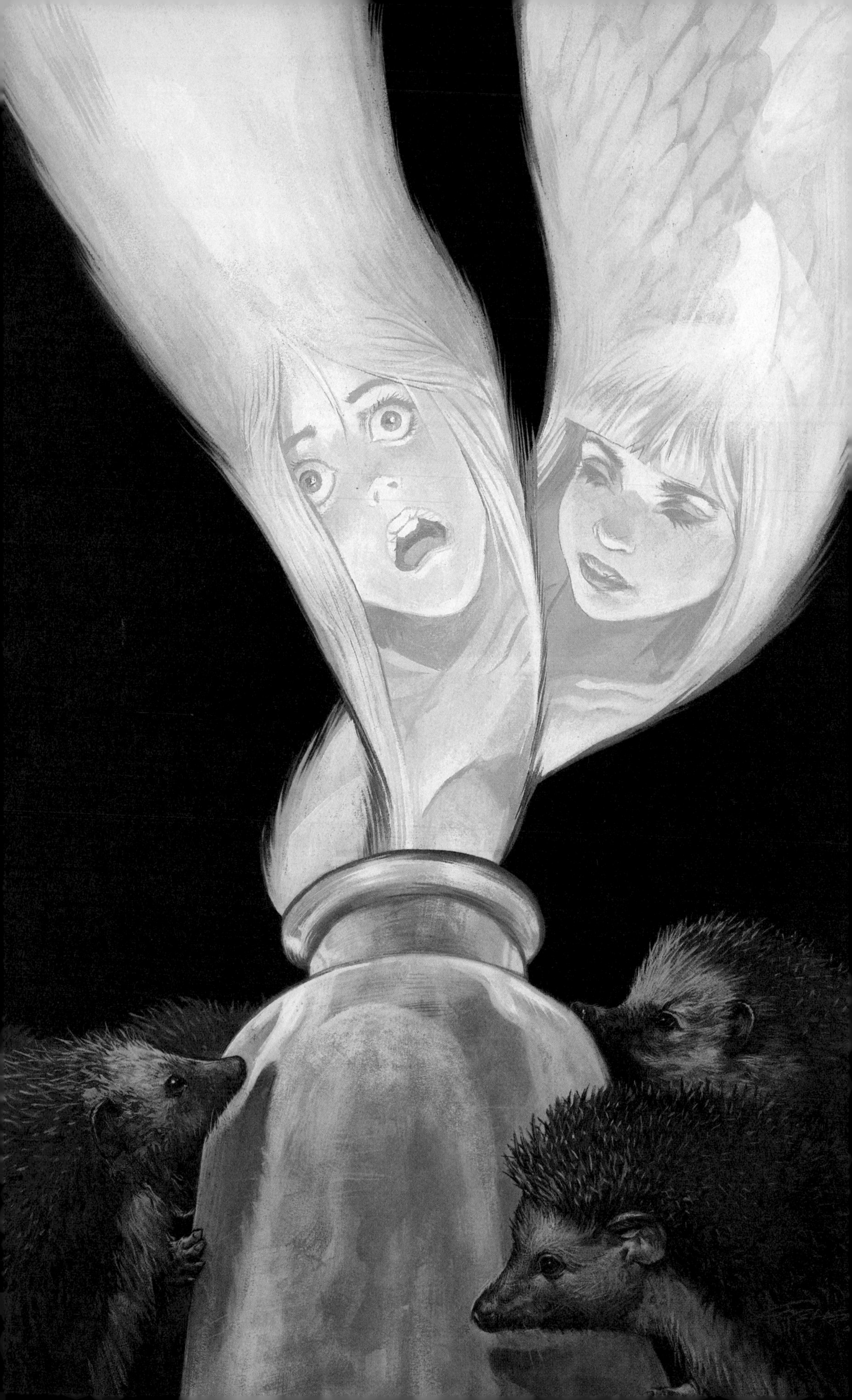

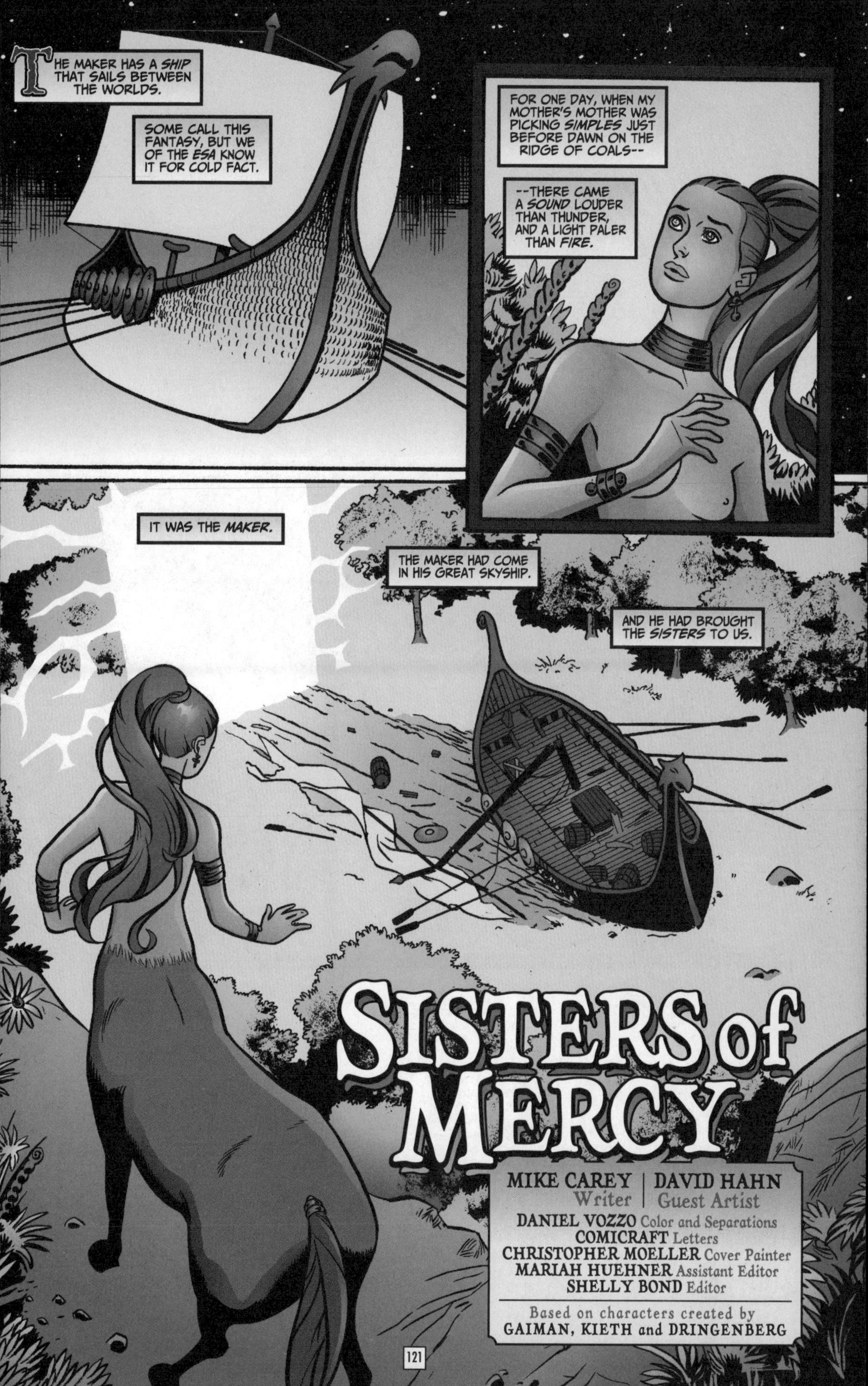
THE MAKER HAS A SHIP THAT SAILS BETWEEN THE WORLDS.
SOME CALL THIS FANTASY, BUT WE OF THE ESA KNOW IT FOR COLD FACT.
FOR ONE DAY, WHEN MY MOTHER'S MOTHER WAS PICKING SIMPLES JUST BEFORE DAWN ON THE RIDGE OF COALS--
--THERE CAME A SOUND LOUDER THAN THUNDER, AND A LIGHT PALER THAN FIRE.
IT WAS THE MAKER.
THE MAKER HAD COME IN HIS GREAT SKYSHIP.
AND HE HAD BROUGHT THE SISTERS TO US.
SISTERS of MERCY
MIKE CAREY Writer
DAVID HAHN Guest Artist
DANIEL VOZZO Color and Separations
COMICRAFT Letters
CHRISTOPHER MOELLER Cover Painter
MARIAH HUEHNER Assistant Editor
SHELLY BOND Editor
Based on characters created by GAIMAN, KIETH and DRINGENBERG

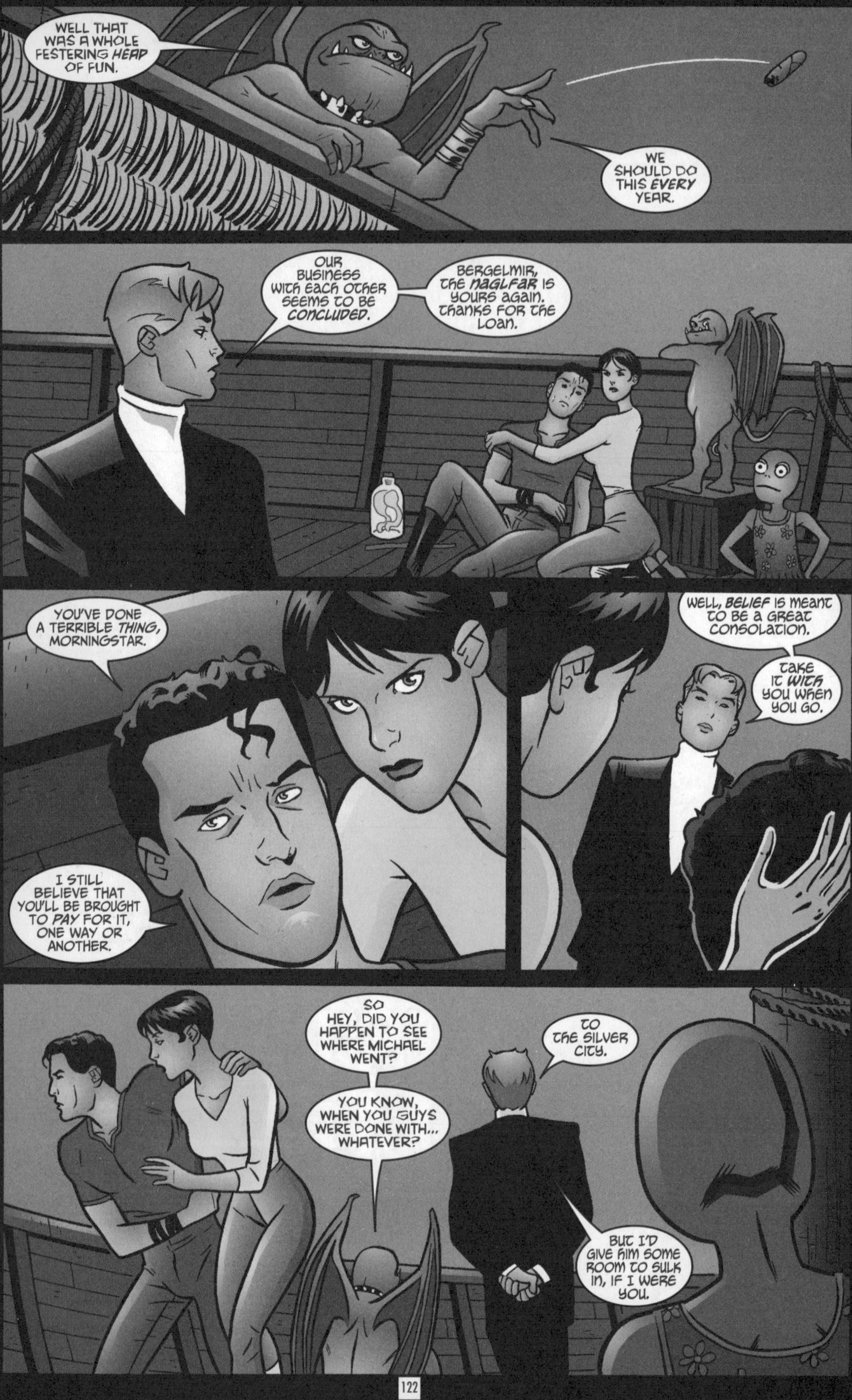
WELL THAT WAS A WHOLE FESTERING HEAD OF FUN.
WE SHOULD DO THIS EVERY YEAR.
OUR BUSINESS WITH EACH OTHER SEEMS TO BE CONCLUDED.
BERGELMIR, THE NAGLFAR IS YOURS AGAIN. THANKS FOR THE LOAN.
YOU'VE DONE A TERRIBLE THING, MORNINGSTAR.
I STILL BELIEVE THAT YOU'LL BE BROUGHT TO PAY FOR IT, ONE WAY OR ANOTHER.
WELL, BELIEF IS MEANT TO BE A GREAT CONSOLATION.
TAKE IT WITH YOU WHEN YOU GO.
SO HEY, DID YOU HAPPEN TO SEE WHERE MICHAEL WENT?
YOU KNOW, WHEN YOU GUYS WERE DONE WITH... WHATEVER?
TO THE SILVER CITY.
BUT I'D GIVE HIM SOME ROOM TO SULK IN, IF I WERE YOU.

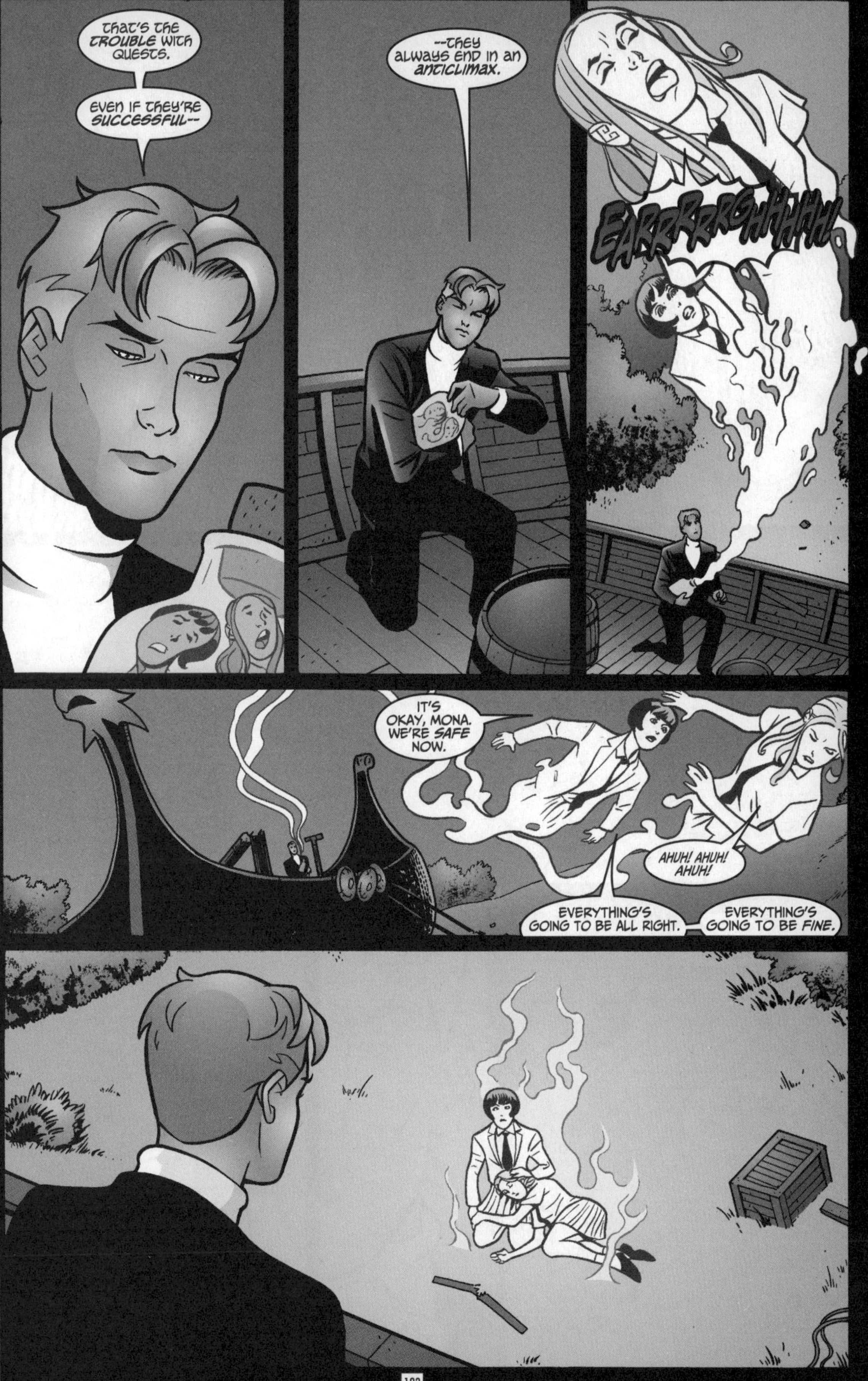
THAT'S THE TROUBLE WITH QUESTS.
EVEN IF THEY'RE SUCCESSFUL--
--THEY ALWAYS END IN AN ANTICLIMAX.
EARRRRRGHHHHH!
IT'S OKAY, MONA. WE'RE SAFE NOW.
AHUH! AHUH! AHUH!
EVERYTHING'S GOING TO BE ALL RIGHT.
EVERYTHING'S GOING TO BE FINE.

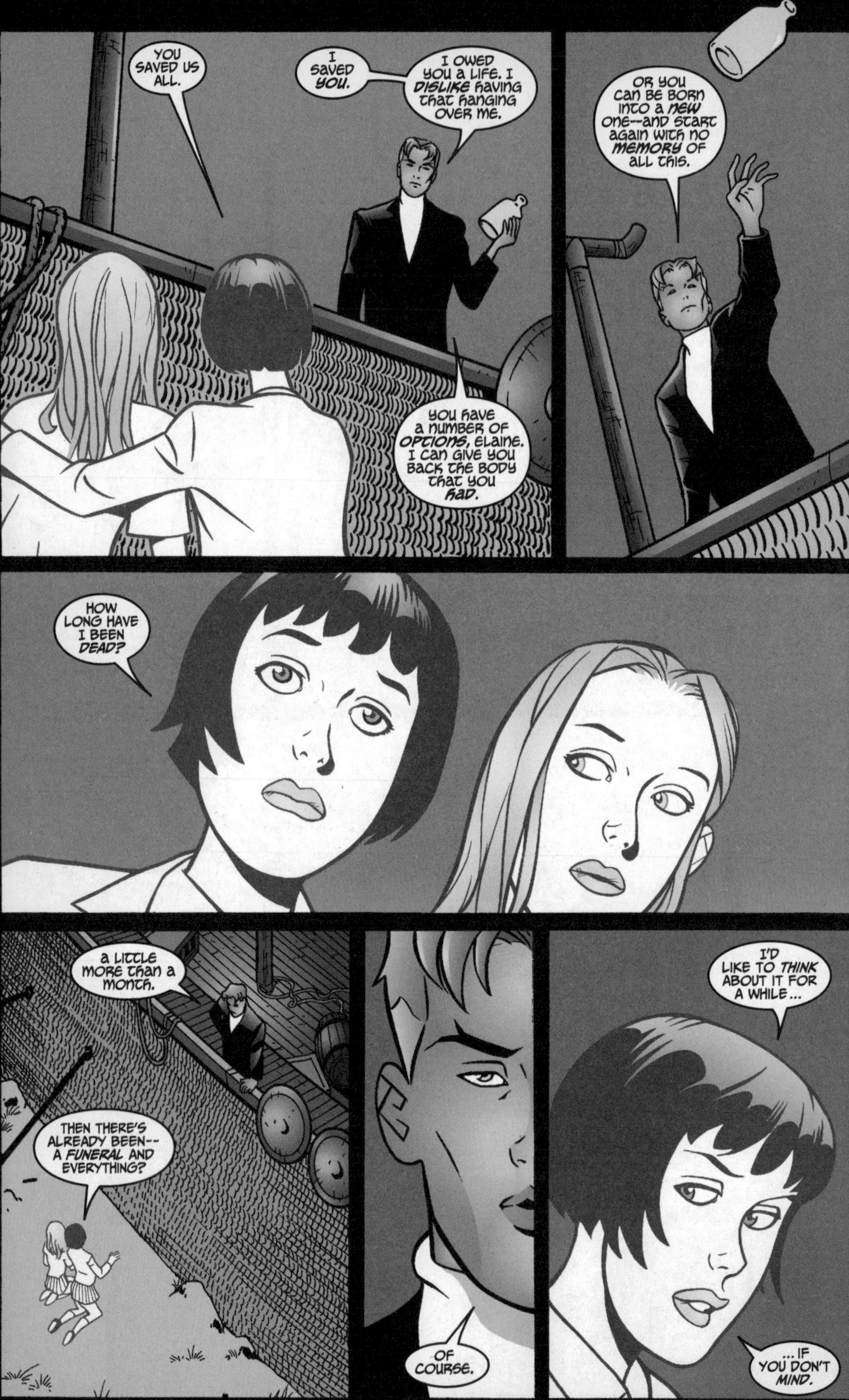
YOU SAVED US ALL.
I SAVED YOU.
I OWED YOU A LIFE. I DISLIKE HAVING THAT HANGING OVER ME.
YOU HAVE A NUMBER OF OPTIONS, ELAINE. I CAN GIVE YOU BACK THE BODY THAT YOU HAD.
OR YOU CAN BE BORN INTO A NEW ONE--AND START AGAIN WITH NO MEMORY OF ALL THIS.
HOW LONG HAVE I BEEN DEAD?
A LITTLE MORE THAN A MONTH.
THEN THERE'S ALREADY BEEN--A FUNERAL AND EVERYTHING?
OF COURSE.
I'D LIKE TO THINK ABOUT IT FOR A WHILE...
...IF YOU DON'T MIND.

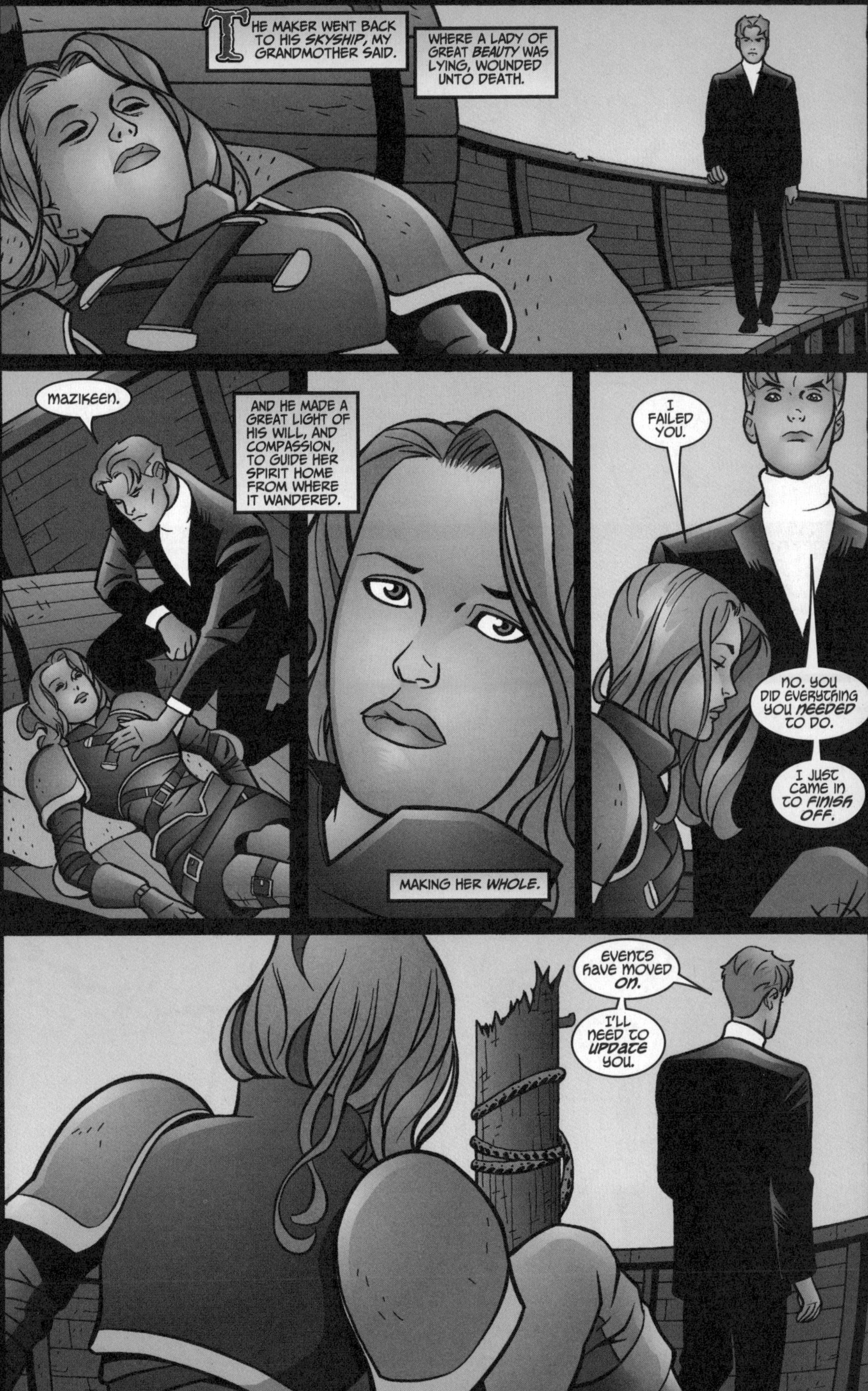
THE MAKER WENT BACK TO HIS SKYSHIP, MY GRANDMOTHER SAID.
WHERE A LADY OF GREAT BEAUTY WAS LYING, WOUNDED UNTO DEATH.
MAZIKEEN.
AND HE MADE A GREAT LIGHT OF HIS WILL, AND COMPASSION, TO GUIDE HER SPIRIT HOME FROM WHERE IT WANDERED.
MAKING HER WHOLE.
I FAILED YOU.
NO. YOU DID EVERYTHING YOU NEEDED TO DO.
I JUST CAME IN TO FINISH OFF.
EVENTS HAVE MOVED ON.
I'LL NEED TO UPDATE YOU.

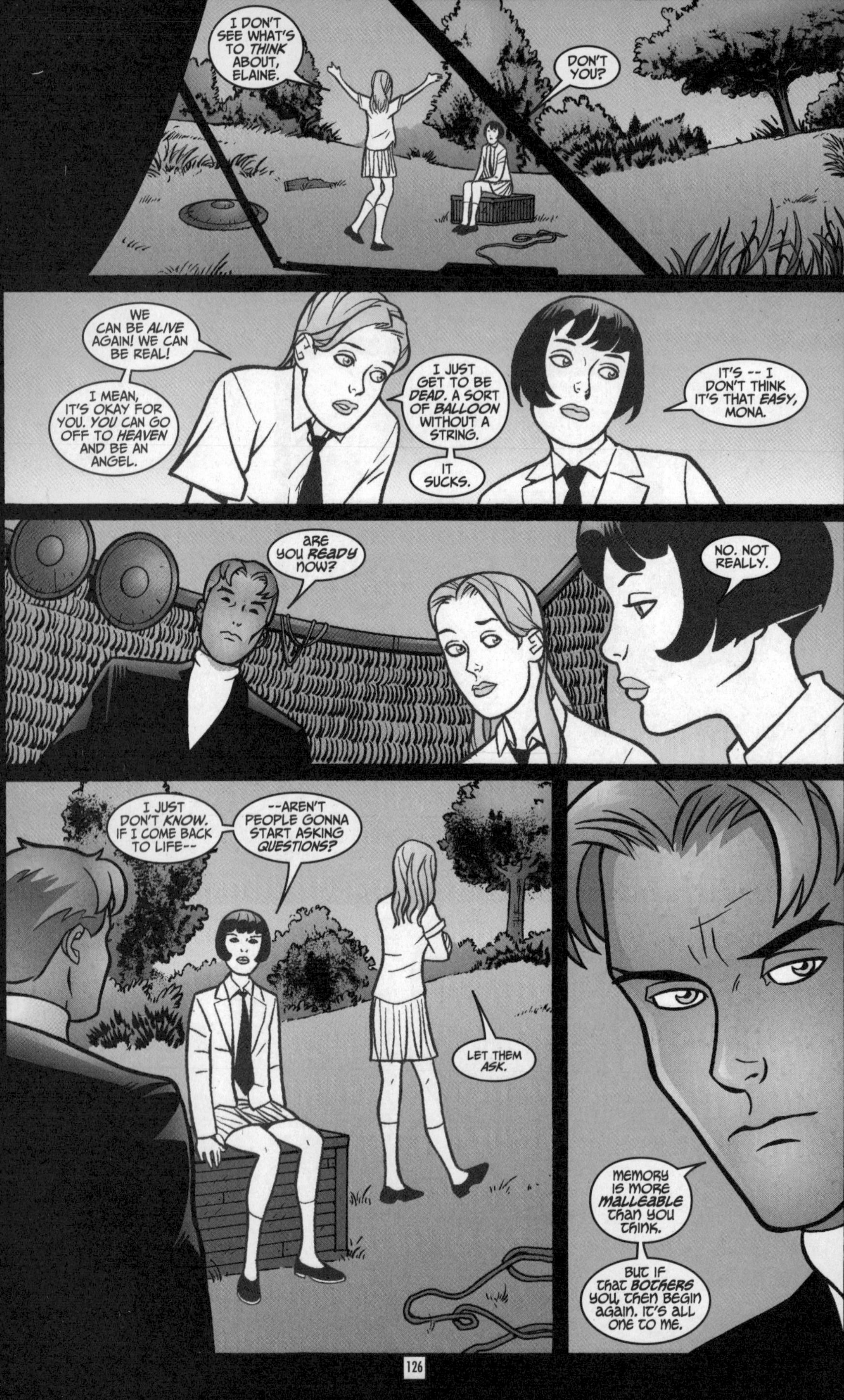
I DON'T SEE WHAT'S TO THINK ABOUT, ELAINE.
DON'T YOU?
WE CAN BE ALIVE AGAIN! WE CAN BE REAL!
I MEAN, IT'S OKAY FOR YOU. YOU CAN GO OFF TO HEAVEN AND BE AN ANGEL.
I JUST GET TO BE DEAD. A SORT OF BALLOON WITHOUT A STRING.
IT SUCKS.
IT'S -- I DON'T THINK IT'S THAT EASY, MONA.
ARE YOU READY NOW?
NO. NOT REALLY.
I JUST DON'T KNOW. IF I COME BACK TO LIFE--
--AREN'T PEOPLE GONNA START ASKING QUESTIONS?
LET THEM ASK.
MEMORY IS MORE MALLEABLE THAN YOU THINK.
BUT IF THAT BOTHERS YOU, THEN BEGIN AGAIN. IT'S ALL ONE TO ME.

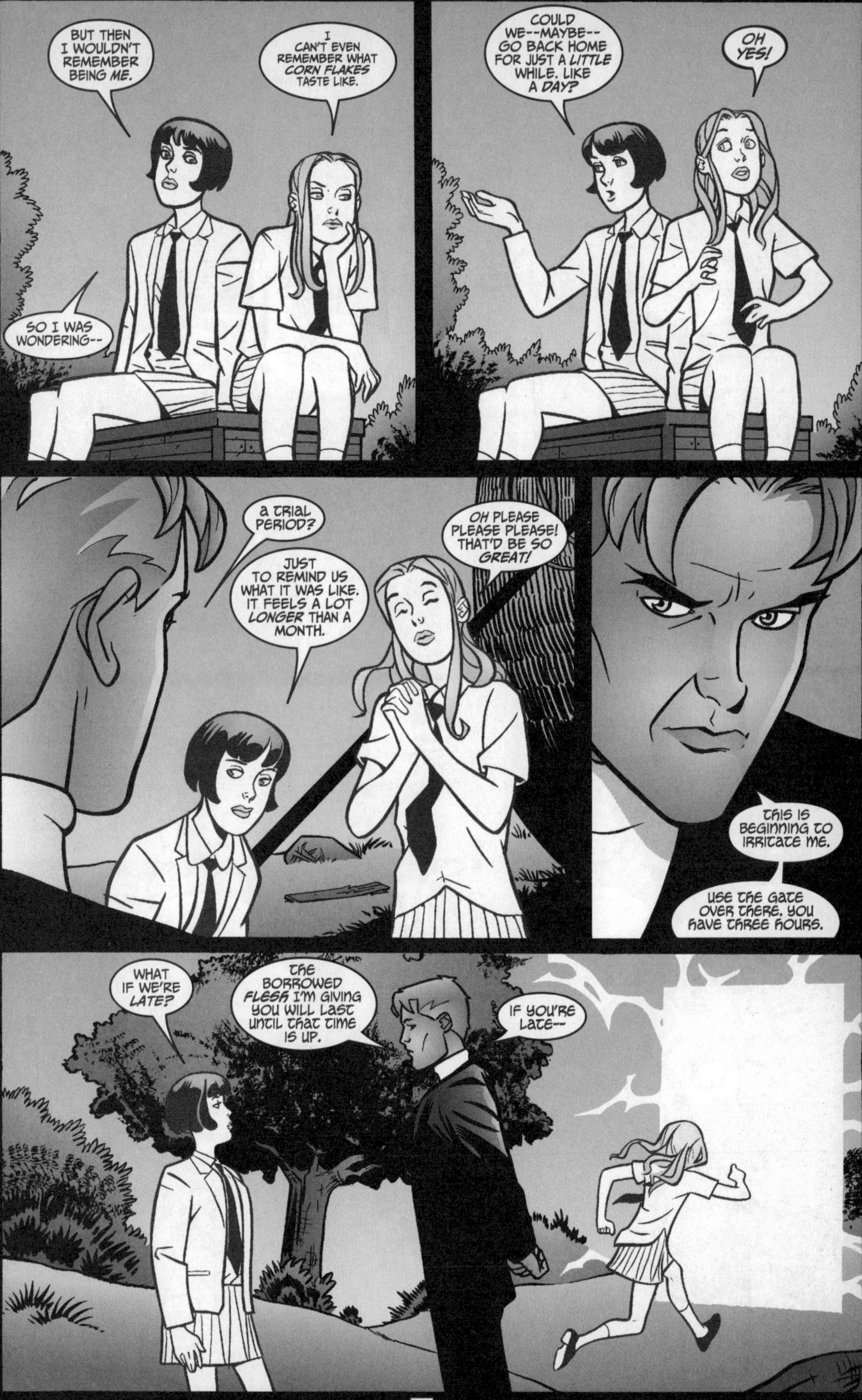
BUT THEN I WOULDN'T REMEMBER BEING *ME*.
I CAN'T EVEN REMEMBER WHAT *CORN FLAKES* TASTE LIKE.
SO I WAS WONDERING--
COULD WE--MAYBE--GO BACK HOME FOR JUST A *LITTLE* WHILE. LIKE A *DAY*?
*OH YES!*
a TRIAL PERIOD?
JUST TO REMIND US WHAT IT WAS LIKE. IT FEELS A LOT *LONGER* THAN A MONTH.
*OH* PLEASE PLEASE PLEASE! THAT'D BE SO *GREAT!*
THIS IS BEGINNING TO IRRITATE ME.
USE THE GATE OVER THERE. YOU HAVE THREE HOURS.
WHAT IF WE'RE *LATE?*
THE BORROWED *FLESH* I'M GIVING YOU WILL LAST UNTIL THAT TIME IS UP.
IF YOU'RE LATE--

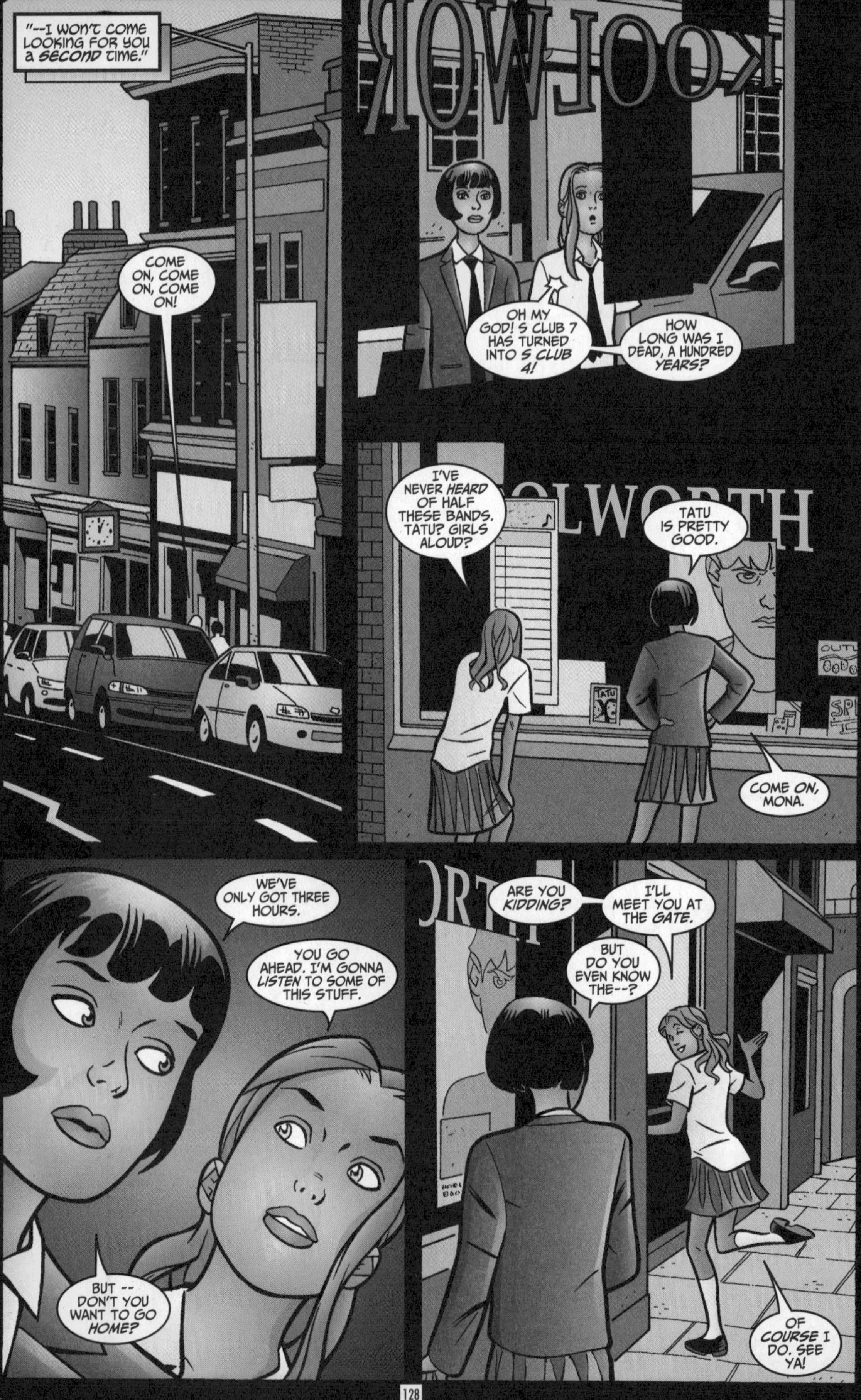
"--I WON'T COME LOOKING FOR YOU A SECOND TIME."
COME ON, COME ON, COME ON!
OH MY GOD! S CLUB 7 HAS TURNED INTO S CLUB 4!
HOW LONG WAS I DEAD, A HUNDRED YEARS?
I'VE NEVER HEARD OF HALF THESE BANDS. TATU? GIRLS ALOUD?
TATU IS PRETTY GOOD.
COME ON, MONA.
WE'VE ONLY GOT THREE HOURS.
YOU GO AHEAD. I'M GONNA LISTEN TO SOME OF THIS STUFF.
BUT -- DON'T YOU WANT TO GO HOME?
ARE YOU KIDDING?
I'LL MEET YOU AT THE GATE.
BUT DO YOU EVEN KNOW THE--?
OF COURSE I DO. SEE YA!

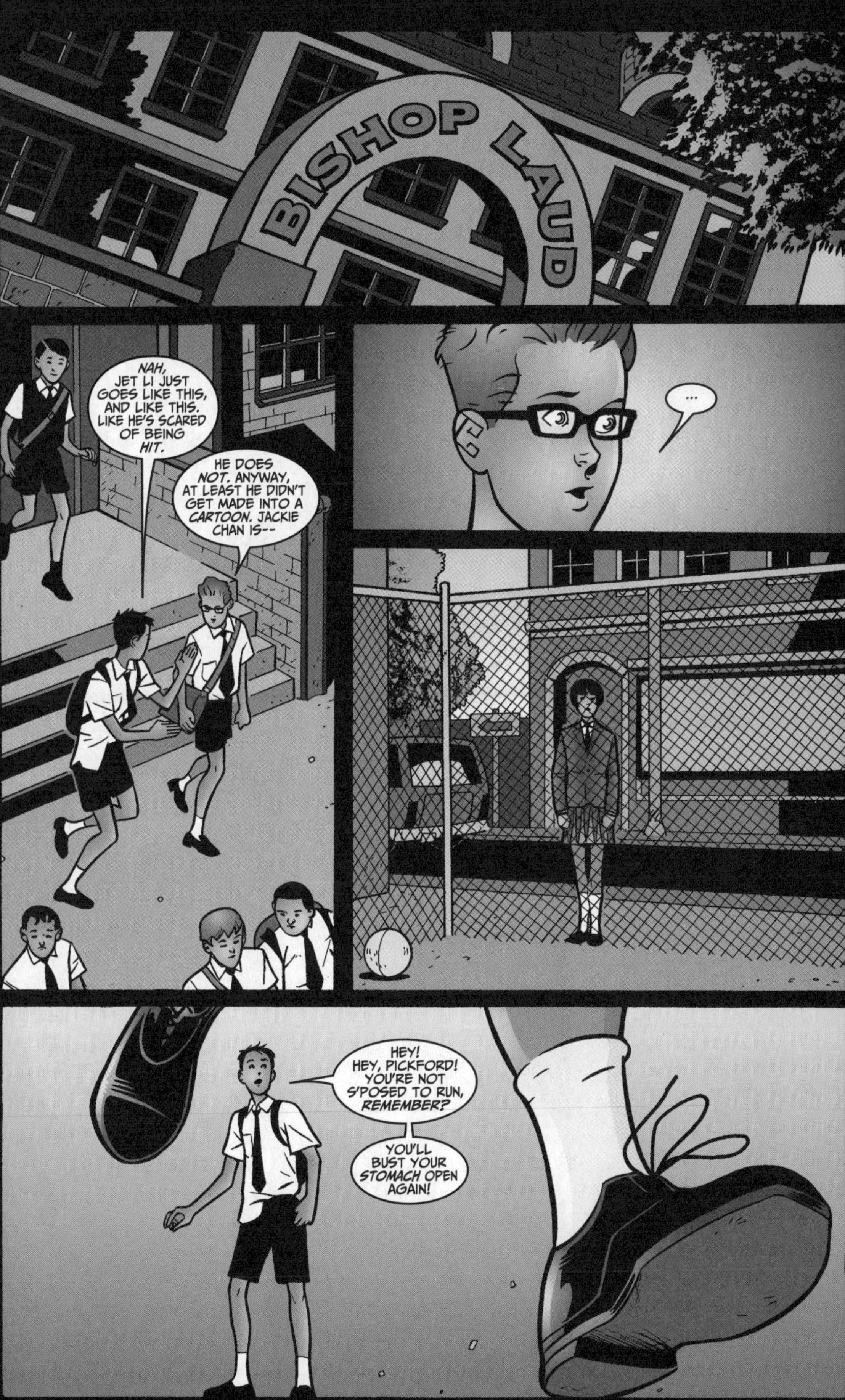
BISHOP LAUD
NAH, JET LI JUST GOES LIKE THIS, AND LIKE THIS. LIKE HE'S SCARED OF BEING *HIT*.
HE DOES *NOT*. ANYWAY, AT LEAST HE DIDN'T GET MADE INTO A *CARTOON*. JACKIE CHAN IS--
...
HEY! HEY, PICKFORD! YOU'RE NOT S'POSED TO RUN, *REMEMBER?*
YOU'LL BUST YOUR *STOMACH* OPEN AGAIN!

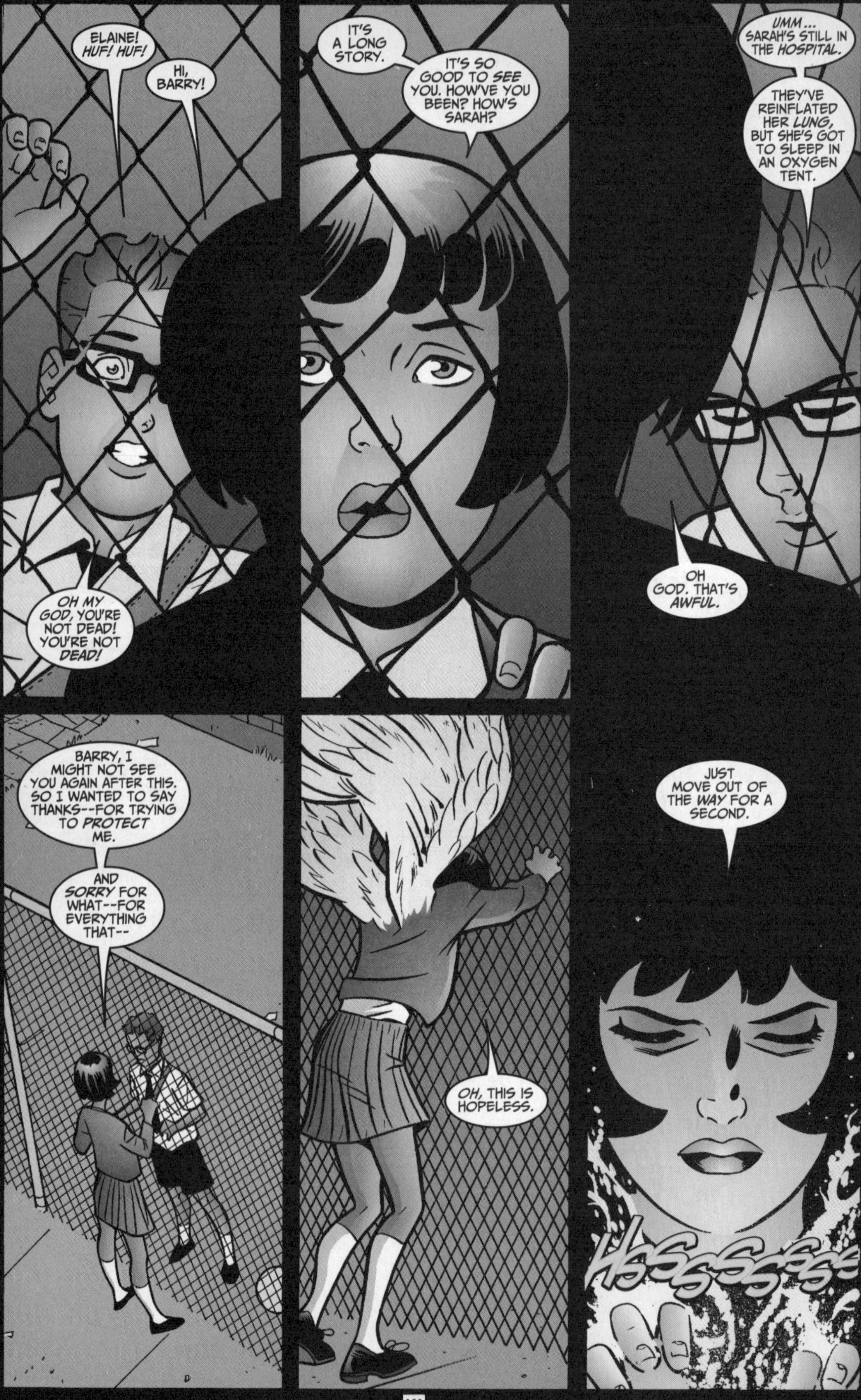

ELAINE! HUF! HUF!
HI, BARRY!
OH MY GOD, YOU'RE NOT DEAD! YOU'RE NOT DEAD!
IT'S A LONG STORY.
IT'S SO GOOD TO SEE YOU. HOW'VE YOU BEEN? HOW'S SARAH?
UMM... SARAH'S STILL IN THE HOSPITAL.
THEY'VE REINFLATED HER LUNG, BUT SHE'S GOT TO SLEEP IN AN OXYGEN TENT.
OH GOD. THAT'S AWFUL.
BARRY, I MIGHT NOT SEE YOU AGAIN AFTER THIS. SO I WANTED TO SAY THANKS--FOR TRYING TO PROTECT ME.
AND SORRY FOR WHAT--FOR EVERYTHING THAT--
OH, THIS IS HOPELESS.
JUST MOVE OUT OF THE WAY FOR A SECOND.
HSSSSSSSS

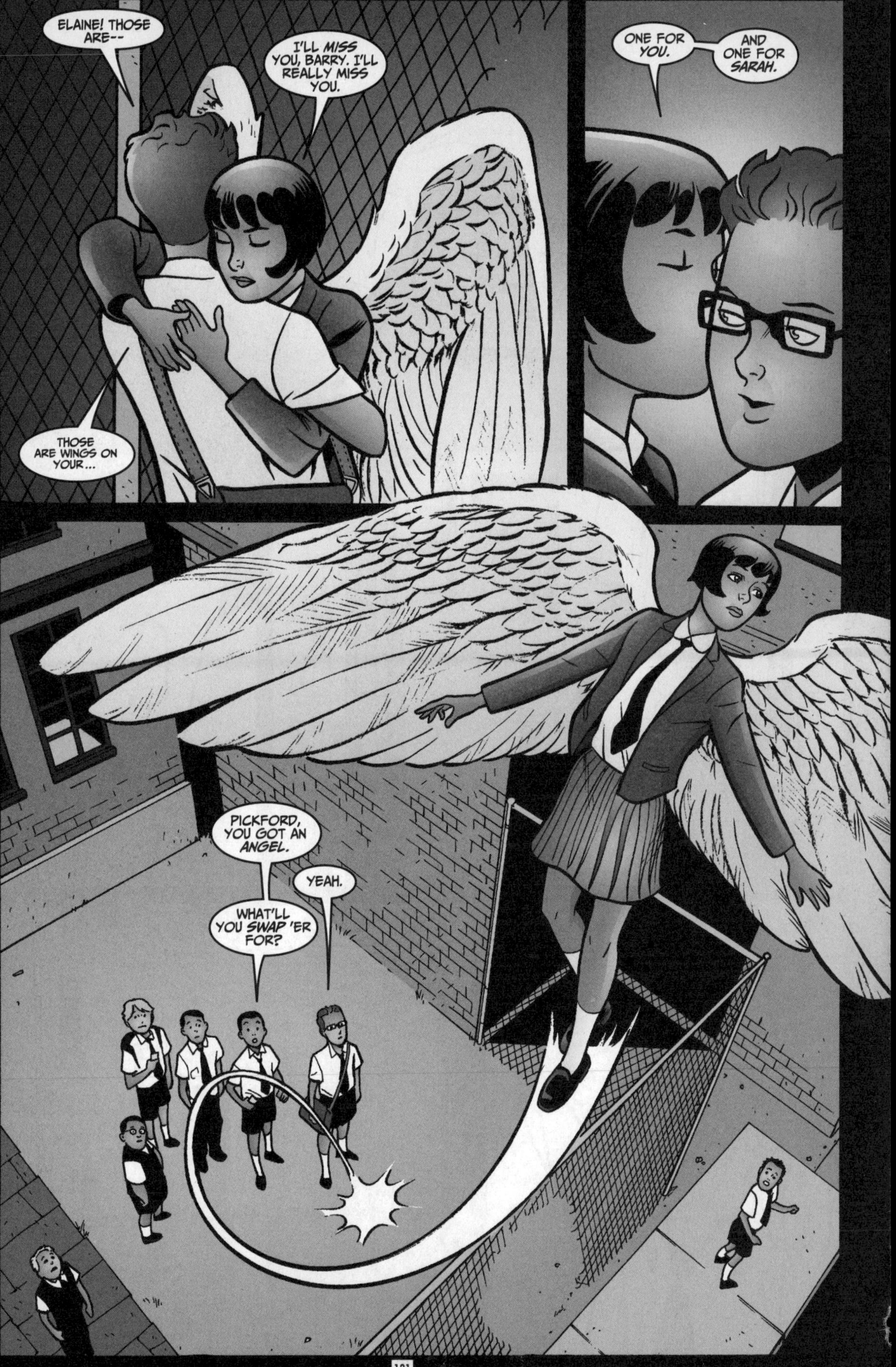

ELAINE! THOSE ARE--
I'LL MISS YOU, BARRY. I'LL REALLY MISS YOU.
THOSE ARE WINGS ON YOUR...
ONE FOR YOU.
AND ONE FOR SARAH.
PICKFORD, YOU GOT AN ANGEL.
YEAH.
WHAT'LL YOU SWAP 'ER FOR?

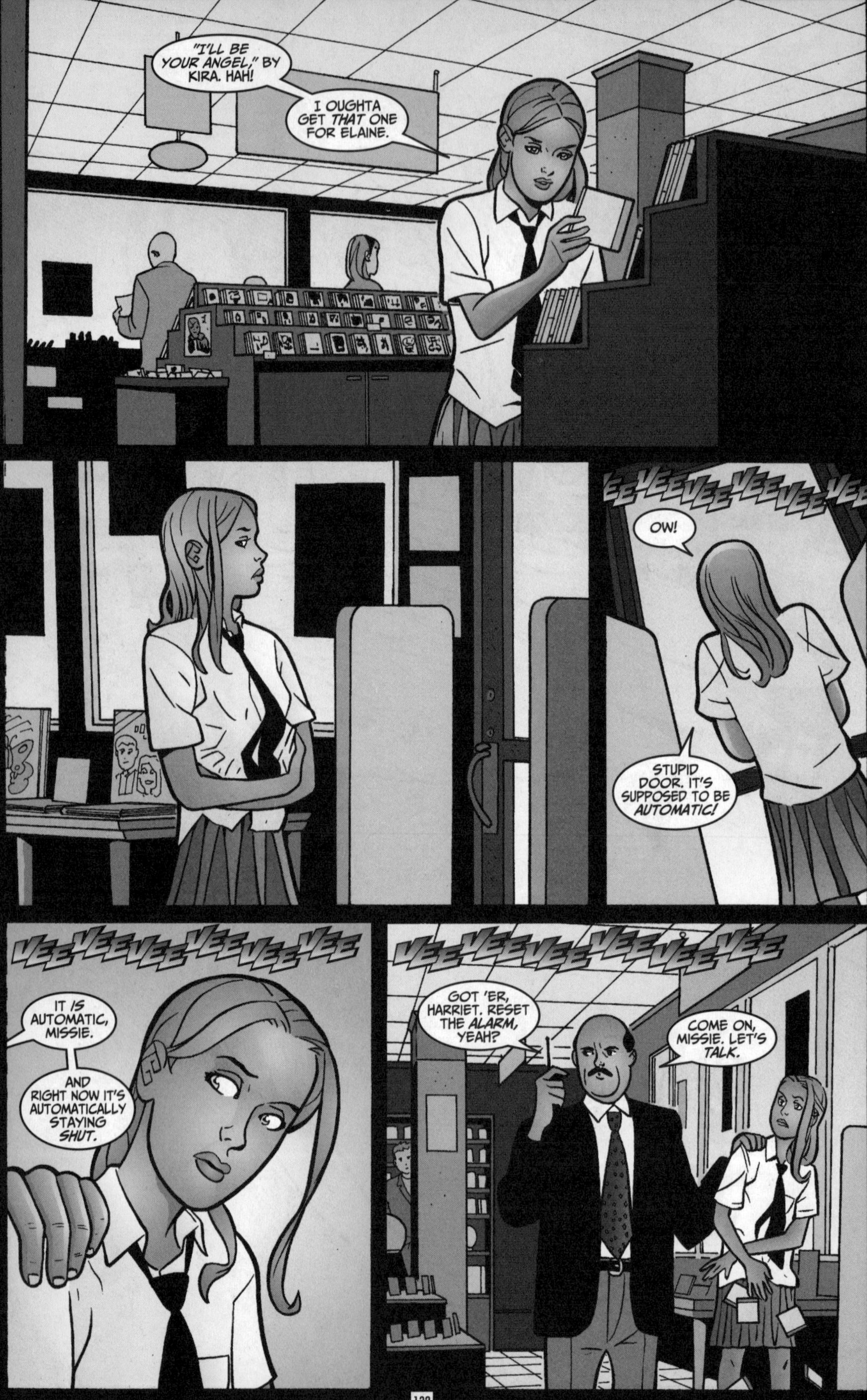
"I'LL BE YOUR ANGEL," BY KIRA. HAH!
I OUGHTA GET THAT ONE FOR ELAINE.
VEEVEEVEEVEEVEEVEEVEE
OW!
STUPID DOOR. IT'S SUPPOSED TO BE AUTOMATIC!
VEEVEEVEEVEEVEEVEEVEE
IT IS AUTOMATIC, MISSIE.
AND RIGHT NOW IT'S AUTOMATICALLY STAYING SHUT.
VEEVEEVEEVEEVEEVEEVEE
GOT 'ER, HARRIET. RESET THE ALARM, YEAH?
COME ON, MISSIE. LET'S TALK.

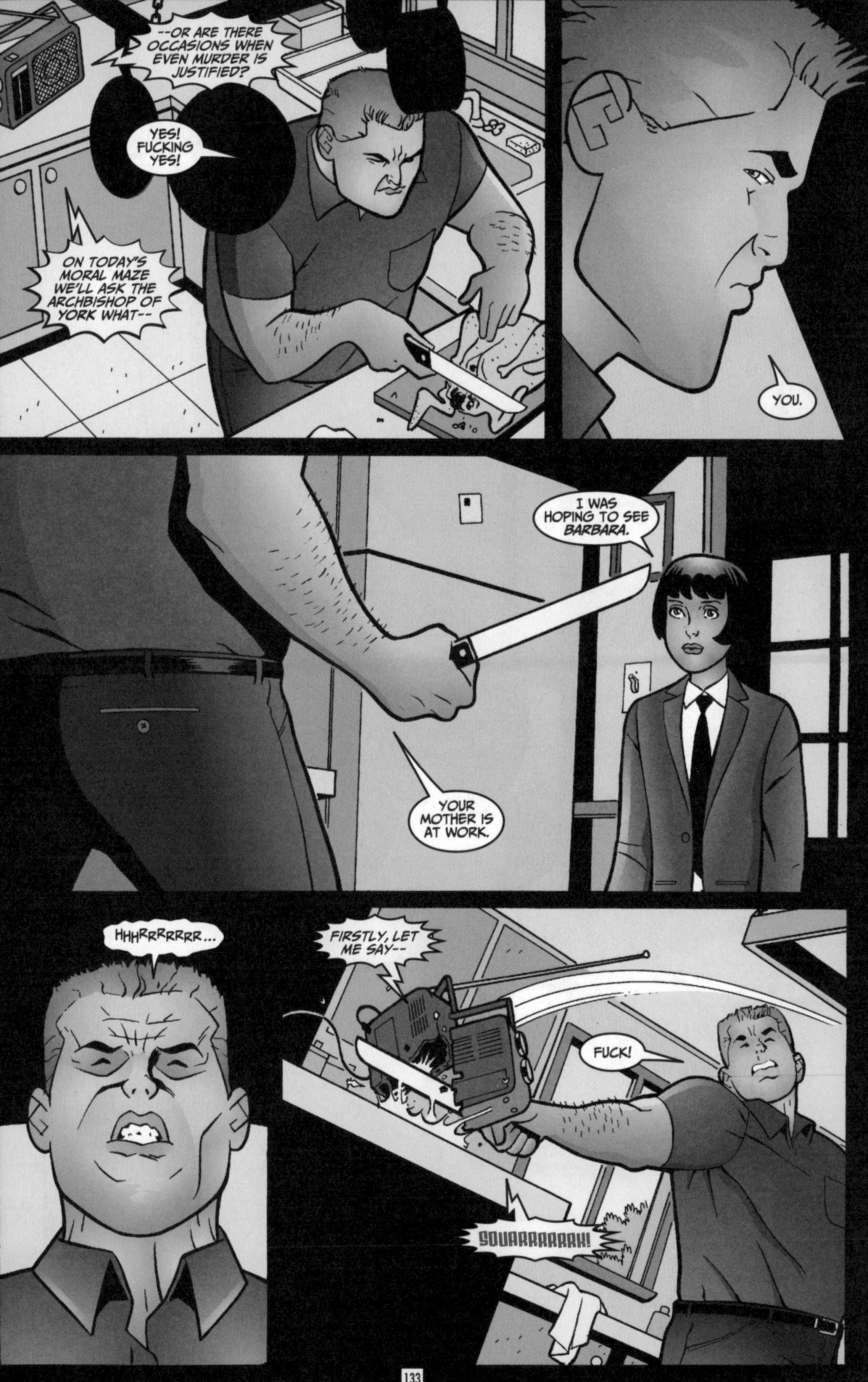
--OR ARE THERE OCCASIONS WHEN EVEN MURDER IS JUSTIFIED?
YES! FUCKING YES!
ON TODAY'S MORAL MAZE WE'LL ASK THE ARCHBISHOP OF YORK WHAT--
YOU.
I WAS HOPING TO SEE BARBARA.
YOUR MOTHER IS AT WORK.
HHHRRRRRR...
FIRSTLY, LET ME SAY--
FUCK!
SQUARRRRRRRK!

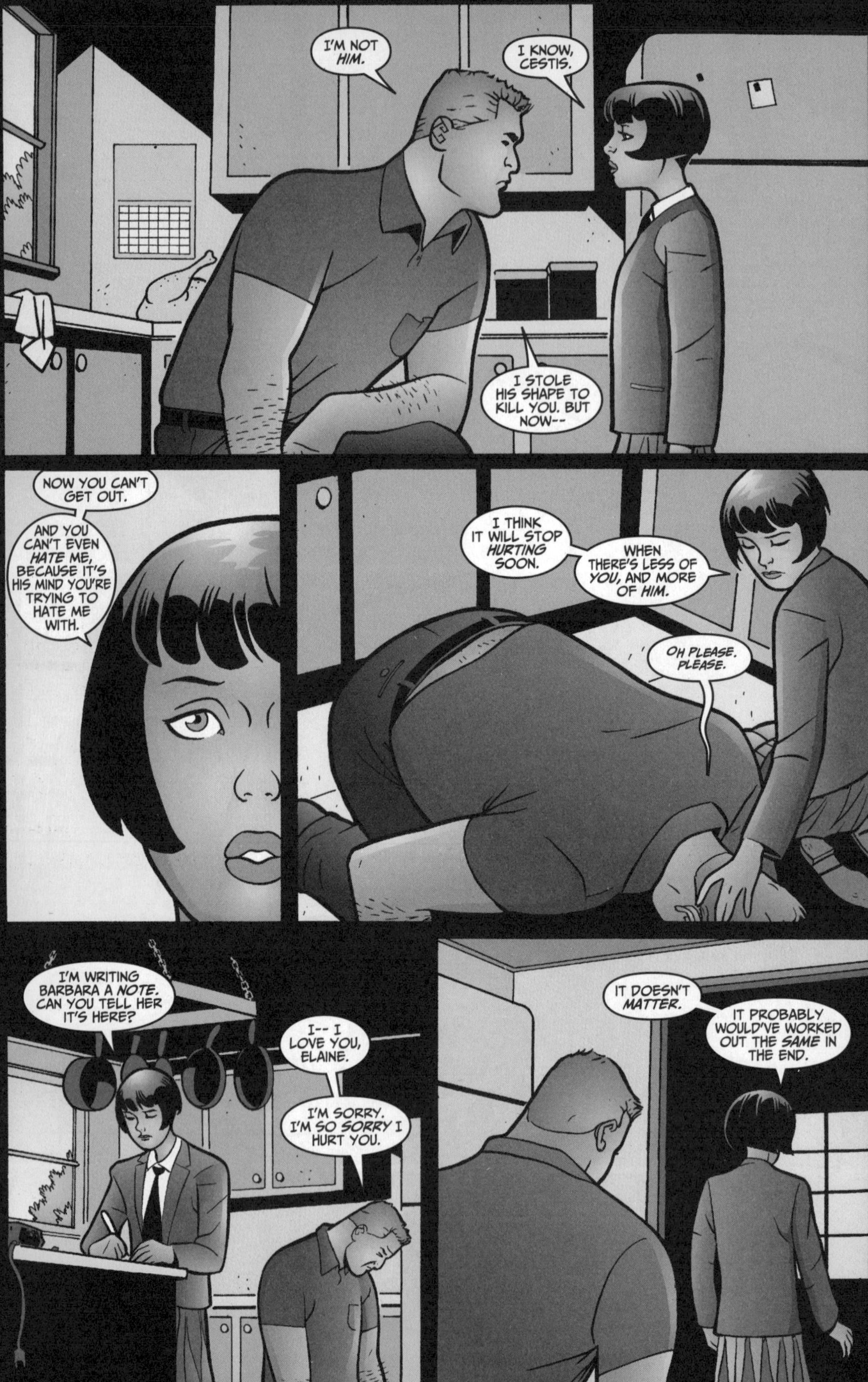
I'M NOT *HIM.*
I KNOW, CESTIS.
I STOLE HIS SHAPE TO KILL YOU. BUT NOW--
NOW YOU CAN'T GET OUT.
AND YOU CAN'T EVEN *HATE* ME, BECAUSE IT'S HIS MIND YOU'RE TRYING TO HATE ME WITH.
I THINK IT WILL STOP *HURTING* SOON.
WHEN THERE'S LESS OF *YOU,* AND MORE OF *HIM.*
*OH PLEASE. PLEASE.*
I'M WRITING BARBARA A *NOTE.* CAN YOU TELL HER IT'S HERE?
I-- I LOVE YOU, ELAINE.
I'M SORRY. I'M SO *SORRY* I HURT YOU.
IT DOESN'T *MATTER.*
IT PROBABLY WOULD'VE WORKED OUT THE *SAME* IN THE END.

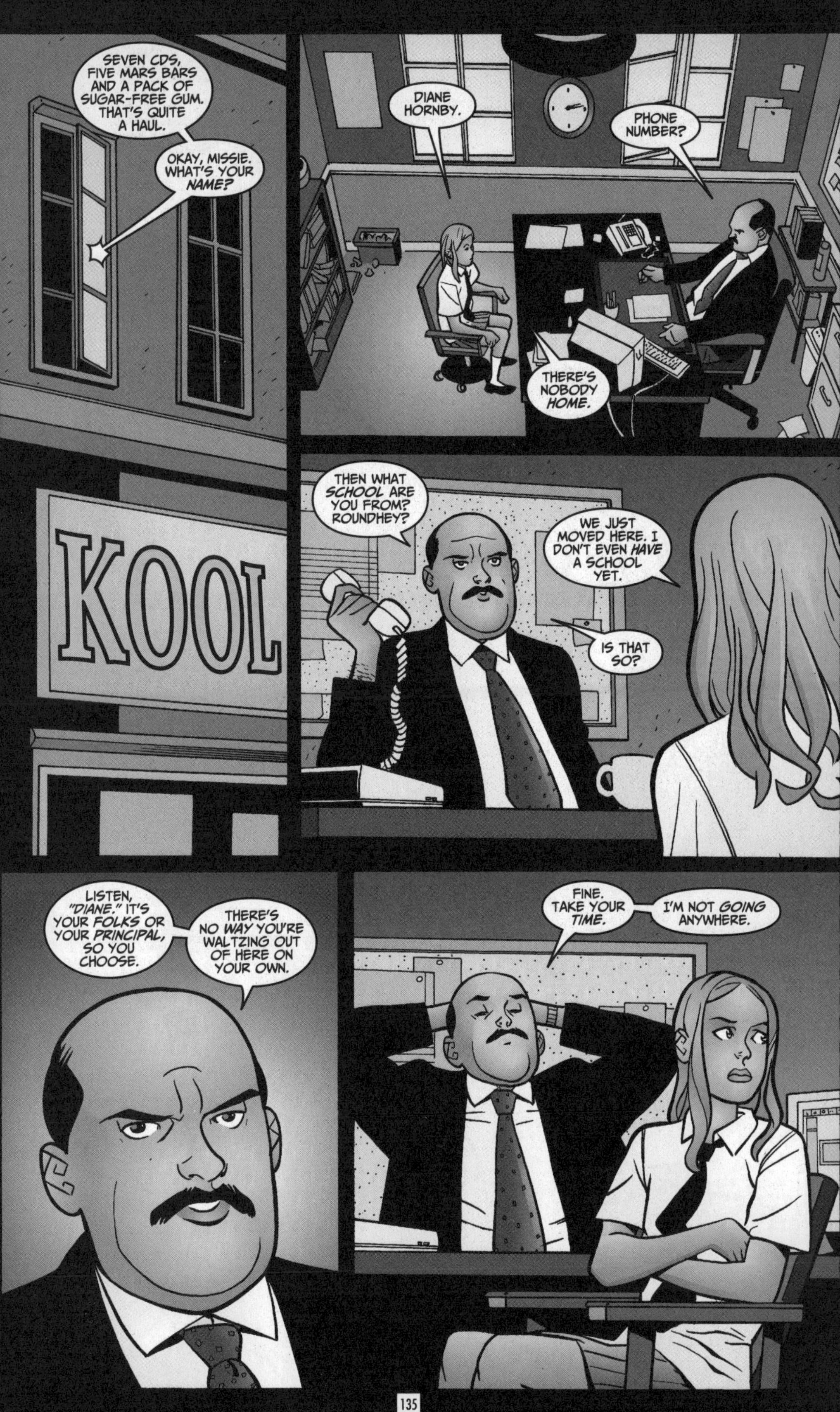
SEVEN CDS, FIVE MARS BARS AND A PACK OF SUGAR-FREE GUM. THAT'S QUITE A HAUL.
OKAY, MISSIE. WHAT'S YOUR NAME?
DIANE HORNBY.
PHONE NUMBER?
THERE'S NOBODY HOME.
KOOL
THEN WHAT SCHOOL ARE YOU FROM? ROUNDHEY?
WE JUST MOVED HERE. I DON'T EVEN HAVE A SCHOOL YET.
IS THAT SO?
LISTEN, "DIANE." IT'S YOUR FOLKS OR YOUR PRINCIPAL, SO YOU CHOOSE.
THERE'S NO WAY YOU'RE WALTZING OUT OF HERE ON YOUR OWN.
FINE. TAKE YOUR TIME.
I'M NOT GOING ANYWHERE.

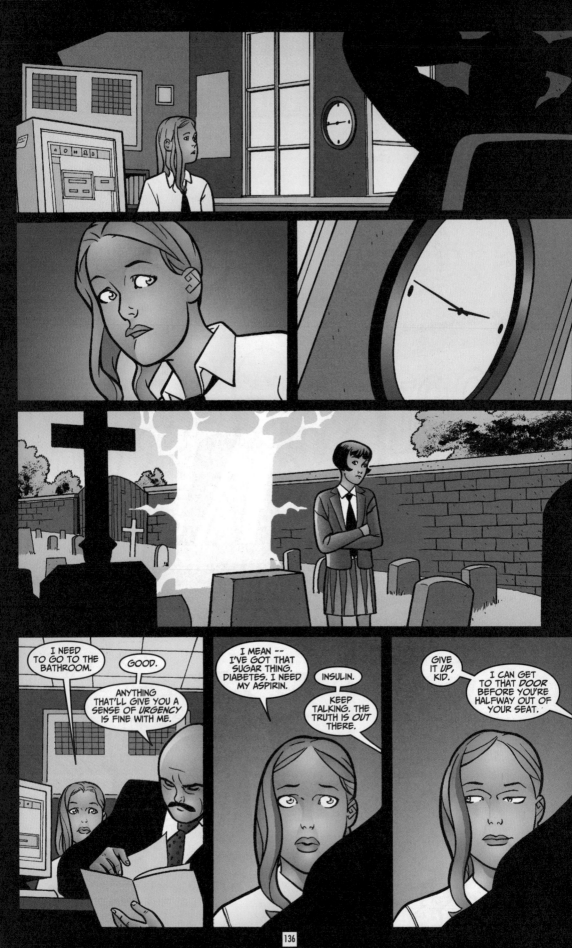

I NEED TO GO TO THE BATHROOM.

GOOD. ANYTHING THAT'LL GIVE YOU A SENSE OF *URGENCY* IS FINE WITH ME.

I MEAN -- I'VE GOT THAT *SUGAR* THING. DIABETES. I NEED MY ASPIRIN.

INSULIN.

KEEP TALKING. THE TRUTH IS *OUT* THERE.

GIVE IT *UP*, KID.

I CAN GET TO THAT *DOOR* BEFORE YOU'RE HALFWAY OUT OF YOUR SEAT.

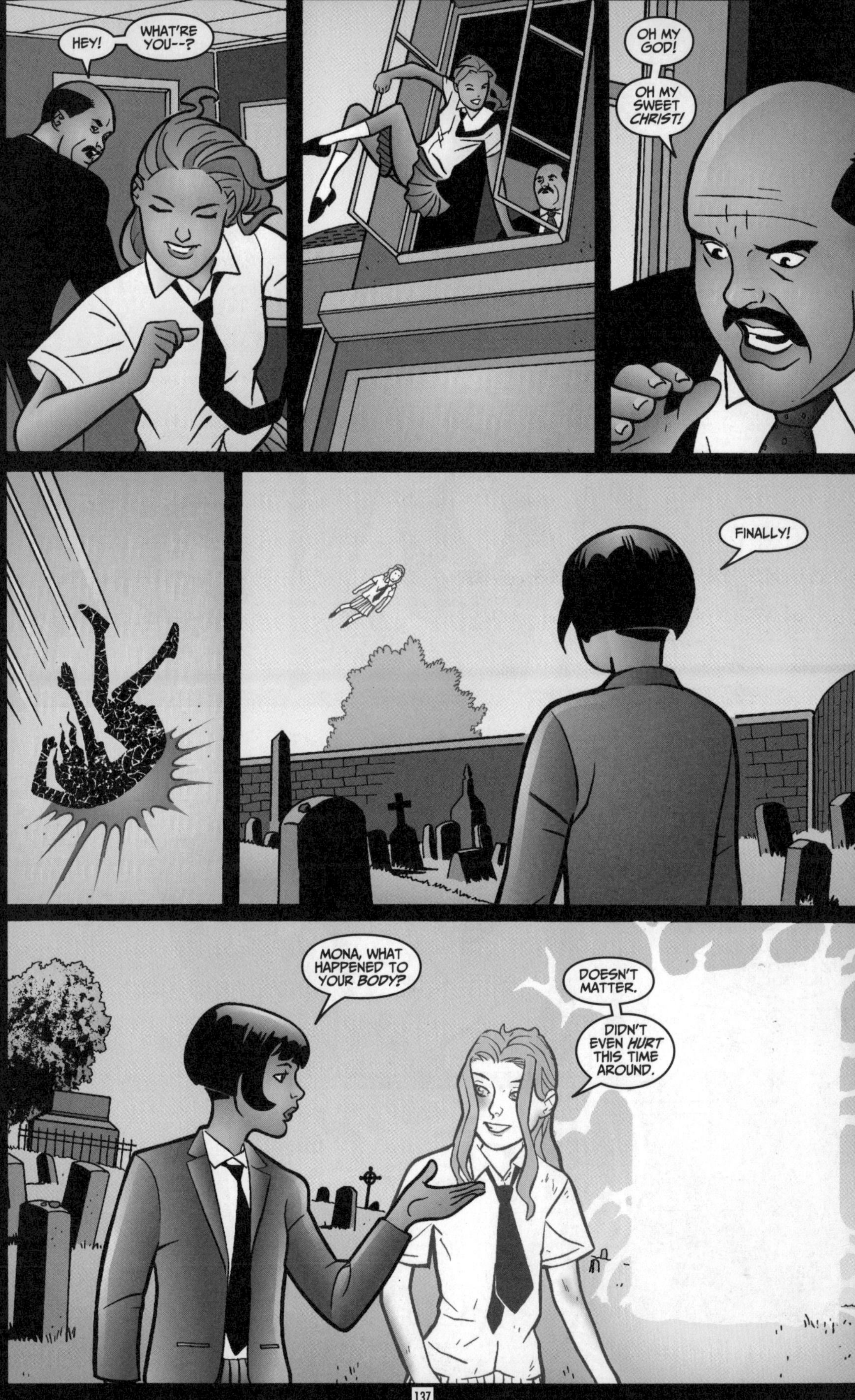
HEY!
WHAT'RE YOU--?
OH MY GOD!
OH MY SWEET CHRIST!
FINALLY!
MONA, WHAT HAPPENED TO YOUR BODY?
DOESN'T MATTER.
DIDN'T EVEN HURT THIS TIME AROUND.

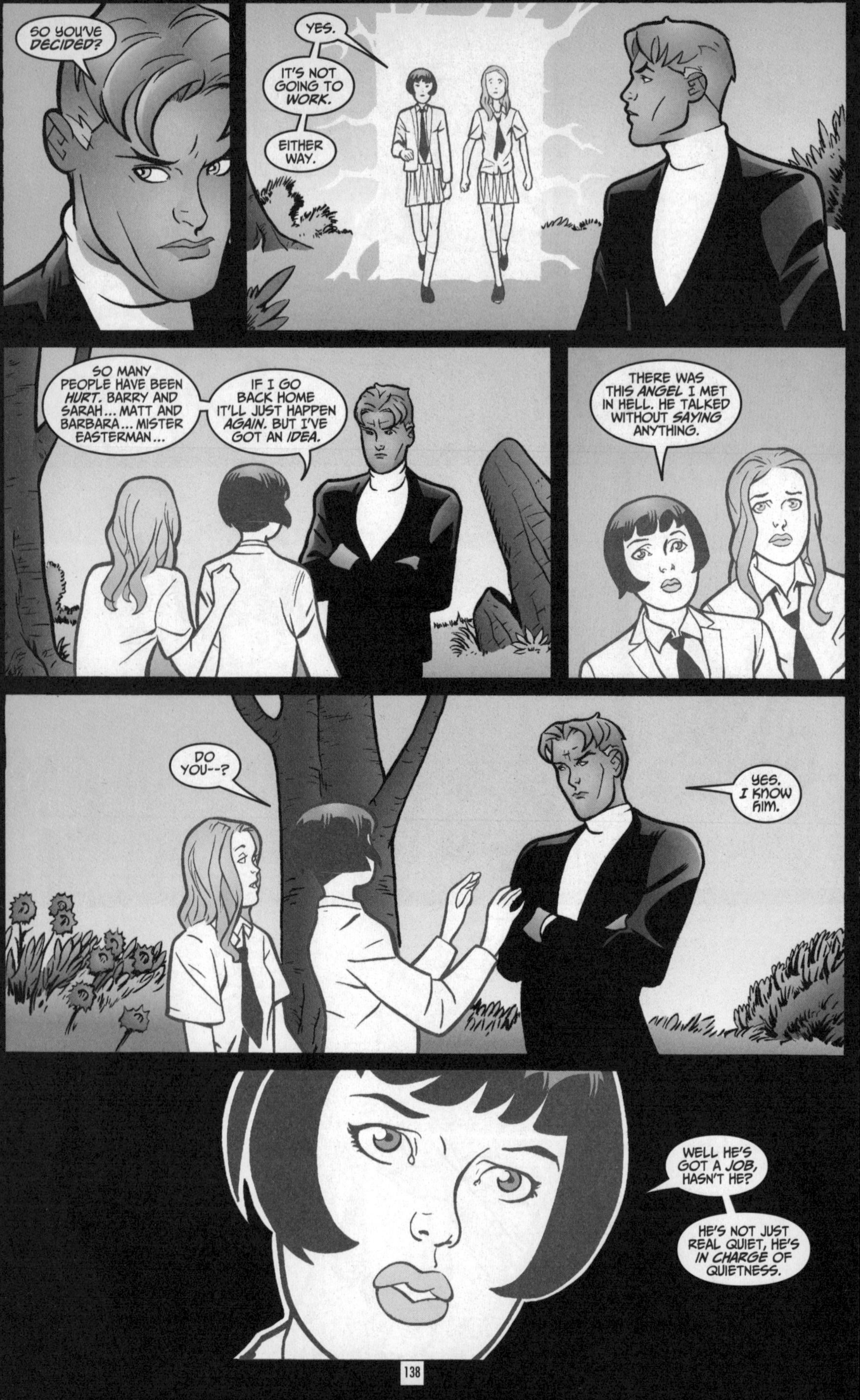
SO YOU'VE DECIDED?
YES.
IT'S NOT GOING TO WORK.
EITHER WAY.
SO MANY PEOPLE HAVE BEEN HURT. BARRY AND SARAH... MATT AND BARBARA... MISTER EASTERMAN...
IF I GO BACK HOME IT'LL JUST HAPPEN AGAIN. BUT I'VE GOT AN IDEA.
THERE WAS THIS ANGEL I MET IN HELL. HE TALKED WITHOUT SAYING ANYTHING.
DO YOU--?
YES. I KNOW HIM.
WELL HE'S GOT A JOB, HASN'T HE?
HE'S NOT JUST REAL QUIET, HE'S IN CHARGE OF QUIETNESS.

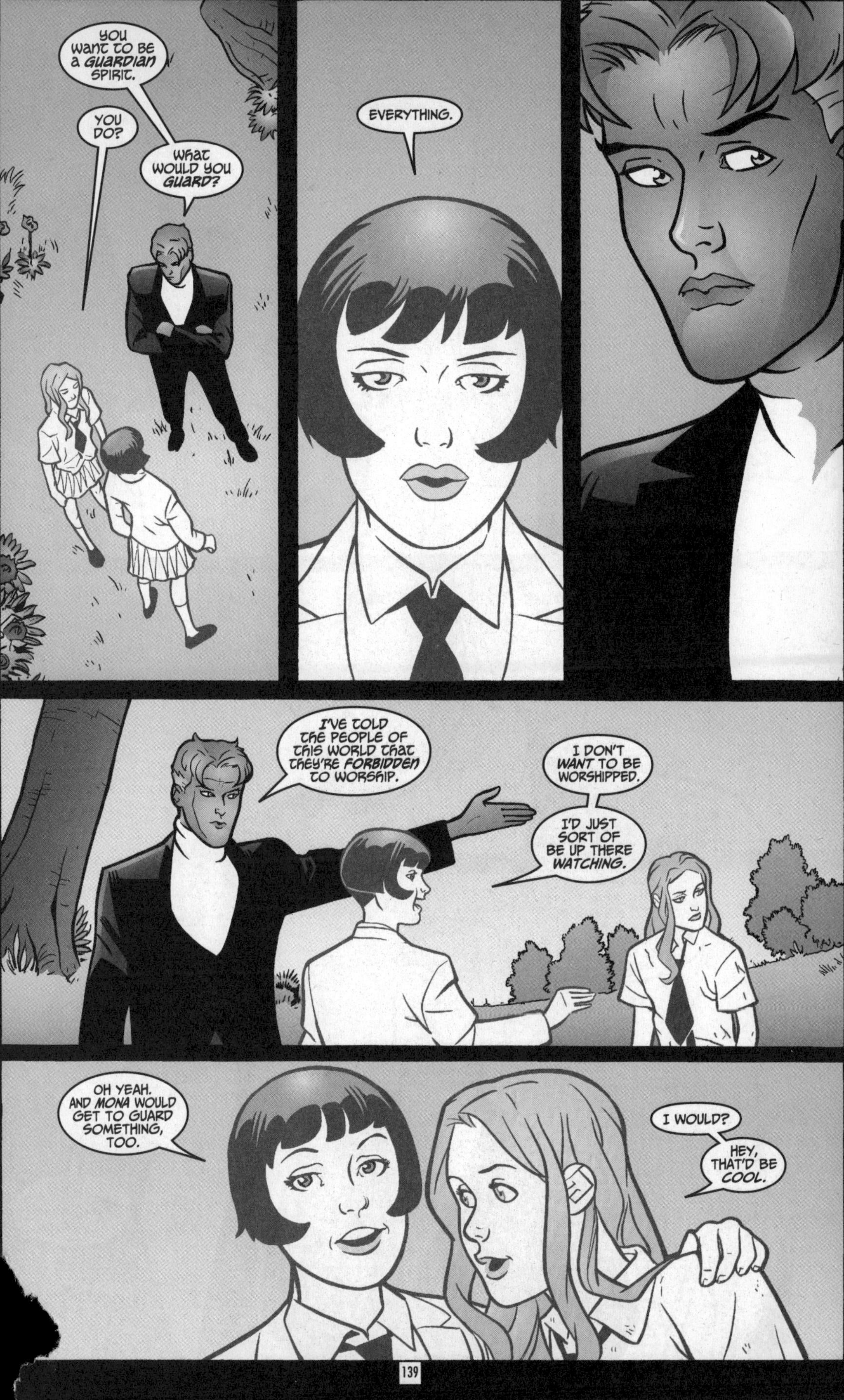

YOU WANT TO BE A GUARDIAN SPIRIT.
YOU DO?
WHAT WOULD YOU GUARD?
EVERYTHING.
I'VE TOLD THE PEOPLE OF THIS WORLD THAT THEY'RE FORBIDDEN TO WORSHIP.
I DON'T WANT TO BE WORSHIPPED.
I'D JUST SORT OF BE UP THERE WATCHING.
OH YEAH. AND MONA WOULD GET TO GUARD SOMETHING, TOO.
I WOULD?
HEY, THAT'D BE COOL.

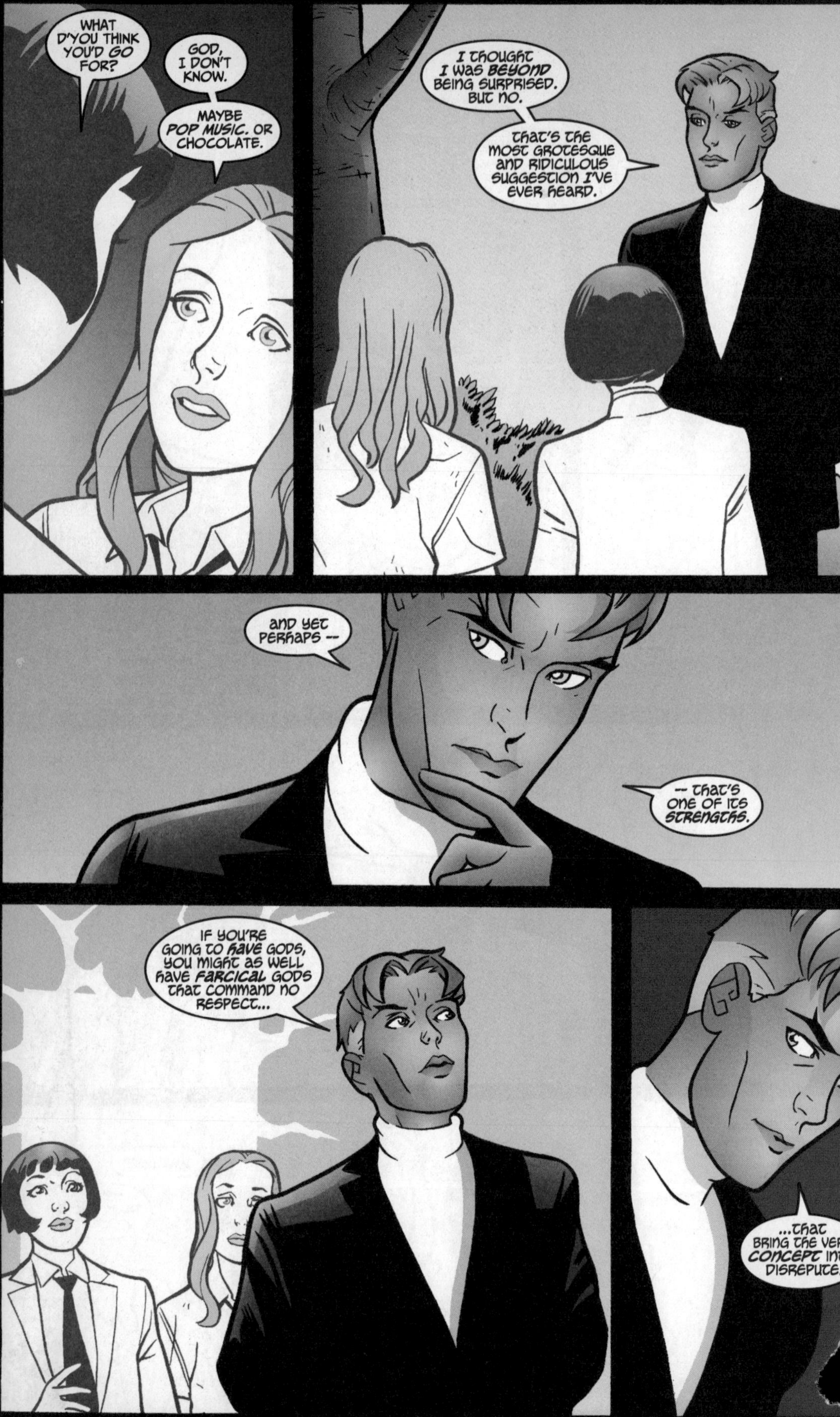
WHAT D'YOU THINK YOU'D GO FOR?
GOD, I DON'T KNOW.
MAYBE POP MUSIC. OR CHOCOLATE.
I THOUGHT I WAS BEYOND BEING SURPRISED. BUT NO.
THAT'S THE MOST GROTESQUE AND RIDICULOUS SUGGESTION I'VE EVER HEARD.
AND YET PERHAPS --
-- THAT'S ONE OF ITS STRENGTHS.
IF YOU'RE GOING TO HAVE GODS, YOU MIGHT AS WELL HAVE FARCICAL GODS THAT COMMAND NO RESPECT...
...THAT BRING THE VERY CONCEPT INTO DISREPUTE.

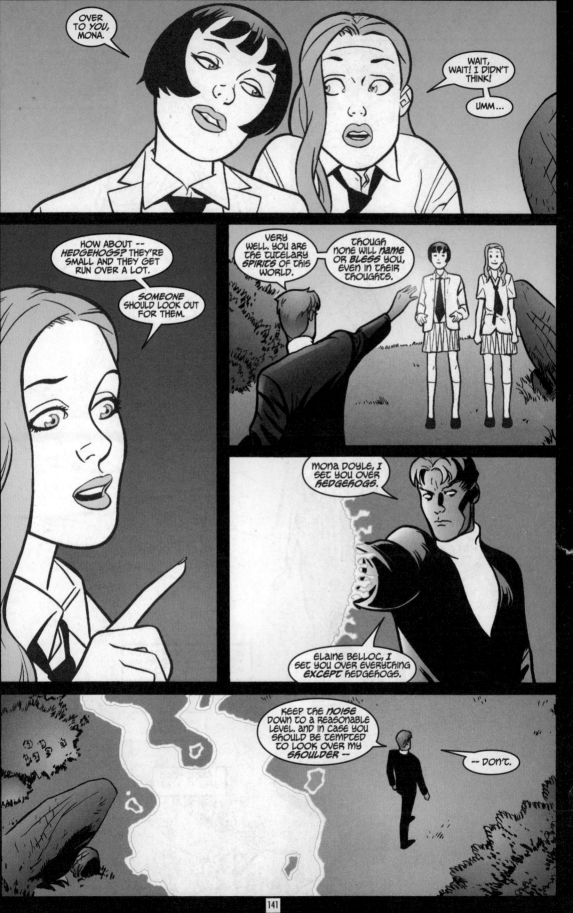

OVER TO *YOU,* MONA.

WAIT, WAIT! I DIDN'T THINK!

UMM...

HOW ABOUT -- *HEDGEHOGS?* THEY'RE SMALL AND THEY GET RUN OVER A LOT.

SOMEONE SHOULD LOOK OUT FOR THEM.

VERY WELL. YOU ARE THE *TUTELARY SPIRITS* OF THIS WORLD.

THOUGH NONE WILL *NAME* OR *BLESS* YOU, EVEN IN THEIR THOUGHTS.

MONA DOYLE, I SET YOU OVER *HEDGEHOGS.*

ELAINE BELLOC, I SET YOU OVER EVERYTHING *EXCEPT* HEDGEHOGS.

KEEP THE *NOISE* DOWN TO A REASONABLE LEVEL. AND IN CASE YOU SHOULD BE TEMPTED TO LOOK OVER MY *SHOULDER* --

-- DON'T.

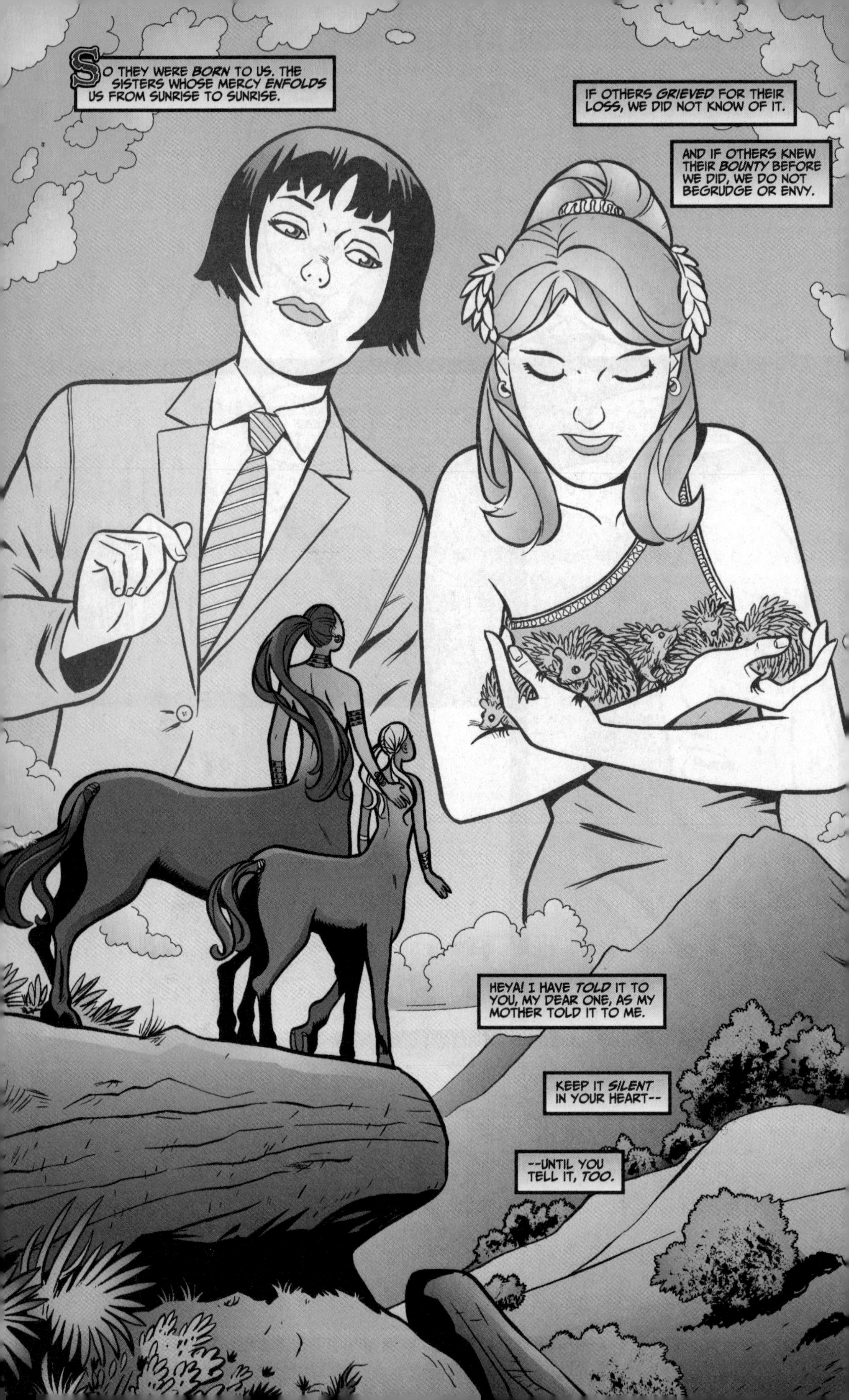
SO THEY WERE BORN TO US. THE SISTERS WHOSE MERCY ENFOLDS US FROM SUNRISE TO SUNRISE.
IF OTHERS GRIEVED FOR THEIR LOSS, WE DID NOT KNOW OF IT.
AND IF OTHERS KNEW THEIR BOUNTY BEFORE WE DID, WE DO NOT BEGRUDGE OR ENVY.
HEYA! I HAVE TOLD IT TO YOU, MY DEAR ONE, AS MY MOTHER TOLD IT TO ME.
KEEP IT SILENT IN YOUR HEART--
--UNTIL YOU TELL IT, TOO.

# THE LUCIFER LIBRARY

**BOOK ONE:**
**DEVIL IN THE GATEWAY**

**BOOK TWO:**
**CHILDREN AND MONSTERS**

**BOOK THREE:**
**A DALLIANCE WITH THE DAMNED**

**BOOK FOUR:**
**THE DIVINE COMEDY**

**BOOK FIVE:**
**INFERNO**

**BOOK SIX:**
**MANSIONS OF THE SILENCE**

**BOOK SEVEN:**
**EXODUS**

**BOOK EIGHT:**
**THE WOLF BENEATH THE TREE**

## Also from writer Mike Carey:

**THE SANDMAN PRESENTS:**
**THE FURIES**
**with John Bolton**

**HELLBLAZER: ALL HIS ENGINES**
**with Leonardo Manco**

**HELLBLAZER: RED SEPULCHRE**
**with Marcelo Frusin, Steve Dillon**
**and Jimmy Palmiotti**

### All titles are suggested for mature readers.